THAILAND
THE BEAUTIFUL COOKBOOK

ในน้ำมีปลา ในนามีข้าว
ไพร่ฟ้า หน้าใส

หลักศิลาจารึกของพ่อขุนรามคำแหงแห่งสุโขทัย ปีพุทธศักราช 1292

"In the water there are fish, in the fields there is rice ...
The faces of the people shine bright."

Stone inscription dated 1292, attributed to King Ramkhamhaeng the Great of Sukhothai

NORTHEAST BARBECUED CHICKEN (LEFT, RECIPE PAGE 124) AND CHARCOAL BEEF (RECIPE PAGE 134)

AUTHENTIC RECIPES FROM THE REGIONS OF THAILAND

THAILAND
THE BEAUTIFUL COOKBOOK

Recipes by

PANURAT POLADITMONTRI
AND JUDY LEW

Text by

WILLIAM WARREN

Photography by

LUCA INVERNIZZI TETTONI
JOHN HAY

HarperCollins*Publishers*

First published in USA 1992 by
Collins Publishers San Francisco.
Reprinted in 1992; 1995; 1998; 1999.

Conceived and produced by Weldon Owen Inc.
814 Montgomery Street, San Francisco, CA 94133, USA
Fax (415) 291 8841
A member of the Weldon International Group of Companies
Sydney • San Francisco • London

Chairman: Kevin Weldon
President: John Owen
General Manager: Stuart Laurence
Publisher: Wendely Harvey
Co-Editions Director: Derek Barton
Project Director: Dawn Low
Editor: Margaret Olds
Assistant Editor: Kate Etherington
Editorial Assistant: Tristan Phillips
Indexer: Susan Leipa – Comsearch Information Services
Picture Editor: Jenny Mills
Designer: John Bull – The Book Design Company
Production Director: Mick Bagnato
Maps: Stan Lamond – Lamond Art & Design
Illustrations: Yolande Bull
Food Stylist: Ann Creber
Food Photography: John Hay
Scenic Photography: Luca Invernizzi Tettoni
Associate Project Director, Thailand: Yvan Van Outrive
Project Coordinator, Thailand: Wongvipa Thephasdin
    Na Ayudhaya

The Library of Congress has catalogued the hardcover
edition as follows:

Poladitmontri, Panurat,
    Thailand the beautiful cookbook; authentic recipes
from the regions of Thailand/recipes by Panurat
Poladitmontri and Judy Lew; text by William Warren;
photography by Luca Invernizzi Tettoni, John Hay.
    p. cm.
    Includes index.
    ISBN 0-00-255029-6
    1. Cookery, Thai. 2. Thailand – Social life and customs.
    I. Lew, Judy. II. Warren, William, 1930- III. Title.
    TX724.5 T5P66 1992
641.59593–dc 20   91-33549

ISBN 0-06-757595-1 (pbk.)

Printed by Toppan in China

A Weldon Owen Production

ENDPAPERS: GRAND STAIRCASE MURAL, THE REGENT OF BANGKOK.
PAINTED BY PAIBOON SUWANNAKUDT TO COMMEMORATE THE
BICENTENNIAL OF BANGKOK AND THE ESTABLISHMENT OF THE
CURRENT CHAKRI DYNASTY
PHOTO: LUCA INVERNIZZI TETTONI/PHOTOBANK

PAGES 2-3: SINGHA, BURMESE STYLE LIONS, LOOK OUT OVER
THE MIST-FILLED MAE HONG SON VALLEY FROM WAT PHRA
THAT DOI KONG MU
PHOTO: LUCA INVERNIZZI TETTONI/PHOTOBANK

PAGES 6-7: RAKING UNHUSKED RICE IN THE FIELDS NEAR AYUTTHAYA
PHOTO: MICHAEL FREEMAN

PAGES 8-9: A FLOATING MARKET IN RATCHABURI PROVINCE, WHERE
VENDORS PADDLE THEIR FLAT-BOTTOMED BOATS ALONG THE CANALS
PHOTO: LUCA INVERNIZZI TETTONI/PHOTOBANK

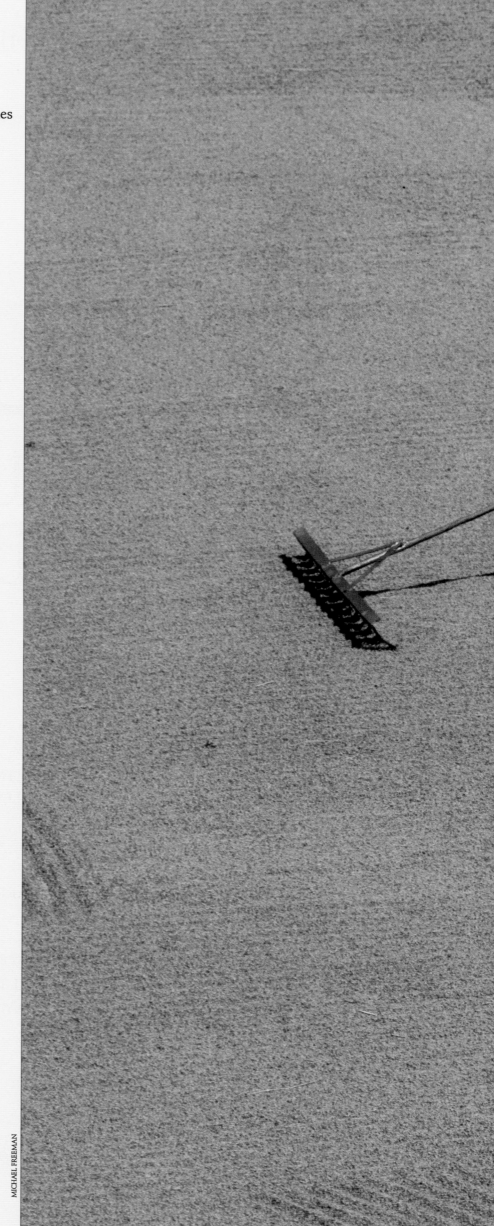

MICHAEL FREEMAN

BARBECUED CHICKEN (RECIPE PAGE 130)

CONTENTS

MONKS IN A MONASTERY IN CHIANG MAI

INTRODUCTION

EXCEPT FOR TWO BRIEF INTERLUDES in the sixteenth and eighteenth centuries, when the Burmese occupied the capital and some other parts of the kingdom, Thailand has enjoyed more than seven hundred years of independence—a distinction that can be claimed by no other country in Southeast Asia—and that has had a powerful effect on its social and political development.

But this is not to say that the Thais have been untouched by outside influences. Indeed, another great distinction, perhaps an even more important one, lies in their remarkable capacity for selective adaptation, taking certain foreign aspects and altering them in ways that make them uniquely Thai. Like the cuisine of the country, with its subtle, sometimes surprising blend of hot, sweet, and sour flavors, Thai culture is an artful amalgam, its individual components often recognizable but its overall effect highly distinctive.

China, where the Thais are generally believed to have originated as a minority ethnic group, certainly provided significant ingredients. So did India, Java, and Cambodia, all of which exerted strong influences on pre-Thai cultures. Later Sri Lanka made contributions, especially to Buddhist art and architecture, and later still there were borrowings from various European countries. The influences may, in the opinion of some historians, go back much further, to the very dawn of history: excavations in northeastern Thailand during the 1960s found evidence of rice cultivation as long ago as 3500 B.C., a thousand years before either China or India.

The earliest Thai principalities were established in the far north, centered around such cities as Chiang Rai and Chiang Mai and forming a loose federation known as Lanna. True independence came in the mid-thirteenth century when two Thai chieftains in the north central region overthrew their Khmer overlords and established the kingdom of Sukhothai, a name that in its Sanskrit form means "Dawn of Happiness". To judge from the scanty records that survive, the appellation was appropriate; for Sukhothai at the height of its short-lived power was indeed a happy place, a mystic Thai version of Camelot, which still continues to exert a potent power over the national imagination.

It had wise paternalistic rulers, who were alert to the needs of their people and very different from the aloof god-kings of the Khmers. It was abundant; "in the water there is fish, in the fields there is rice" reads part of a famous inscription of 1292. Its power, for a time at least, was

THE GOLDEN STUPA OF A LAKESIDE WAT AT MAE HONG SON
PREVIOUS PAGES: THIS TRADITIONAL DANCE OF THE NORTHEAST, PERFORMED AT A FESTIVAL IN UBON RATCHATHANI, MIMES FISHING

considerable; less by means of conflict than through strategic alliances it managed to forge a sphere of influence that covered nearly all of present-day Thailand. And it was extraordinarily creative; the Buddhist architecture and art of Sukhothai, all produced in a few centuries, were never to be equalled for originality and sheer beauty.

We know little about the food of Sukhothai, though one familiar present-day ingredient certainly not in use was the chili pepper, which reached Southeast Asia from its Central American homeland a few centuries later. On the other hand, there is no reason to think that the early Thai view differed much from that given by a contemporary writer: "Wherever we are and whatever we are doing, we like first and best to eat." Very likely, ordinary people sat down to the basic fare described by a French visitor to Ayutthaya, the next capital. "A Siamese," he wrote, "makes a very good meal with a pound of rice a day, which amounts to not more than a farthing; and with a little dry or salt fish, which costs no more... Their sauces are plain, a little water with some spices, garlic, or some sweet herb. They do very much esteem a liquid sauce, like mustard, which is only crayfish corrupted because they are ill-salted; they call it Kepi."

By contrast, it is interesting to note the Thai opinion of French cuisine at about the same time, as recorded by an envoy from Ayutthaya to the court of King Louis XIV in 1684. When he was given some wine at a reception in his honor, he noted that it "helps give taste to the food which would otherwise be insipid to our palates; here are few spices and much meat, and an attraction of quantity replaces piquant wholesomeness."

With the rise of Ayutthaya in the fourteenth century, perhaps the most cosmopolitan of all cities in the region, other ingredients were added to the Thai blend. At the peak of its power in the seventeenth century, Ayutthaya had a population of more than a million, among them Laotians, Cambodians, Chinese, Indians, Japanese, Persians, Dutch, Portuguese, English, and French, many of whom left some kind of lasting imprint. Thai sweets based on sugar and egg yolks, for instance, are nearly all derived from the Portuguese,

THAI CLASSICAL DANCE, OF INDIAN ORIGIN, HAS TWO
MAIN FORMS: KHON—MASKED DRAMA; AND LAKON—DRAMA

LUCA INVERNIZZI TETTONI / PHOTOBANK

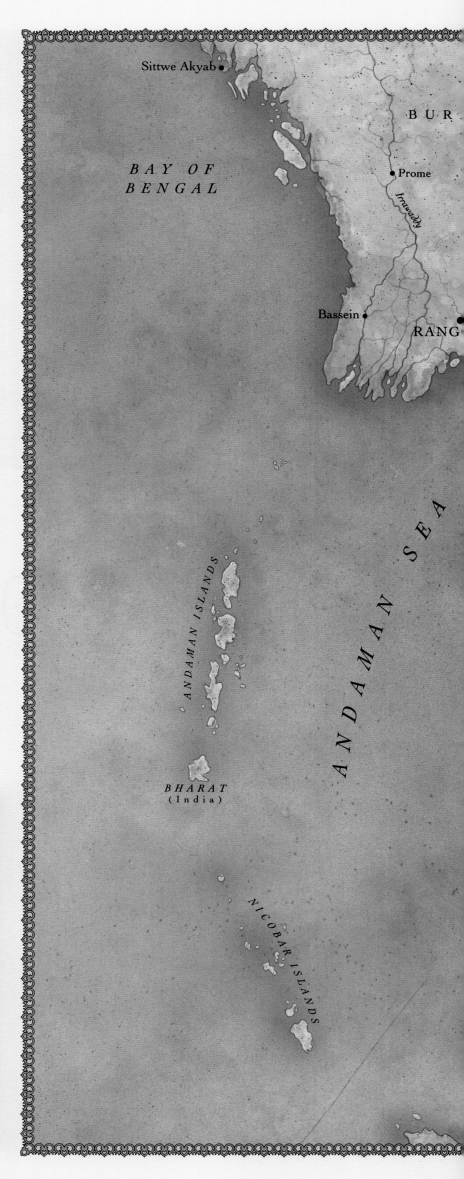

VIETNAM

GULF OF TONKIN

LAOS

Chiang Rai
Menam Khong

Mae Hong Son
Phayao

CHIANG MAI
Nan

Lamphun

VIENTIANE
Nong Khai

Lampang
Phrae

Mae Nam Khong

NORTH

Loei

Udon
Thani
Nakhon Phanom

Sakon Nakhon

Sukhothai

Tak
Khon Kaen
Kalasin
Savannakhet
HUE

Phitsanulok

Roi Et

Mekong

Phetchabun

NORTHEAST

Nakhon Sawan

CENTRAL
PLAINS
Chaiyaphum

Ubon Ratchathani

Ang Thong
Lop
Buri

Nakhon Ratchasima
Surin

Chao Phraya

Pra Nakhon Si Ayutthaya

THON BURI
BANGKOK

Arangya
prathet

Ratchaburi
Samut Sakhon

Chon Buri

KAMPUCHEA

Phetchaburi

Pattaya

Hua Hin
Rayong

THAILAND

Trat

Mekong

Prachuap
Khiri Khan

*GULF OF
THAILAND*

PHNOM PENH

SAIGON
HO CHI MIN

Chumphon
My Tho

Ranong
Rach Gia

Can Tho

Surat Thani

Phangnga
Nakhon Si Thammarat

Krabi

Phuket
SOUTH

Trang

SOUTH CHINA SEA

Songkhla

Hat Yai
Pattani

Yala

Narathiwat

Satun

MOULMEIN

Salween

WAT RATBURANA AT AYUTTHAYA, ONCE THE CAPITAL OF SIAM.
THE CITY WAS DESTROYED BY BURMESE INVADERS IN 1767

UPCOUNTRY, RURAL PEOPLE LEAD A SIMPLE LIFE. HERE A MAN
CARRIES HIS WARES ON A POLE OVER HIS SHOULDER

and the Indians contributed a milder form of curry. The Portuguese were also probably responsible for introducing that now-essential ingredient, the chili pepper, shortly after they opened relations with Ayutthaya in 1511, and may have brought the tomato as well.

Surrounding Ayutthaya and stretching all the way to the gulf was the real source of Thailand's wealth: the vast, fertile Chao Phraya River valley, an ancient checkerboard of paddy fields, fruit orchards, and waterways, which not only fed most of the kingdom but also supplied most of its foreign exchange. This great resource remained after Ayutthaya was destroyed by the Burmese in 1767 and sustained subsequent capitals established further down the river, first at Thonburi and finally, in 1782, across the river on the site of a small trading port called Bangkok.

Visitors today, as in the past, often fail to perceive Thailand's cultural and geographical variety—confined as so many of them are to cities and resort areas, where Western

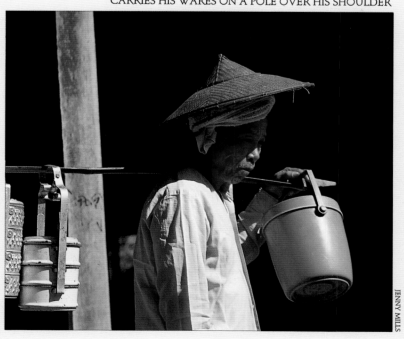

JENNY MILLS

A JUNK ON PHANGNGA BAY. CHINESE STYLE
SAILING BOATS ARE NOW USED BY TOURISTS

and other influences (mainly Chinese) tend to predominate. The overwhelming majority of Thais, however, still live in rural areas, mostly in villages of between 100 and 150 households, and still abide by regional mores that are only superficially affected by modern changes.

Geographically the country is divided into four main regions. The North, sharing borders (and many cultural affinities) with Burma and Laos, has mountains and secret valleys that until fairly recent years were all but inaccessible. It experiences temperatures that drop sufficiently in the winter months to permit cultivation of temperate-zone fruits and vegetables. The Northeast is a rolling plateau stretching to the Mekong River which separates Thailand from Laos, and also, in its southern part, bordering on Cambodia. Once densely forested and fertile, it is now semi-arid, a condition that influences both the psychology and cuisine of its inhabitants. The Central Plains region, which includes the provinces along the eastern coast of the gulf, is one of the

19

JENNY MILLS

LONG-TAILED BOATS TAKE VISITORS TO THE ISLANDS
OF THE ANDAMAN SEA IN THAILAND'S SOUTHWEST

world's greatest rice-growing areas and has been the scene of Thailand's most intense cultural and economic development. The South, a peninsula stretching like a long finger all the way down to Malaysia, is characterized by craggy limestone mountains, dense jungles, and a rich abundance of seafood from the waters off its two coastlines.

Equally varied are the approximately 56 million people who live in Thailand. In addition to the Thai majority the population includes numerous other ethnic groups—semi-nomadic hill tribes, Chinese, Vietnamese, Laotians, Malays, Cambodians, Indians and Burmese, to mention only some—nearly all of whom have been politically assimilated, yet who also display marked cultural differences.

Buddhism is the faith followed by most, reflected not only by the country's 27,000 temples, dazzling creations that manage to be at once fantastical and serene, but also, less visibly, by countless modes of instinctive behavior that range from a fatalistic acceptance of misfortune to a passion for social harmony. The domed Muslim mosque, however, is almost as common as the Buddhist monastery in the far south; astrologers and fortune tellers figure prominently in daily life; and every village and town has its shrines to the countless far more ancient spirits who bring rain, prosperity, fecundity, or even a winning ticket in the lottery.

As a country, as a culture, Thailand can be likened to one of its most popular traditional arts, that of fitting countless fragments of brightly colored glass or porcelain to form mosaics for the adornment of such celebrated structures as Bangkok's Wat Arun, the Temple of Dawn. From a distance the effect is that of a seamless pattern of sparkling jewel-like hues, shading imperceptibly into one another. Only on closer inspection do the individual parts of the design become clear; only then can the outsider begin to appreciate the ingenuity that has produced this remarkably complex creation.

THE COUNTRY SWARMS WITH BICYCLES AND MOTORBIKES.
HERE NEIGHBORS STOP FOR A CHAT OUTSIDE CHIANG MAI

JOHN HAY

THE ROYAL PALACE AND THE TEMPLE OF
THE EMERALD BUDDHA IN BANGKOK
LUCA INVERNIZZI TETTONI / PHOTOBANK

EATING A THAI MEAL

THE THAIS TAKE THEIR REPASTS seated on a mat or carpet," reported Bishop Jean-Baptiste Pallegoix, a missionary who lived in Bangkok during the early nineteenth century. "The dishes are great brazen vases with a cover, over which a red cloth is placed; the meat is cut into small pieces, and the rice is kept apart in a deep porringer on one side of the floor, while a great basin of water is on the other, having in it a drinking cup. The guests have neither knives or forks, but use a mother-of-pearl spoon to dip into the various dishes, of which having eaten a sufficiency, they drink pure water or tea. To help themselves one after another from the same plate, to drink one after another from the same cup, has nothing strange."

Though the Bishop clearly moved in lofty circles, in which accoutrements like brazen vases and mother-of-pearl spoons were taken for granted, certain features of the Thai meal he describes will be familiar to any contemporary diner.

Almost always, eating Thai style will involve a number of people, usually a family group, for being forced to eat alone ranks high on the Thai scale of misfortunes.

A visit to a Thai house for dinner begins with the warm welcome that is the hallmark of Thai hospitality. The host will likely offer some refreshing cool water as a prelude to a session of light-hearted conversation— Thai people enjoy telling jokes and teasing each other so that talk, not food, may occupy much of the early part of the visit. But then comes the time to enjoy a meal together.

Dishes are usually comprised of bite-sized portions, and meal service typically includes only a fork and a spoon. In fact a century or so ago no cutlery (apart from serving utensils) was used at traditional meals. The rice, whether ordinary or glutinous, was pressed into small balls with fingers and then dipped into the other dishes. European spoons and forks appeared during the nineteenth century, at first in royal circles and later taken up by the general population; the custom today is to actually eat with a dessert-sized spoon, using the fork mainly to move food around on the plate. A Chinese-style ceramic spoon is often provided if there is a soup, in which case each guest will have a small bowl as well as a plate. Knives are rarely used, since meats are already cut into bite-sized pieces, and chopsticks only when Chinese-type noodles are included.

Almost always there will be a variety of dishes, for it takes more than one or two preparations to achieve the blend of flavors Thais like. An ample supply of rice is always the centerpiece. Traditionally all of the dishes are served at the same time. The Thai cook strives for a balance of flavors, textures and colors.

Ideally, a Thai meal offers a combination of flavors: sweet, hot, sour, salty and bitter. Sometimes several of these are present in a single creation, subtly blending, while in other dishes one flavor predominates. Most often, in addition to the obligatory bowl of rice, there will be a soup of some kind, a curry, a steamed dish, a fried one, a salad, and one or more of the basic sauces, probably based on *nam prik* and/or *nam pla*.

There is generally enough food to accommodate any unexpected guests who may drop in. All the dishes are placed on the table at the same time and can be eaten in no particular order. Nor are there any rigid rules about what goes with what: diners are free to mix dishes according to individual taste. Diners at the table serve themselves only one or two mouthfuls of a dish at a time, allowing everyone

A TRADITIONAL KITCHEN IN NORTHERN THAILAND

to share the same dishes. Serving plates are replenished as they empty. Dessert for a formal meal often consists of several dishes—usually fruit of some kind as well as a solid and a liquid sweet. Water and tea are still the most common liquid accompaniments, though a bottle of Thai whisky is often present at festive gatherings, to be drunk with soda and fresh lime juice.

The preferences of individual cooks will dictate how strongly the various flavors are emphasized. When using these recipes Western cooks may wish to alter them so that the flavors are sweeter, less salty or less hot. In the event that some of the ingredients may not be available outside Thailand (such as specific noodles), alternative suggestions and explanations are provided for the cook's benefit.

OUTDOOR RESTAURANTS ARE POPULAR WITH THAIS AND TOURISTS ALIKE

THE NORTH

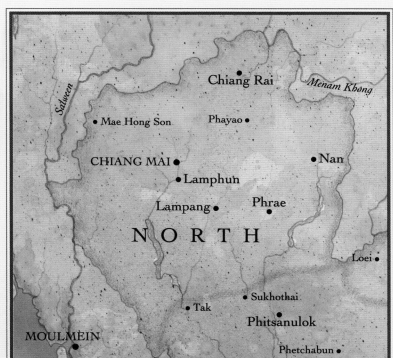

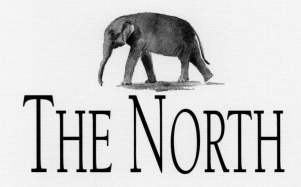

THE NORTH

L IKE OTHER PARTS OF MODERN THAILAND, the North is currently undergoing dramatic changes, most vividly apparent in the construction boom in once-quiet provincial capitals such as Chiang Mai and Chiang Rai and the network of new highways reaching far into the surrounding countryside. At the same time, however, the North retains a large measure of its traditional culture, in part because of geography but equally perhaps because of a long history that provides its people with a strong sense of their own identity. Even the most casual visitor immediately senses that there is something "different" about the North—not just its weather, which is often much cooler than the rest of the country, but also its crafts, architecture, food, language, and everyday social behavior.

Bordered by Burma and Laos, the North is a rugged mountainous region rising to 8,451 feet (2,576 meters) at its highest point on the summit of Doi Inthanon and watered by a number of rivers including the Ping, the Wang, the Yom, the Nan, and the mighty Mekong. Once it was thickly forested with hardwood trees, particularly teak, and timber was a major source of wealth for Thai princes and, later, European companies which were granted concessions; but indiscriminate logging, together with an increasing demand for more arable land, has resulted in the destruction of much of the old-growth forest, though some tracts are preserved in national parks and serious efforts at reafforestation are being undertaken by the government.

CELEBRATING THAI NEW YEAR, SONGKRAN

PREVIOUS PAGES: LIMESTONE OUTCROPPINGS ON THE WAY FROM PHAYAO TO CHIANG RAI

JOHN HAY

A RICE PLANTER WEARS A BROAD-BRIMMED HAT
FOR PROTECTION FROM THE SUN

PLANTING RICE SEEDLINGS IN CHIANG RAI PROVINCE

LUCA INVERNIZZI TETTONI / PHOTOBANK

It is a region of precipitous slopes, accessible only by good-weather trails, and verdant valleys where hamlets and rice fields are clustered along rivers and streams, of Buddhist temples flashing in the sunlight, and thick mists that roll suddenly down from the hills, obscuring everything. Nearly a thousand species of orchids are native to the North, festooning trees in the dry summer months with a spectrum of colors ranging from bright gold to rare blue. There are elephants, too, no longer roaming wild or being used for transport as in the not-so-distant past but still playing a vital role in what remains of the timber industry; a Young Elephant Training Center in Lampang province has a five-year course to teach student pachyderms such skills as dragging, carrying, pushing and stacking huge logs. In a few less-populated areas, especially near the Burmese border, there are still secret fields of pink opium poppies, tended by people in bizarre costumes that might have been taken from a medieval illustration.

Historically the culture of northern Thailand goes back to the seventh century when the Mons, an ethnic group who had already established important city-states in the Central Plains region, founded a kingdom called Haripunchai in the valley of the Ping River. Located on the site of the present-day town of Lamphun, this was an important religious center whose artistic influence continued long after its power waned. The Thais began arriving later—exactly when is a matter of scholarly dispute—and became predominant in the

CHIANG MAI AT DUSK. THE CITY STILL RETAINS
PARTS OF THE OLD WALLS AND MOATS

mid-thirteenth century, when one of them, King Mengrai, embarked on an ambitious campaign to unite the whole of the northern region under his rule.

Beginning in his home principality on the bank of the Mekong River, King Mengrai moved southward, founding first Chiang Rai as his capital in 1262 and then Chiang Mai in 1297. According to northern chronicles he was killed by a bolt of lightning in 1317, having ruled for more than fifty years and having established a kingdom that would control the region for the next two centuries.

Chiang Mai was the heart of Lanna, as the kingdom was known, and during its golden age around the middle of the fifteenth century it was celebrated for its Buddhist scholarship, its splendid temples, and the skills of its superb artisans. The famous Emerald Buddha, a small green jadeite image now enshrined at Wat Phra Keo in Bangkok, is believed to be of Lanna origin, probably produced by a Chiang Mai sculptor. Even today Chiang Mai has an exceptionally large number of monasteries—more than a hundred scattered through the metropolitan area—and it is also still the principal source of Thailand's best handicrafts.

Despite its cultural achievements, the Lanna kingdom was often at war, sometimes with another rising Thai state of Ayutthaya to the south, but more often with neighboring Burma. Beginning in 1558 the North entered two centuries of domination by the Burmese who, while they never actually occupied the region in the military sense, neverthe-

less appointed local chiefs to carry out their orders and exerted a strong cultural influence which is reflected today in northern art and food. In 1774 King Kawila of Lampang, a city not far from Chiang Mai, managed to regain Lanna independence, but only for a short time; he soon pledged his allegiance to King Rama I, founder of Bangkok, and technically at least the North became a part of the Thai kingdom.

Administrative control, however, remained weak during most of the nineteenth century and to some degree well into the twentieth. This was mainly because of the difficulty of getting from Bangkok to Chiang Mai, which lay on the other side of a formidable mountain chain that effectively sealed off the North from the Central Plains region. During the rainy season the journey took fifty-five days by river, buffalo cart, and elephant back, and even in the dry months it required thirty-five days of hard travel.

Among the few outsiders willing to undergo such discomforts were a small group of American Protestant missionaries, who established the first schools and hospitals while also managing to convert more locals to Christianity than anywhere else in Thailand. Another early visitor, in 1883, was a Danish traveler named Carl Bock, who referred to Chiang Mai as "the most powerful of all the Lao states" and found that real power remained in the hands of local princes, descendants of the ancient Lanna royalty. Bock paid a visit to the daily Chiang Mai market, where "as in the island of Bali, the women do all the selling. They all sit on the ground, with a basket on each side of them, sometimes with the contents emptied out and spread on a couple of plantain-leaves. The principal articles offered for sale are provisions, fruits and vegetables; tobacco, betel-nuts, and lime; fish, dried salted, and stewed, but always more or less stinking; buffalo-meat, and pieces of buffalo-hide, also eaten and considered good; ... mushrooms, of which the Laotians are very fond; wax and cotton; earthenware pots, jars and jugs, so brittle they almost break at a touch; and always a good stock of flowers that would be the envy of a Parisian."

Later during his stay Carl Bock was invited to dinner with the highest ranking "Chow", or prince. He was surprised to find that the meal included potatoes, "which had been introduced along with other vegetables into this country by the American missionaries, and which the Chow ate with great relish, helping himself to them sans ceremonie, in the good old-fashioned peasant style, and blowing his fingers to keep them cool".

Not until the northern railway line reached Chiang Mai in 1921—a major feat of engineering by any standard—did central Thais begin to come north in any appreciable numbers, and it was not until 1928 that the people of the North gained their first glimpse of their ruler, when King Rama VII came on a royal visit, riding through the city on a splendidly caparisoned elephant.

This long period of isolation explains many of the characteristics that so impress visitors to the North today, for it meant that its people were relatively unexposed to the changes going on elsewhere in the country, and their own customs and traditions remained strong for much longer.

BRIGHTLY PAINTED PAPER UMBRELLAS ARE MADE BY LOCALS ON THE OUTSKIRTS OF CHIANG MAI

Language and manners are two notable examples. Northern Thai even today differs from that spoken in the Central Plains region (about as much as Spanish does from Portuguese), and as used in daily life it contains a greater number of polite expressions and sounds much more soothing to the ear. Northern Thais themselves are renowned for their gentle ways and hospitality to strangers; an old custom of the region, still widely practiced, is the placing of an earthenware jar of cool water outside houses so any thirsty passerby can refresh himself. Observe, too, the smiles that still flash so readily even in busy cities, the friendliness of vendors in marketplaces, the willingness to assist in countless small ways. On the rare occasion when impolite behavior is encountered, the offender will almost always turn out to be an outsider, and when northerners have to go to Bangkok for one reason or another they are usually shocked by its brash impersonal ways. The people of Chiang Mai in particular have a tendency to look down disapprovingly on the bumptious residents of the far younger capital, often protesting loudly (sometimes successfully) when the latter attempt to intrude with their money-making innovations.

All Thais attach great importance to the pursuit of *sanuk*—a term usually translated as "fun", though in fact covering a far wider range of pleasures—but northerners seem to go much further and with more exuberance than almost anybody else. Loi Krathong, for instance, the loveliest of traditional Thai festivals, when little lighted boats are set adrift in rivers and canals to pay homage to the water spirits, is in other regions merely a one-night affair in November—*sanuk*, to be sure, but not a major interruption to daily life. In Chiang Mai, three full days are devoted to the festivities and almost the entire city participates in some way, along with thousands of visitors who book hotel rooms months in advance. Similarly, both the Western and the old Thai New Year's celebrations are major events in the North, with shows, gala parades, and contests to select a beauty queen. Some occasions are purely local and give the impression of having been organized mainly to provide a pleasant break in routine: the Chiang Mai Flower Festival, for instance, when blossom-bedecked floats stop city traffic; or the Lamphun

TAPAE ROAD IS THE BUSIEST STREET IN CHIANG MAI, NORTHERN THAILAND'S CULTURAL AND COMMERCIAL CENTER

MONKS SWEEPING THE COURTYARD AT WAT PHRA DOI KHONG MU IN MAE HONG SON

A GROUP OF YOUNG GIRLS IN EMBROIDERED COSTUMES
AT ONE OF THE MANY REGIONAL FESTIVALS

EATING A KHANTOKE DINNER, THE TRADITIONAL NORTHERN
MEAL. SOMETIMES A RED LACQUERWARE TABLE IS USED

Garlic Festival, where the climax comes with the choice of *Nang Kratiem*, or "Miss Garlic", and her crowning with a garland of pungent bulbs.

Even religious observances there have an added zest. About a third of Thailand's 27,000 Buddhist temples are in the North, and at the end of the rainy season it is hard to go anywhere in the region without coming across one or more *thot kathin*, merit-making ceremonies when groups of people present new robes and other necessities to monks, usually in out-of-the-way monasteries. Solemn as they are essentially, these too are nevertheless still opportunities for *sanuk* in the form of music, dancing, and convivial meals prepared by outstanding local cooks.

Like nearly all traditional Thai houses, those of the North are elevated from the ground on stout pillars, offering protection from floods and wild animals as well as a working area below, but they differ from the airy Central Plains style in a number of significant respects. The prefabricated walls slant outward rather than inward, the windows are smaller, and the overall effect is that of a sturdier structure built for life in a cooler climate. The roof-peaks, especially of houses in the Chiang Mai area, are often adorned with a graceful V-shaped decoration which is unique to the region and may once have had magical significance. Temples are often different, too, with their lavish woodcarvings and frequent use of Burmese ornamental techniques.

Northern cuisine also remains quite distinctive. Instead of the soft, boiled rice of the Central Plains region, northerners

A HILLTRIBE VILLAGE ON DOI MAE SALONG, THE NORTHERNMOST
POINT OF THAILAND, AT THE BORDER WITH BURMA

A YOUNG MONK PLAYS WITH A ROOSTER DURING
A QUIET MOMENT AT A CHIANG MAI TEMPLE

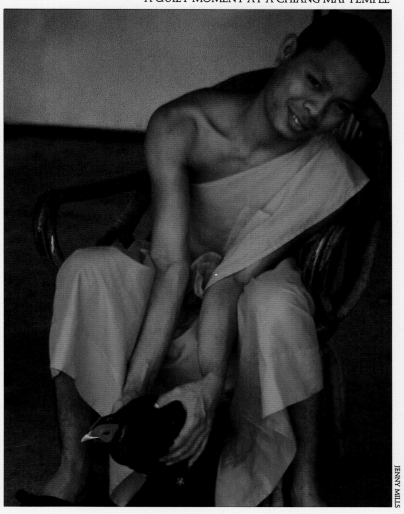

prefer a steamed glutinous variety and traditionally eat it with the fingers, kneading small handfuls into balls with which to scoop up more liquid dishes. (As well as the white variety of glutinous rice there is also one with black grains, which has a nutty flavor reminiscent of American wild rice, but Thais usually eat this sweetened as a dessert.)

Coconut milk, which is widely used as an ingredient in much of central and southern Thai cooking, plays an insignificant role in the North, where the curries tend to be clear rather than thickened.

The fondness for *khao neow,* or "steamed sticky rice", reflects the influence of neighboring Laos, as do the northern versions of *nam prik,* that basic sauce that accompanies every Thai meal, which range from a relatively mild minced pork and tomato mixture (*nam prik ong*) to a fiery *nam prik tadaeng* composed mainly of dried red chilies. Burmese influence is evident as well, particularly in such popular dishes as *gaeng hang lay,* a pork curry that employs ginger, tamarind and turmeric for its distinctive flavor, and *khao soi,* a curry broth with egg noodles and chicken, pork or beef, topped with shallots, pickled vegetables and slices of lime. One of the favorite regional specialties is *naem,* a spicy pork sausage eaten in a wide variety of ways and probably the delicacy northerners miss most when they move away. While some are highly seasoned, the curries and salads (*yams*) of the North are generally milder than those of central and northeastern Thailand, although chili-hot sauces are always available for those who want a stronger flavor.

JENNY MILLS

33

JENNY MILLS

THE NAGA IS THE MYTHICAL KING OF SERPENTS. THESE TWO
CARVED NAGAS ARE ON A CHIANG MAI TEMPLE BALUSTRADE

Other northern foods are perhaps best appreciated by true connoisseurs: crisply fried cicadas, for example, or cow's placenta (a much-prized treat in Phayao province), or a version of *laab* consisting of minced raw buffalo meat, pulverized rice, chilies, mint and a dash of buffalo bile to provide the bitter flavor common to many traditional dishes of the region. Popular, too, is the giant waterbeetle called *maengda*, which when pounded in a mortar adds an aromatic flavor to certain dishes; the beetles are also eaten fried or, when out of season, pickled. Some of the tribal people who live in the mountains are quite partial to dog meat and raise a black chow-like variety in order to have a guaranteed supply on hand for feast days.

The traditional form of meal in the North, especially when guests are being entertained, is the *khantoke* dinner—*khan*, meaning "bowl", and *toke* a low round table made of woven bamboo, or, in a fancier version, red lacquerware. Diners sit on the floor around the table and help themselves to assorted dishes placed on it, in no particular order. Glutinous rice is always provided, and nowadays ordinary rice as well, along with one or two curries, a minced-meat dish, a salad, raw and pickled vegetables, fried pork rind, and a variety of sauces and condiments. Dessert will generally be fruit—most memorably, if it is in season, the succulent lychee-like longan, harvested from the trees that grow in almost every compound. Longan, known in Thai as *lamyai*, is sent all over the country during August and September and also exported by air to fanciers in Singapore and Hong Kong.

In central Thailand, particularly in Bangkok, one significant result of increased relations with the West during the nineteenth century was a rapid decline of local handicrafts. Wealthy families who had once maintained their own personal groups of artisans—weavers and woodcarvers, goldsmiths and jewelers—turned to the European goods that began flooding the markets, prompted partly by a desire for novelty and partly by the fact that their rulers were urging Westernization as proof that Thailand was a "civilized" country and thus not ripe for colonization.

Few of these innovations reached the remote North, where artisans continued to produce their ancient crafts and to hand down their skills through the generations. There were the silversmiths who hammered out the thin, exquisitely decorated bowls used in so many regional rituals; the woodcarvers who produced the elaborate panels, sometimes inlaid with pieces of colored glass, that adorned every temple; the lacquerware makers who wove delicate objects of bamboo and then patiently applied coat after coat of thin resin to achieve the desired thickness; the weavers who used primitive looms to create shimmering lengths of brocaded silk, often in patterns so intricate that months were required to complete a single piece. Moreover, there were specialists in pottery and fine rice paper, jewelry and hand-painted umbrellas, embroidery and bronze-casting.

All these have survived to the present day, often in the same villages that produced them a century ago. Chiang Mai's famous Night Bazaar offers a wide selection of northern crafts, which has made it one of the region's leading tourist attractions, and there are numerous "factories"—often nothing more than a few simple sheds—in which the various processes can be observed. Such skills are playing a significant role in the modern regional economy, as evidenced by a visit to the subdistrict of Hang Dong, just outside Chiang Mai, where hundreds of artisans are busily turning out furniture and woodcarvings for wholesale exporters with clients throughout the world.

Among the most exotic sights of the far North are the tribal people who live in the hills. There are seven principal tribes—Karen, Hmong (Meo), Akha, Lahu, Lawa, Lisu, and Yao—and their numbers have been variously estimated at somewhere between 250,000 and 500,000. Arriving at a precise figure would be all but impossible, however, for by nature most of the groups are nomadic and move more or less freely across national borders. Each has its own distinctive culture, differing not only in language and racial origin, but also, most vividly, in their costumes. Yao women, for instance, are noted for their skill at embroidery and wear elaborately decorated loose trousers, huge indigo turbans, and a bright pink boa-like puff around the neck. Those of the Lisu tribe favor bold red and turquoise dresses and, during festivals, spectacular silver jewelry that covers them almost like a suit of armor, while the Hmong are gifted at producing subtly patterned batik cloth and display their wealth by wearing masses of silver ornaments.

In previous times the members of these tribes rarely descended to towns from their lofty homes, and only a few intrepid missionaries bothered to learn much about their lifestyles. Today they are far more visible, partly because of a growing demand for their distinctive crafts but more because their presence has given rise to a number of problems, both social and ecological.

LUCA INVERNIZZI TETTONI / PHOTOBANK

ELEPHANTS ARE NO LONGER USED AS PACK ANIMALS, BUT
IN THE HILLS THEY ARE STILL SOMETIMES USED TO HAUL LOGS

The traditional tribal cash crop—indeed, for many, the only means of earning any money at all—was opium poppy, refined in secret factories by middlemen and smuggled out as heroin to dealers of the West. Equally harmful in terms of Thailand's future was their slash-and-burn method of clearing forests for the poppy fields, working the thin soil until it was exhausted and then moving on to a new location, leaving behind a trail of wasted, eroded slopes.

It was Thailand's King Bhumibol Adulyadej who first called attention to these destructive practices in the late 1960s. Traveling extensively by helicopter, jeep, and foot through the region from his palace atop Doi Suthep overlooking Chiang Mai, the King visited numerous tribal sites and eventually established a pioneering Royal Project to bring them better social welfare and introduce alternative crops to replace the poppy. As a result, although opium continues to be grown in Burma and Laos (and to transit illegally through Thailand), Thai production has fallen from a high of about 250 tons (250 tonnes) a year during the 1970s to only about 15–30 tons (15–30 tonnes). More and more hill tribes have now settled in permanent villages with schools and adequate medical services, and they earn a better living through the cultivation of coffee, strawberries, peaches, and such temperate-zone vegetables as asparagus, kidney beans, and lettuce. Thanks to processing facilities and improved transportation, these are now adding to the variety of Bangkok markets as well as being exported as fresh and canned products and so earning money for the country.

In addition the hill tribes have been assisted by Queen Sirikit, who popularized their crafts by using them prominently in her own fashions and also opened training centers for artisans through her SUPPORT Foundation.

Tourism is now the major source of income in the North, with Chiang Mai as the focal point. Whereas three decades ago there were only one or two proper hotels in the city, now there are dozens, along with an even greater number of condominiums and housing projects catering to people from Bangkok who want a place for holidays during the cool winter months. The impact is also being felt much further afield: in the once-mysterious "Golden Triangle", where warlords battled for control of the opium traffic and where resorts with views of three national borders are now rising; and in the scenic valley of Mae Hong Som, formerly known as "the Siberia of Thailand" because it was regarded as a suitably remote place to exile erring officials, although now it is only a short plane trip from Chiang Mai. Trekkers with backpacks are exploring the slopes of Doi Inthanon, and tour groups are thrilling to the novelty of a two-hour elephant ride in the jungle.

For all its recent development, however, the North is still probably Thailand's most distinctive region, with a culture that has so far proved remarkably resistant to change. Its "differences", which derive in part from Burmese and Lao influences, are undoubtedly its most valuable asset, making it a place where Thais as well as foreign visitors go in search of traditional customs that have been diluted elsewhere.

PREPARING SNACKS AT A BUSY MARKET

SOUPS AND APPETIZERS

THE THAIS "snack" all through the day and into the night and so in the city and village markets streetside vendors offer a multitude of good things to eat. Some dishes are small, others, like the popular noodle dishes, are more substantial and can even make a meal in themselves: all can be regarded as snacks to eat separately or as appetizers forming the first part of a meal. Appetizers, snacks, hors d'oeuvres—however you treat them, they are delicious.

Stir-fried Thai noodles (*pad thai*) are often served as an appetizer in Thai restaurants. This is a colorful dish of fried rice noodles and shrimp accompanied by fresh vegetables like crispy bean sprouts and banana blossoms.

Another appetizer which will tantalize the palate is fish cakes (*taud man pla*), which are especially good when served with refreshing cucumber salad (*tam taeng*).

Satay, yet another popular appetizer, consists of curry-marinated chicken or beef strips charcoal-broiled on skewers. They are usually served with a peanut dipping sauce (*nam jim satay*) although other sauces can be served.

The huge variety of appetizers means that, whatever dishes are served later in the meal, a complementary appetizer can be served first, to ready the diner for the taste sensations to follow. Unlike Western-style cuisine, soup is not served as an appetizer in a Thai meal.

While a soup dish is included in a full Thai meal to provide liquid refreshment throughout the meal, soup is

PREVIOUS PAGES: SPICY MIXED VEGETABLE SOUP (TOP, RECIPE PAGE 40), CHICKEN COCONUT SOUP (BOTTOM, RECIPE PAGE 40) AND RICE SOUP WITH SHRIMP (RIGHT, RECIPE PAGE 41)

38

A WOMAN SELLING HATS ON A KLONG TAKES A FEW MOMENTS OFF TO ENJOY A BOWL OF SOUP

also used as a snack or a meal on its own. Rice soup is a favorite light nourishment at both the beginning and end of the day. Rice soup with pork (*khao tom moo*) and glass noodle soup (*gaeng jued woon sen*) are popular for breakfast. These and other light soups like Thai wonton soup (*geow nam moo*) are also used as snacks or as a light luncheon dish. Thai wonton soup contains wontons cooked in a thin salty stock, with bok choy and bean sprouts spiced up with green onions, cilantro and fried garlic.

Other soups served at lunchtime are more substantial. Red Sea noodles (*yen ta fo*), for example, is a striking noodle soup. A mouthful initially resonates with a salty and sour tone, punctuated by a slight note of sweetness. *Yen ta fo* contains pork, fish cakes, squid and fried wontons and is garnished with fried garlic.

A soup dish is also an essential part of a full Thai meal. Diners refresh their palates with small sips in-between the flavors of the various other dishes. A full Thai meal is an ensemble of distinctive flavors: the citrus freshness of lemon grass, mint and kaffir lime leaf; the aromatic freshness imparted by spices such as cardamon, star anise, turmeric and cinnamon; the pungency of garlic, ginger, cilantro and basil; and the fierce bite of chilies and pepper.

Soups play an important role in this symphony of flavors. Hot and sour shrimp soup (*tom yam goong*), for example, gives a taste that is sour, savory and hot. This

TRAYS OF BITE-SIZED SAVORY APPETIZERS FOR SALE
ON A ROADSIDE CART IN BANGKOK

refreshing and tart soup includes lemon grass and fresh lime juice. Tamarind flavor soup (*gaeng som pla chon*) is an orange-colored fish soup containing swamp cabbage. The color derives from dried chili peppers and the subtle sourness comes from tamarind juice. Another popular soup, chicken coconut soup (*tom kha gai*) bathes tender pieces of chicken in the silky creaminess of coconut milk. The "kha" in the name refers to galangal, a root which resembles ginger in appearance but its inimitable flavor contains a mint-like jolt.

FRIED EGG SOUP

Bangkok and the Central Plains

GAENG JUED KAI

แกงจืดไข่

Fried Egg Soup

Easy to prepare, this mild-flavored soup is a good accompaniment for any meal.

¼ cup (2 fl oz/60 ml) oil
4 garlic cloves (*kratiem*), chopped
½ cup chopped onions
6 eggs, beaten
6 cups (1½ qt/1.5 l) water
8 oz (250 g) pork, thinly sliced in 2-in (5-cm) lengths
⅓ cup (3 fl oz/90 ml) fish sauce (*nam pla*)
1 cup sliced cabbage
2 green onions/scallions/spring onions, cut into 1-in (2.5-cm) slices
¼ teaspoon white pepper

▨ Heat a small skillet and add half the oil. Fry the garlic until golden brown. Set aside the garlic, then fry the onion.
▨ In another small skillet, add the rest of the oil and fry the beaten eggs until golden brown, about 2 minutes on each side. Remove carefully, keeping in one piece, and set aside. When cool, cut into 1-in x 2-in (2.5-cm x 5-cm) strips.
▨ In a large saucepan, heat the water to boiling and add the pork. Reheat to boiling and when the pork is cooked add the egg strips, onion and the remaining ingredients. Remove to a serving bowl and top with the fried garlic before serving.

SERVES 4

Bangkok and the Central Plains

TOM KHA GAI

ต้มข่าไก่

Chicken Coconut Soup

A rich, aromatic dinner soup, which is enjoyed throughout the meal. Whenever possible, fresh kaffir lime leaves should be used, and their flavor and aroma is increased when they are torn instead of cut with a knife. Young galangal (kha orn) is pale yellow, with firm unwrinkled pink shoots. Fresh young ginger can be substituted if necessary, but the flavor will not be quite the same.

2 cups (16 fl oz/500 ml) coconut milk
6 thin slices young galangal (*kha orn*)
2 stalks lemon grass/citronella (*ta-krai*), lower ⅓ portion only, cut into 1-in (2.5-cm) lengths and crushed
5 fresh kaffir lime leaves (*bai ma-grood*), torn in half
8 oz (250 g) boned chicken breast, sliced
5 tablespoons (2½ fl oz/75 ml) fish sauce (*nam pla*)
2 tablespoons sugar
½ cup (4 fl oz/125 ml) lime juice
1 teaspoon black chili paste (*nam prik pow*) (see page 241)
¼ cup cilantro/coriander leaves (*bai pak chee*), torn
5 green Thai chili peppers (*prik khee noo*), crushed

▨ Combine half the coconut milk with the galangal, lemon grass and lime leaves in a large saucepan and heat to boiling. Add the chicken, fish sauce and sugar.
▨ Simmer for about 4 minutes, or until the chicken is cooked. Add the remaining coconut milk to the saucepan and heat just to boiling.
▨ Place the lime juice and chili paste in a serving bowl then pour the soup into the serving bowl.
▨ Garnish with the torn cilantro leaves and crushed chili peppers, and serve.

SERVES 4   *Photograph pages 36–37*

Bangkok and the Central Plains

GAENG LIANG

แกงเลียง

Spicy Mixed Vegetable Soup

A traditional soup, which in some variations is extremely hot and spicy. This version, however, is quite mild.

½ cup fresh shrimp/prawn meat, chopped
½ cup dried shrimp/prawns, chopped
8 shallots, chopped
2 tablespoons shrimp paste (*gapi*)
1 teaspoon white pepper
⅓ cup (3 fl oz/90 ml) fish sauce (*nam pla*)
4 cups (1 qt/1 l) water
½ cup chopped spinach, in 3-in (7.5-cm) lengths
½ firm fresh yellow gourd, cut into ½-in (1-cm) wedges
¼ cup bush basil leaves (*bai manglak*)

▨ Place the fresh and dried shrimp, shallots, shrimp paste and pepper in a mortar. Pound with a pestle until smooth. A blender can also be used.
▨ Place the fish sauce and water in a large saucepan, heat to boiling and add the blended mixture and the other ingredients. Stir thoroughly, bring to the boil and cook for 3 minutes. Remove to a soup tureen and serve.

SERVES 4   *Photograph pages 36–37*

DRIED FISH BELLY SOUP, GARNISHED WITH DRIED PUFFY PORKSKIN

Bangkok and the Central Plains

KHAO TOM GOONG

ข้าวต้มกุ้ง

Rice Soup with Shrimp

Rice soups are easy to prepare. Cooked rice is usually used, although uncooked rice will produce the same result, only over longer time. The use of different types of shellfish or fish can provide endless variations of this flavorful dish.

2 cups (16 fl oz/500 ml) water
2 stalks celery, chopped
¼ teaspoon white pepper
1 tablespoon Maggi seasoning
8 oz (250 g) shrimp/prawns, shelled, deveined
   and butterflied
1 cup steamed jasmine rice *(khao suay)* (see page 98)
2 tablespoons fish sauce *(nam pla)*
2 tablespoons oil
1 teaspoon thinly sliced garlic cloves *(kratiem)*
cilantro/coriander leaves *(bai pak chee)*, for garnish

✻ Heat the water to boiling in a large saucepan and add the chopped celery, white pepper and Maggi seasoning.
✻ Add the shrimp, rice and fish sauce.
✻ Heat to boiling and cook for 3 minutes, or until shrimp are cooked.
✻ Heat the oil in a small skillet and sauté the garlic until golden brown.
✻ Serve the soup with the fried garlic sprinkled over it and garnished with cilantro leaves.

SERVES 4   *Photograph pages 36–37*

Bangkok and the Central Plains

KAPAW PLA

กระเพาะปลา

Dried Fish Belly Soup

If fish belly is difficult to find you can substitute with dried puffy porkskin instead.

4 cups (1qt/l 1) water
1 whole chicken breast, about 1 lb (500 g)
8 oz (250 g) dried fish belly/fish maw, soaked in hot
   water until soft
⅓ cup (3 fl oz/90 ml) light soy sauce
1 tablespoon sweet soy sauce
½ cup bamboo shoot strips (see glossary)
¼ teaspoon white pepper
4 small hard-cooked/hard-boiled eggs, shelled and sliced
¼ cup cilantro/coriander leaves *(bai pak chee)*, minced

✻ Heat the water to boiling in a large saucepan and simmer the chicken breast for about 10–15 minutes or until done. Reserve the chicken stock.
✻ Place the cooked chicken breast in cold water to•cool. Remove the meat from the bone and discard the skin. Shred the meat and set aside.
✻ Drain the dried fish belly, squeeze out any excess water and cut into 1-in (2.5-cm) pieces.
✻ Heat the chicken stock to boiling, add the dried fish belly and all the remaining ingredients except the eggs and the cilantro. Stir in the shredded chicken and cook until hot. Pour into a serving bowl and garnish with egg slices and cilantro.

SERVES 4

41

CRISPY FISH SPICY SOUP

Bangkok and the Central Plains

TOM YAM PLA GROB

ต้มยำปลากรอบ

Crispy Fish Spicy Soup

In earlier times catfish were brought in from Cambodia. Today the grilled crispy fish are sold in markets throughout Thailand.

3 cups (24 fl oz/750 ml) water
8 oz (250 g) grilled crispy fish (see glossary)
4 thin slices galangal (*kha*)
4 shallots
4 dried jalapeño peppers (*prik chee fa haeng*)
2 garlic cloves (*kratiem*)
2 stalks lemon grass/citronella (*ta-krai*), halved
⅓ cup (3 fl oz/90 ml) fish sauce (*nam pla*)
½ cup (4 fl oz/125 ml) tamarind juice (*ma-kaam piag*)
  (see glossary)

▧ Heat the water to boiling in a large saucepan. Meanwhile, break the fish into 2-in (5-cm) pieces.
▧ Place the galangal, shallots, peppers, garlic and lemon grass on top of a charcoal grill and broil/grill until they are slightly burned. Allow to cool then crush using a mortar and pestle.
▧ Add with the fish and all the other ingredients to the boiling water and simmer for 20 minutes.

SERVES 4

Bangkok and the Central Plains

GAENG JUED PAKKAAD DONG

แกงจืดผักกาดดอง

Chinese Mustard Pickle Soup

Sips of soup between other dishes cleanse the palate for the interplay of flavors that is so much a part of a Thai meal. This one is a very refreshing soup. Chinese mustard pickles are available from Asian food stores.

1 tablespoon oil
4 garlic cloves (*kratiem*), minced
4 cups (1 qt/1 l) water
1 lb (500 g) pork ribs, cut into 2-in (5-cm) pieces
1 lb (500 g) Chinese mustard pickle, cut into 2-in
  (5-cm) pieces
¼ cup (2 fl oz/60 ml) fish sauce (*nam pla*)
¼ teaspoon white pepper

▧ Heat a small skillet and add the oil. Stir-fry the garlic until golden brown. Reserve the garlic.
▧ Heat the water to boiling and add the pork ribs. Cover and simmer for 15 minutes.
▧ Mix in the Chinese mustard pickle pieces, the fish sauce and the pepper, stirring until warmed through.
▧ Remove to a serving bowl and top with the fried garlic.

SERVES 4

CHINESE MUSTARD PICKLE SOUP (BOTTOM) AND
THAI WONTON SOUP (TOP, RECIPE PAGE 44)

Bangkok and the Central Plains

GEOW NAM MOO

เกี๊ยวน้ำหมู

Thai Wonton Soup

Wonton soup is a delicious light meal. Both the wonton fillings and the soup vegetables can be varied according to personal preference.

2 tablespoons oil
2 tablespoons chopped garlic cloves (*kratiem*)

FILLING FOR WONTONS

8 oz (250 g) ground/minced pork
1 teaspoon chopped garlic cloves (*kratiem*)
¼ teaspoon white pepper
1 teaspoon Maggi seasoning
2 tablespoons fish sauce (*nam pla*)

8 oz (250 g) wonton wrappers
6 cups (1½ qt/1.5 l) water
1 lb (500 g) pork or chicken bones
3 tablespoons fish sauce (*nam pla*)
1 teaspoon salt
8 oz (250 g) bok choy, cut into 1-in (2.5-cm)
    lengths, diagonally
8 oz (250 g) bean sprouts
2 green onions/scallions/spring onions, cut into 1-in
    (2.5-cm) lengths
¼ cup chopped cilantro/coriander leaves (*bai pak chee*)

▓ Heat the oil in a small skillet and fry the garlic until golden brown. Set aside.
▓ Combine the filling ingredients. Fill each wonton wrapper with 1 heaped teaspoon of filling then fold it in half, sealing the edges with water. To complete the wonton, form some pleats by pinching the edge above the meat filling.
▓ Heat the water to boiling in a large saucepan and simmer the pork bones for 5 minutes. Discard the bones, reserving the stock.
▓ Heat another large pot of water to boiling. Add the wontons and cook for 30 seconds, then remove them with a strainer and add directly to the stock from the bones. Add the fish sauce and salt.
▓ Add the bok choy and reheat the soup to boiling.
▓ To serve, put a small bed of bean sprouts in a soup tureen. Spoon in the wonton soup and garnish with green onions and cilantro. Sprinkle with the fried garlic.

SERVES 4   *Photograph page 43*

Bangkok and the Central Plains

POH TAEK

โป๊ะแตก

Seafood Combination Soup

Vary this dish by adding or substituting other seafoods and adapting the number of chili peppers to taste. Its lovely aroma comes from the galangal and kaffir lime leaves.

2 ½ cups (20 fl oz/625 ml) water
2 stalks lemon grass/citronella (*ta-krai*), cut into 1-in
    (2.5-cm) slices
6 thin slices galangal (*kha*)
6 kaffir lime leaves (*bai ma-grood*), torn in half

TAMARIND FLAVOR SOUP (LEFT) AND
SEAFOOD COMBINATION SOUP (RIGHT)

3–4 green Thai chili peppers (*prik khee noo*)
2 green jalapeño peppers (*prik chee fa*)
4 oz (250 g) white fish fillets, cut into ½-in x 2-in (1-cm x
    5-cm) pieces
4 oz (250 g) squid, cleaned, scored and sliced
4 oz (250 g) large shrimp/prawns, with shells
4 oz (250 g) small crabs (2 small crabs), cleaned and cut in
    half with top shell removed
4 oz (250 g) mussels
4 oz (250 g) clams
3 oyster mushrooms, sliced
¼ cup (2 fl oz/60 ml) fish sauce (*nam pla*)
¼ cup (2 fl oz/60 ml) lime juice

▓ In a large saucepan heat the water, lemon grass, galangal, lime leaves and peppers to boiling.
▓ Add the prepared fish fillets, squid, shrimp, crabs, mussels, clams and mushrooms and boil for 30 seconds. Reduce the temperature and add the fish sauce and lime juice and stir carefully.
▓ Remove to an attractive serving bowl.

SERVES 4

Bangkok and the Central Plains

GAENG SOM PLA CHON

แกงส้มปลาช่อน

Tamarind Flavor Soup

Gaeng som pla chon is orange in color, with a sour and sweet taste given by the tamarind used in the recipe. This should be served with fried sun-dried fish (pla kem taud), *on page 122, and steamed jasmine rice* (khao suay), *on page 98.*

1½ lb (750 g) whole snapper
4 cups (1 qt/1 l) water
4 garlic cloves (*kratiem*)
8 shallots
6 large dried red jalapeño peppers (*prik chee fa haeng*)
1 teaspoon shrimp paste (*gapi*)
1 teaspoon salt
¼ cup (2 fl oz/60 ml) fish sauce (*nam pla*)

2 tablespoons sugar
⅓ cup (3 fl oz/90 ml) tamarind juice (*ma-kaam piag*)
  (see glossary)
8 oz (250 g) swamp cabbage or spinach, cut in 1-in
  (2.5-cm) lengths

▒ Clean the snapper and discard the head of the fish. Cut the fish in half and cut 4 steaks from the top half.
▒ Heat the water to boiling in a large pot and cook the tail half of the fish for about 5 minutes. Remove the fish, keeping aside the stock. Take the flesh off the fish and discard the other parts.
▒ Combine the flesh from the fish with the garlic, shallots, peppers, shrimp paste and salt in a processor and blend well.
▒ Heat the fish stock to boiling and add the fish steaks and the blended ingredients along with the fish sauce, sugar and tamarind juice. Cook at a slow boil until the fish steaks are done. When the fish steaks are cooked, add the swamp cabbage and cook until just done (about 15 seconds).
▒ Serve in individual bowls.

SERVES 4

RICE SOUP WITH PORK (LEFT) AND GLASS NOODLE SOUP (RIGHT)

Bangkok and the Central Plains

GAENG JUED WOON SEN

แกงจืดวุ้นเส้น

Glass Noodle Soup

The glass, or cellophane, noodles become translucent when cooked, giving this soup a most attractive appearance.

MARINADE

1 tablespoon fish sauce (*nam pla*)
1 tablespoon Maggi seasoning
2 garlic cloves (*kratiem*), minced
¼ teaspoon white pepper
1 teaspoon cornstarch/cornflour

8 oz (250 g) ground/minced pork
1 tablespoon oil
2 garlic cloves (*kratiem*), minced
4 cups (1 qt/1 l) water
2 oz (60 g) dried cellophane noodles (*woon sen*), soaked in
    warm water until soft
¼ cup (2 fl oz/60 ml) fish sauce (*nam pla*)
1 cup sliced cabbage
2 green onions/scallions/spring onions, cut into 1-in
    (2.5-cm) pieces
¼ cup minced cilantro/coriander leaves (*bai pak chee*)
¼ teaspoon white pepper

Mix together the ingredients for the marinade, then combine with the pork. Form the mixture into 1-in (2.5-cm) diameter meatballs, and set aside.
Heat the oil in a small skillet and fry the garlic until light golden brown. Remove, drain, and set aside.
Heat the water to boiling in a large saucepan, add the meatballs and reheat to boiling. Continue to cook until the meatballs rise to the surface. Add all the remaining ingredients except the fried garlic and heat to boiling. Carefully pour into a soup tureen and scatter the fried garlic on top.

SERVES 4

Bangkok and the Central Plains

KHAO TOM MOO

ข้าวต้มหมู

Rice Soup with Pork

A rice soup such as this one is usually the most substantial part of a Thai breakfast.

2 cups (16 fl oz/500 ml) water
1 tablespoon Maggi seasoning
¼ teaspoon white pepper
½ teaspoon galangal powder (*kha pon*)
2 stalks celery, chopped
8 oz (250 g) ground/minced pork
1 cup steamed jasmine rice (*khao suay*) (see page 98)
2 tablespoons fish sauce (*nam pla*)
2 tablespoons oil
1 teaspoon sliced garlic (*kratiem*)
cilantro/coriander leaves (*bai pak chee*), for garnish

Heat the water to boiling in a large pot and add the Maggi seasoning, white pepper, galangal powder and chopped celery.
Add the pork, rice and fish sauce. Stir thoroughly so that the ground pork is broken up, then heat to boiling and simmer until the pork is cooked.
Heat the oil in a small skillet and fry the garlic on medium-high heat until golden brown.
Carefully pour the rice soup into a serving bowl. Sprinkle the fried garlic slices over the top of the soup, and garnish with the cilantro leaves.

SERVES 4

Bangkok and the Central Plains

KHAO TOM PLA GAPONG

ข้าวต้มปลากะพง

Rice Soup with Red Snapper

This is a good dish for a light luncheon or snack, providing energy without being too heavy.

3 tablespoons oil
6 garlic cloves (*kratiem*), chopped
4 cups (1 qt/1 l) water
½ teaspoon powdered galangal (*kha pon*)
1 lb (500 g) red snapper or other firm-fleshed fish fillets,
    cut in 1-in (2.5 cm) slices
2 cups cooked rice
1 cup chopped celery
½ teaspoon white pepper
⅓ cup (3 fl oz/90 ml) fish sauce (*nam pla*)
¼ cup chopped green onions/scallions/spring onions
¼ cup chopped cilantro/coriander leaves (*bai pak chee*)

Heat a small saucepan and add the oil and garlic. Stir-fry the garlic until golden brown, remove the pan from the heat and set aside.
Add the water to a large saucepan and heat to boiling. Add the remaining ingredients except the green onions and cilantro and heat to boiling. Simmer until the fish is cooked.
Pour carefully into a serving bowl and garnish with the fried garlic and oil spread on the surface. Sprinkle with the green onions and cilantro.

SERVES 4

Bangkok and the Central Plains

Tom Yam Goong

ต้มยำกุ้ง

Hot and Sour Shrimp Soup

A subtle blend of hot and sour with citrus overtones, tom yam goong *is the most famous of all Thai soups. Each region has its own particular variation of the recipe.*

8 oz (250 g) shrimp/prawns, shelled and deveined, with
 shells reserved
3 cups (24 fl oz/750 ml) water
2 garlic cloves (*kratiem*), minced
5 kaffir lime leaves (*bai ma-grood*)
3 thin slices fresh or dried galangal (*kha*)
¼ cup (2 fl oz/60 ml) fish sauce (*nam pla*)

2 stalks lemon grass/citronella (*ta-krai*), lower ⅓ portion only,
 cut into 1-in (2.5-cm) lengths
2 shallots, sliced
½ cup sliced straw mushrooms
5 green Thai chili peppers (*prik khee noo*), optional
¼ cup (2 fl oz/60 ml) lime juice
1 teaspoon black chili paste (*nam prik pow*) (see page 241)
1 tablespoon chopped cilantro/coriander leaves (*bai pak chee*)

Rinse the prawn shells and place them in a large pot with the water. Heat to boiling, strain the broth and discard the shells.

Add the garlic, lime leaves, galangal, fish sauce, lemon grass and shallots to the stock, then the mushrooms and chili peppers, if using. Cook gently for 2 minutes.

Add the shrimp to the soup, and reheat to boiling. When the shrimp are cooked, place the lime juice and black chili paste in a serving bowl. Pour the soup into the bowl, stir, garnish with the cilantro leaves, and serve.

SERVES 4

SHRIMP PASTE FRIED RICE (LEFT) AND CRISPY OMELETS (RIGHT)

Bangkok and the Central Plains

KANOM BUENG YUAN

ขนมเบื้องญวน

Crispy Omelets

Originally from Vietnam, the Thai version of this recipe varies according to the availability of ingredients for the filling.

FILLING FOR OMELETS

2 tablespoons oil
8 garlic cloves (*kratiem*), chopped
1 lb (500 g) shredded coconut meat
1 lb (500 g) shelled shrimp/prawns
½ cup chopped salted dried turnip
½ cup (4 oz/125 g) ground roasted peanuts
½ cup chopped fried tofu (see glossary)
½ teaspoon white pepper
¼ cup cilantro/coriander leaves (*bai pak chee*)
1 cup bean sprouts

CRISPY OMELET BATTER

1½ cups (6 oz/185 g) rice flour
½ teaspoon baking soda/bicarbonate of soda

1½ cups (12 fl oz/375 ml) coconut milk
2 eggs
½ cup (4 fl oz/125 ml) water
1 teaspoon turmeric
¼ teaspoon salt
¼ cup (2 fl oz/60 ml) oil

▨ Heat a large skillet and add the oil, garlic, coconut meat, and shrimp and cook until the shrimp are almost done. Add all the remaining filling ingredients except the bean sprouts and continue to cook for 3 more minutes. When the filling is cooked, stir in the bean sprouts and remove from the heat. Set filling aside.

▨ Mix the omelet batter by combining all the ingredients and gently beating until smooth.

▨ Heat a 10-in (25-cm) skillet on medium-high heat and add just enough oil to coat the skillet, pouring out any excess.

▨ Pour in enough of the batter to coat the surface of the skillet, reducing the temperature if necessary. When the omelet is cooked remove it from the pan. Repeat until all the batter is used—makes 6–8 omelets.

▨ When all the omelets are cooked, divide the filling between them. Arrange it on one half of each omelet so that the rest of the omelet can be folded over to cover the filling.

▨ Carefully remove the omelets to a serving plate and serve with northeast cucumber salad (*tam taeng*), on page 176.

SERVES 6–8

Bangkok and the Central Plains

KHAO CLOOK GAPI

ข้าวคลุกกะปิ

Shrimp Paste Fried Rice

The salty shrimp paste which gives this fried rice its unique flavor is an essential ingredient in many Thai recipes.

½ cup (2 fl oz/60 ml) oil
½ cup (1 oz/30 g) dried shrimp/prawns
2 eggs, beaten
4 shallots, sliced
4 garlic cloves (*kratiem*), thinly sliced
½ cup shredded green mango
4 wedges lime
2 tablespoons oil
4 cups cooked rice
2 tablespoons shrimp paste (*gapi*)
3 tablespoons fish sauce (*nam pla*)

❧ Heat the oil to 375°F (190°C). Fry the shrimp for 30 seconds then remove and set aside.

❧ Pour out most of the oil, leaving 1 tablespoon. Pour the eggs into the pan and cook without stirring on medium heat. Carefully remove in one piece and set aside. Roll the egg sheet into a cylinder and slice thinly.

❧ Arrange the fried shrimp on the side of a serving plate and pile the egg strips on another section of the plate. Arrange the shallots, garlic, mango and lime wedges attractively on the same plate.

❧ Heat a large skillet, add the oil and then the rice, shrimp paste and fish sauce. Stir-fry until all the ingredients are well combined and heated through. Remove to a serving platter and serve with the condiment plate.

SERVES 4

Bangkok and the Central Plains

KHAO GRIAB PAAK MAW

ข้าวเกรียบปากหม้อ

Folded Rice Skin Dumplings

A very common and popular dish offered at the street markets of Bangkok and in the surrounding villages, this is a perfect snack for any time of day.

FILLING

1 tablespoon oil
8 oz (250 g) ground/minced pork
½ cup (4 oz/125 g) ground roasted peanuts
4 garlic cloves (*kratiem*), minced
¼ cup chopped cilantro/coriander leaves (*bai pak chee*)
½ teaspoon white pepper
3 tablespoons fish sauce (*nam pla*)
2 tablespoons sugar

6 garlic cloves (*kratiem*), chopped
¼ cup (2 fl oz/60 ml) oil
24 Thai rice papers
½ cup coriander/cilantro leaves (*bai pak chee*)

❧ Heat a medium skillet and add the oil, then add the rest of the filling ingredients. Cook on medium-high heat until the pork is cooked and the liquid is all reduced and clinging to the other ingredients. Set aside.

❧ Using a small skillet, fry the garlic cloves in the ¼ cup of oil until golden, then discard the garlic, reserving the garlic oil.

❧ Prepare a steaming pot using a large pot of boiling water 2–3 in (5–7.5 cm) deep. Cover the top of the pot with a piece of wet muslin cloth and tie around the rim with string to keep the surface taut. Cut a 2-in (5-cm) opening near the edge to release the steam.

❧ Moisten each sheet of rice paper with water and cut to size, making circles 5 in (12.5 cm) in diameter, and then place on the muslin surface to heat for 1–2 minutes. Remove and place on a plate. Repeat, stacking with a layer of wax/greaseproof paper between each one.

❧ When the rice skins are ready, spoon on 1 teaspoon of the filling on each. Use a small paddle or the handle of a spoon to fold the rice skin in half to cover the filling. Overlap the sides and crimp around the edges softly to give it shape. As each dumpling is made, remove it to a plate and brush with the garlic oil to keep it from sticking to the others.

❧ To serve, wrap each dumpling in a small piece of lettuce and eat with cilantro on the side.

SERVES 4

CRISPY NOODLES (TOP, RECIPE PAGE 50) AND
FOLDED RICE SKIN DUMPLINGS (BOTTOM)

Bangkok and the Central Plains

MEE GROB

หมี่กรอบ

Crispy Noodles

Originally a village favorite, this dish then became popular in the cities.

4 cups (1 qt/1 l) oil
6 oz (200 g) rice vermicelli *(sen mee)*

SAUCE

½ cup (4 fl oz/125 ml) vinegar
½ cup (4 oz/125 g) sugar
1 teaspoon salt
1 teaspoon tomato paste
3 tablespoons garlic pickle *(kratiem dong)* (see page 245)

GARNISH

2 eggs, beaten (optional)
¼ cup chopped green onions/scallions/spring onions
¼ cup chopped red bell pepper/capsicum
⅛ cup 1-in (2.5-cm) lengths chopped chives
4 oz (125 g) fried tofu, cut into small pieces (see glossary)
1 tablespoon chopped cilantro/coriander leaves *(bai pak chee)*

In a deep-fryer or wok, heat the oil to 375°F (190°C) and fry the rice vermicelli until puffed. Remove and set aside.
Combine the sauce ingredients in a large skillet and cook for 4 minutes over medium heat, until of syrupy consistency.
If desired, fry the beaten eggs in a small pan. When cooked remove carefully and slice into thin strips. Set aside.
Add the noodles to the pan and mix quickly with the sauce so that they are evenly coated. Place on a serving dish and sprinkle with the garnish. Serve immediately.

SERVES 4   *Photograph page 49*

Bangkok and the Central Plains

PO PIA SOD

ปอเปี๊ยะสด

Fresh Spring Rolls

These rolls are not fried and so are ideal for the health-conscious.

12 spring roll wrappers
12 leaves green leaf lettuce/Chinese lettuce
3 Chinese sausages, cut into ½-in (1-cm) cubes
1 cup fried tofu (see glossary)
1 cucumber, peeled, cut into ½-in (1-cm) strips
2 cups bean sprouts, blanched
2 cups spinach, blanched
½ cup (4 fl oz/125 ml) peanut sauce *(nam jim satay)*
  (see page 238)

Steam the spring roll wrappers. Place one wrapper on a flat surface, then place a 6-in (15-cm) square piece of lettuce leaf on the lower portion of the wrapper. Arrange a twelfth of each of the Chinese sausage, tofu, cucumber, bean sprouts and spinach on top of the lettuce leaf.
Roll the bottom of the wrapper up, bring the sides in and continue to roll all the way up. Repeat for the rest of the wrappers.
Slice the rolls and serve with the peanut sauce.

SERVES 4

FRESH SPRING ROLLS (LEFT) AND SPRING ROLLS (RIGHT, RECIPE PAGE 52)

Bangkok and the Central Plains

PO PIA TAUD

ปอเปี๊ยะทอด

Spring Rolls

These spring rolls are a perfect appetizer for any meal and they are also a favorite when entertaining.

2 tablespoons oil
1 teaspoon minced garlic *(kratiem)*
8 oz (250 g) ground/minced pork
2 cups grated carrots
2 cups chopped celery
¼ cup (2 fl oz/60 ml) fish sauce *(nam pla)*
1 tablespoon Maggi seasoning
2 tablespoons sugar
⅛ teaspoon white pepper
1 cup bean sprouts
20 spring roll wrappers
2 egg yolks, beaten
3 cups (24 fl oz/750 ml) oil, for deep-frying

▓ Heat a large skillet and add the oil, garlic and pork. Sauté until the pork is cooked.
▓ Add the carrots, celery, sauces, sugar and pepper. Cook for 1 minute on high heat to reduce the sauce. Drain whatever liquid is left from the pan.
▓ Allow the filling to cool, then add the bean sprouts to the filling.
▓ Place a wrapper as a diamond with a corner towards you. Place 2 tablespoons of the filling in the lower portion of the wrapper. Fold the corner up, rolling once. Bring the sides in and brush the upper portion of the wrapper with egg yolk.
▓ Roll the wrapper up, sealing the entire spring roll. Fill and roll up the rest of the wrappers in the same way.
▓ Heat the oil to 350°F (180°C) and deep-fry the spring rolls in batches until golden brown all over, turning as needed.
▓ Serve with a sweet and sour sauce or other dip of your choice.

SERVES 4   *Photograph page 51*

Bangkok and the Central Plains

MEE GA-THI

หมี่กะทิ

Coconut Noodles

Vendors with carts sell these noodles around Bangkok. People can buy a little to eat as a snack or buy more for a complete meal.

1 lb (500 g) rice vermicelli *(sen mee)*
2 tablespoons oil
1 cup (8 oz/250 g) wedged tomatoes
1 lb (500 g) shrimps/prawns, shelled and deveined
½ lb (250 g) pork, cut in 1-in (2.5-cm) slices
3 cups (24 fl oz/750 ml) coconut milk
¼ cup (2 fl oz/60 ml) yellow bean sauce *(tao jeow)*
5 shallots, sliced
½ cup tofu, cut in 1-in (2.5-cm) cubes
2 tablespoons fish sauce *(nam pla)*
½ cup (4 oz/125 g) sugar
1 lb (500 g) bean sprouts
½ cup 1-in (2.5-cm) lengths chopped chives

▓ Soak the rice vermicelli for 30 minutes in water to cover, then drain and set aside.

COCONUT NOODLES

▓ Heat a large skillet and add the oil and tomatoes; cook on medium-high heat for 5 minutes and add the noodles. Cook until the noodles are soft, then set aside in a large serving dish.
▓ Combine the remaining ingredients, except the chives, in a large skillet and cook on medium-high heat for 5 minutes. Garnish with the chives and pour the mixture over the noodles.

SERVES 8

Bangkok and the Central Plains

PAD THAI

ผัดไทย

Stir-Fried Thai Noodles

One of Thailand's best known noodle dishes. It is eaten as a light meal at any time of the day or night, and is especially popular at the night markets throughout the country.

8 oz (250 g) rice noodles *(sen lek)*
3 tablespoons oil
3 garlic cloves *(kratiem)*, minced
¼ cup dried shrimp/prawns
¼ cup (2 fl oz/60 ml) fish sauce *(nam pla)*
¼ cup (2 oz/60 g) sugar
2 tablespoons tamarind juice *(ma-kaam piag)* (see glossary)
1 tablespoon paprika
½ cup fried tofu (see glossary)
2 tablespoons dried unsalted turnip, cut into small pieces
1 egg, beaten
¼ cup 1-in (2.5-cm) lengths chopped chives
¼ cup (2 oz/60 g) ground roasted peanuts
1 cup bean sprouts

STIR-FRIED THAI NOODLES

GARNISH

½ cup bean sprouts
½ cup chopped chives
¼ small banana blossom, cut into strips
½ lime, cut into wedges

▧ Soak the rice noodles in cold water for 30 minutes, or until soft. Drain, and set aside.

▧ Heat a large skillet until hot, then add the oil. Add the garlic and dried shrimp, and stir-fry. Add the noodles and stir-fry until translucent. It may be necessary to reduce the heat if the mixture is cooking too quickly and the noodles stick.

▧ Add the fish sauce, sugar, tamarind juice and paprika. Stir-fry the mixture until thoroughly combined. Stir in the tofu, turnip and egg.

▧ Turn the heat to high and cook until the egg sets, stirring gently. Thoroughly combine the mixture, and continue cooking over medium-high heat for about 2 minutes until most of the liquid is reduced.

▧ Mix in the chives, peanuts and bean sprouts. Place on a serving dish, arrange the bean sprouts, chives, banana blossom and lime attractively and serve.

SERVES 4

COCONUT RICE

The North

KHAO SOI

ข้าวซอย

Chiang Mai Noodles

These fine egg noodles, which also come in a flat form, are a favorite fresh noodle dish from Lam Poon Lam Pang to Chiang Mai. They can be eaten as part of a luncheon or just as a light snack.

2 tablespoons oil
3 garlic cloves (*kratiem*), crushed
3 shallots, chopped
4 cups (1 qt/1 l) coconut milk
2 tablespoons curry powder
1 tablespoon red curry paste (*nam prik gaeng ped*)
  (see page 236)
8 oz (250 g) beef, cut into 1-in (2.5-cm) cubes
½ cup (4 fl oz/125 ml) fish sauce (*nam pla*)
¼ cup (2 oz/60 g) sugar
½ teaspoon turmeric
1 tablespoon lime juice
3 cups (24 fl oz/750 ml) water
6 oz (185 g) fresh thin egg noodles (*ba mee*)
1 green onion/scallion/spring onion, chopped
1 tablespoon chopped cilantro/coriander leaves (*bai pak chee*)

GARNISH

2 shallots, sliced
½ lime, cut into wedges
¼ cup sliced Chinese mustard pickles

▒ Heat a large saucepan and add the oil. When the oil is hot, stir-fry the garlic and shallots for 30 seconds. Add the coconut milk, curry powder, red curry paste and then the beef. Heat to boiling, reduce to medium heat and simmer for approximately 30 minutes.

▒ Add the fish sauce, sugar, turmeric and lime juice. Stir to combine all the ingredients and bring to a slow boil. Continue to cook for 10 minutes.
▒ In a medium saucepan, heat the water to boiling. Stir in the fresh noodles and cook for 1 minute in rapidly boiling water. Drain the noodles and place in a serving bowl.
▒ Pour the curry mixture over the noodles and top with the green onion and the cilantro. Serve with the garnish ingredients arranged on the side.

SERVES 4

Bangkok and the Central Plains

KHAO MAN

ข้าวมัน

Coconut Rice

When this dish is served it is usually accompanied by papaya salad (som tam Esan) on page 172, with dried shrimp served on the side. A lunch dish only, this is an example of palace style dining.

4 cups jasmine rice
1 cup (8 fl oz/250 ml) water
3 cups (24 fl oz/750 ml) coconut milk
1 teaspoon salt
2 tablespoons sugar

▒ Rinse the rice in running water until the water stays clear. Place the water, coconut milk, salt and sugar in a large saucepan.
▒ Add the rice and heat to boiling on high heat, stirring to prevent the rice from sticking to the bottom of the pan.
▒ Cover and simmer until the rice is tender and cooked through.

SERVES 4

Bangkok and the Central Plains

GUAY TEOW RAAD NAA

ก๋วยเตี๋ยวราดหน้า

Wide Noodles with Cream Sauce

This recipe produces a dish similar to Western fettucine dishes. The stir-fry method is easy, while other meat and vegetable combinations can be used to take advantage of regional abundances.

MARINADE

1 tablespoon cornstarch/cornflour
1 egg
2 teaspoons Oriental sesame oil
½ teaspoon white pepper
1 tablespoon Maggi seasoning

8 oz (250 g) pork loin, thinly sliced
8 oz (250 g) wide rice noodles (*sen yai*) or other noodles
¼ cup (2 fl oz/60 ml) oil
2 tablespoons sweet soy sauce
1 tablespoon crushed garlic (*kratiem*)
1 cup (8 fl oz/250 ml) water
3 tablespoons fish sauce (*nam pla*)
2 tablespoons sugar
2 tablespoons cornstarch/cornflour, mixed in a little water
1 cup broccoli flowerets
½ cup sliced carrots
¼ cup sliced red bell pepper/capsicum
½ cup sugar peas/snow peas
¼ cup straw mushrooms
1 green onion/scallion/spring onion, cut in 1-in (2.5-cm) pieces

Mix together the marinade ingredients and pour over the pork slices, turning to make sure all surfaces are coated. Marinate pork for 10 minutes.
Soak the noodles in warm water until soft—about 10 minutes—then drain.
Heat a large skillet, add half the oil and stir-fry the noodles with the sweet soy sauce. Stir continually as these noodles are apt to stick. When thoroughly mixed, remove and set aside.
Heat a large saucepan, add the rest of the oil, garlic, water, fish sauce and sugar. Add the pork and heat the mixture to boiling. Add enough cornstarch mixture to form a medium-thick sauce.
Add all the remaining ingredients and reheat the mixture to boiling, cooking for 3 more minutes. Pour the mixture over the noodles and serve.

SERVES 4

Bangkok and the Central Plains

GUAY TEOW NUEA

ก๋วยเตี๋ยวเนื้อ

Noodles with Meatballs

A hearty noodle dish, this can also be served as a complete meal. Either use the instructions for meatballs contained in the recipe for glass noodle soup (gaeng jued woon sen) on page 46 or purchase the meatballs from an Asian grocery store.

3 tablespoons oil
6 garlic cloves (*kratiem*), minced
1 lb (500 g) wheat noodles
1 lb (500 g) bean sprouts, blanched
1 cup chopped celery, blanched

SAUCE

6 cups (1½ qt/1.5 l) water
1 lb (500 g) meatballs
8 oz (250 g) beef, cut into ⅛-in (3-mm) thick slices
8 garlic cloves (*kratiem*), minced
½ cup chopped cilantro/coriander roots (*raak pak chee*) and leaves (*bai pak chee*)
½ teaspoon white peppercorns
6 clusters of star anise (about 8 pods per cluster)

56

6 whole cardamon
2 sticks cinnamon
1 teaspoon salt
2 tablespoons Maggi seasoning
¼ cup (2 fl oz/60 ml) light soy sauce
2 tablespoons sweet soy sauce
3 oz (90 g) palm sugar (*nam taan peep*)

Heat the oil in a small skillet and fry the garlic until golden brown. Remove contents from pan and set aside.

Cook the noodles in boiling water and drain, then place into a serving bowl and top with the bean sprouts and celery.
Heat the water to boiling and add the meatballs and beef. Secure the raw garlic, coriander, peppercorns, anise, cardamon and cinnamon in a piece of muslin and place in the same pot. Simmer for 20 minutes then remove the seasonings.
Stir in the remaining ingredients, and pour the mixture over the noodles. Sprinkle the fried garlic over the top before serving.

SERVES 6–8

NOODLES WITH MEATBALLS (LEFT), WIDE NOODLES WITH CREAM SAUCE (RIGHT)

RED SEA NOODLES

Bangkok and the Central Plains

YEN TA FO

เย็นตาโฟ

Red Sea Noodles

A favorite dish for lunch served by many restaurants and street vendors, this is a flavorful noodle dish which could also be used to make a complete and healthy meal for four. This is a good way to use up leftover wontons, fish balls and fish cakes, but they can also be purchased ready-made at Asian food stores.

8 wontons
1 cup (8 fl oz/250 ml) oil, for deep-frying
4 garlic cloves (*kratiem*), minced

SOUP

6 cups water
8 oz (250 g) pork loin, in one piece
1 teaspoon salt
8 oz (250 g) fish balls
4 oz (125 g) cleaned sliced squid
4 oz (125 g) sliced fish cakes

1 lb (500 g) wheat noodles
1 lb (500 g) swamp cabbage or spinach, cut into 4-in (10-cm) lengths and blanched
½ cup (4 fl oz/125 ml) fish sauce (*nam pla*)
½ cup (4 fl oz/125 ml) chili in vinegar (*prik dong*) (see page 241)
½ cup (4 oz/125 g) sugar
1 cup (8 fl oz/250 ml) ketchup/tomato sauce
2 cups fried pork skin/pork rind (*kaep moo*) (see page 74)

▩ Deep-fry the wontons in the oil at 350°F (180°C) for 2 minutes or until golden brown. Set aside.

▩ Pour 2 tablespoons of the oil into a small skillet and fry the garlic until golden brown. Remove the garlic and set it aside.
▩ Heat the water to boiling and cook the pork for 15 minutes or until done. Remove the pork and slice into thin pieces. Set aside, reserving the stock.
▩ Add the salt, fish balls, squid and fish cakes to the stock. Heat to boiling.
▩ While the pork is cooking, heat another large pot of water to boiling to cook the noodles. Boil the noodles just until tender, remove and divide between eight individual bowls. Add the cabbage to the individual bowls, dividing into eight equal servings.
▩ Place in each bowl 1 tablespoon each of the fish sauce, vinegar and sugar and 2 tablespoons ketchup. Stir to combine, adding an eighth of the soup and sliced pork. Top each bowl with a fried wonton and some fried pork skin. Serve immediately with the fried garlic sprinkled on top.

SERVES 8

Bangkok and the Central Plains

KANOM JEEN NAM PRIK

ขนมจีนน้ำพริก

Noodles in Sweet Curry Sauce

Celebrations, whether religious or personal, are an important part of Thai life. This is a dish served at celebrations like weddings or house-warmings.

1 cup (8 oz/250 g) dried mung beans, soaked in water to cover overnight
6 cups (1½ qt/1.5 l) water
1 lb (500 g) dried thin wheat noodles or fresh noodles
1 cup shrimp/prawn meat
4 cups (1 qt/1 l) coconut milk
¼ cup (2 fl oz/60 ml) red curry paste (*nam prik gaeng ped*) (see page 236)
½ cup (4 fl oz/125 ml) fish sauce (*nam pla*)
¼ cup (2 oz/60 g) sugar
¼ cup (2 fl oz/60 ml) lime juice
2 kaffir limes (*ma-grood*), cut into halves
½ cup chopped green onions/scallions/spring onions, in 1-in (2.5-cm) pieces
½ cup sliced garlic (*kratiem*), fried in oil until golden brown
1 cup chopped blanched swamp cabbage or spinach
¼ banana blossom, sliced thinly lengthwise
¼ cup dried Thai chili peppers (*prik khee noo haeng*), fried in oil until golden brown

▩ Drain the mung beans and steam in a steamer for 15 minutes or until soft. Remove and set aside.
▩ Heat the water to boiling and boil the noodles until soft, then drain and rinse in cold water. Lift a small amount of noodles up and twist them into a bundle. Repeat until all the noodles are in bundles and set aside on a large plate.
▩ Using a mortar and pestle, grind the steamed mung beans and shrimp meat together to form a smooth paste.
▩ Heat a large saucepan and add the coconut milk, red curry paste, fish sauce, sugar and shrimp and bean mixture and heat to boiling. Add the lime juice and limes and reheat to boiling.
▩ Toss in the green onions and half of the fried garlic.
▩ Arrange the swamp cabbage, banana blossom, chilies and the rest of the fried garlic over the bundles of noodles.
▩ Pour the curry sauce, including the limes, over the noodles and serve.

SERVES 4

NOODLES IN SWEET CURRY SAUCE (TOP) AND
STIR-FRIED WIDE NOODLES (BOTTOM, RECIPE PAGE 60)

Bangkok and the Central Plains

GUAY TEOW PAD SE-IEW

ก๋วยเตี๋ยวผัดซีอิ๊ว

Stir-Fried Wide Noodles

A popular luncheon dish in Bangkok, this is a drier, though equally delicious, version of the cream sauce style.

MARINADE

1 garlic clove (*kratiem*), minced
1 egg, beaten
1 tablespoon cornstarch/cornflour
1 tablespoon wine
1 tablespoon fish sauce (*nam pla*)
1 tablespoon oyster sauce
1 tablespoon sugar
1 teaspoon Oriental sesame oil
1/2 teaspoon white pepper

8 oz (250 g) beef, thinly sliced
8 oz (250 g) fresh rice noodles (*sen yai*), 1/2 in (1 cm) wide
2 tablespoons oil
1 tablespoon fish sauce (*nam pla*)
1 tablespoon sugar
1 tablespoon oyster sauce
1 tablespoon sweet soy sauce
1 cup broccoli flowerets
1/8 cup sliced carrot

▨ Mix together all the ingredients for the marinade, then combine with the beef. Marinate the beef for 10 minutes.
▨ Cook the noodles until tender in a large pot of boiling water.
▨ Heat a large skillet and add the oil. Stir-fry the beef until done.
▨ Add the noodles and all remaining ingredients. Continue to cook until liquid is reduced slightly and all ingredients are hot.

SERVES 4   *Photograph page 59*

Bangkok and the Central Plains

POO JAA

ปูจ๋า

Crab in Shell

A dish elegant enough for any party, showcasing the rich crab meat.

2 large whole crab shells, cleaned and cut in halves,
    or 4 small crab shells, cleaned
1 lb (500 g) crab meat
1 lb (500 g) ground/minced pork
6 garlic cloves (*kratiem*), minced
1/2 teaspoon white pepper
3 tablespoons Maggi seasoning
2 tablespoons fish sauce (*nam pla*)
6 eggs, beaten
4 cups (1 qt/1 l) oil, for deep-frying

▨ Dry the cleaned crab shells. Combine all the remaining ingredients except the eggs and oil.
▨ Stuff the filling mixture into the crab shell and place in a steamer. Steam for 20 minutes or until the filling is cooked. Remove the crab shells from the steamer.
▨ Heat the oil in a wok or deep skillet to 350°F (180°C). Dip each crab shell into the beaten egg and then deep-fry until golden brown.

SERVES 4

60

CRAB IN SHELL (TOP) AND BROILED MUSSELS WITH CHILI SAUCE (BOTTOM, RECIPE PAGE 62)

The South

HOI MA-LAENG POO POW

หอยแมลงภู่เผา

Broiled Mussels with Chili Sauce

Broiling over charcoal is a common method of cooking seafood. Because the cooking method is very simple it is the sauce that makes each dish unique.

2 lb (1 kg) mussels

DIPPING SAUCE

6 garlic cloves (*kratiem*), finely minced
8 green Thai chili peppers (*prik khee noo*), finely chopped
⅓ cup (3 fl oz/90 ml) fish sauce (*nam pla*)
½ cup (4 fl oz/125 ml) lime juice
3 tablespoons sugar
2 tablespoons chopped cilantro/coriander root
  (*raak pak chee*)
2 tablespoons chopped mint
2 tablespoons thinly sliced green onion/scallion/spring
  onion

▦ Clean the mussels well by scrubbing the shells and removing the beards. Broil/grill the mussels over charcoal until they open. Then turn each one over to broil the other side until the mussel is heated through.
▦ Combine all the dipping sauce ingredients.
▦ Each mussel is removed from its shell and dipped into the sauce before eating.
▦ Serve hot.

SERVES 4   *Photograph pages 60–61*

SHRIMP CAKES (TOP) AND SUN-DRIED SHRIMP (BOTTOM)

The South

GOONG HAENG YAM

กุ้งแห้งยำ

Sun-Dried Shrimp

These sun-dried shrimp act as a very good substitute for meat when a lighter dish is desired. Frequently they are served with a rice soup or just as a light meal with rice.

8 oz (250 g) dried shrimp
4 shallots, sliced
2 garlic cloves (*kratiem*), sliced
1 tablespoon sliced green Thai chili pepper (*prik khee noo*)
3 tablespoons fish sauce (*nam pla*)
¼ cup (2 fl oz/60 ml) lime juice
1 tablespoon sugar

▦ Soak the dried shrimp in water for 10 minutes, then drain.
▦ Combine the shrimp with the remaining ingredients and toss. Transfer to a serving plate.

SERVES 4

Bangkok and the Central Plains

TAUD MAN GOONG

ทอดมันกุ้ง

Shrimp Cakes

This is a dish not usually sold by the Bangkok street vendors—more often it is served in restaurants or in private homes.

1 lb (500 g) shrimp/prawns, shelled, deveined and cleaned
3 tablespoons red curry paste (*nam prik gaeng ped*)
  (see page 236)
2 eggs, beaten
3 tablespoons fish sauce (*nam pla*)
¼ cup (1 oz/30 g) cornstarch/cornflour
4 cups (1 qt/1 l) oil, for deep-frying

▦ Place the shrimp in a food processor with all the other ingredients, except the oil, and blend into a smooth paste.
▦ Heat the oil to 375°F (190°C). Form the paste into about 24 patties, each 2 in (5 cm) in diameter and ½ in (1 cm) thick. Drop the patties into the hot oil and deep-fry until they are golden brown and puffed.
▦ Serve with cucumber salad (*tam taeng*), on page 176.

SERVES 4

Bangkok and the Central Plains

PLA DOOK FOO NAM PRIK MA-MUANG

ปลาดุกฟูน้ำพริกมะม่วง

Puffy Catfish with Mango Sauce

A favorite deep-fried fish dish which is usually served as a first course. The mango sauce is a perfect accompaniment to the crispy flesh.

1 catfish, about 1½ lb (750 g), cleaned, retaining the head
1 egg, beaten
¼ cup (1 oz/30 g) cornstarch/cornflour
3 cups (24 fl oz/750 ml) oil, for deep-frying

MANGO SAUCE

½ cup shredded green mango
¼ cup sliced shallots
2 tablespoons chopped green Thai chili peppers
(*prik khee noo*)
3 tablespoons fish sauce (*nam pla*)
2 tablespoons lime juice
2 tablespoons palm sugar (*nam taan peep*)

green leaf lettuce/Chinese lettuce

Cook the catfish by steaming or broiling/grilling.

Shred the meat along either side of the backbone with a fork so that the surface is rough, then brush the fish with the beaten egg and roll it in the cornflour.

Heat the oil in a deep skillet to 350°F (180°C). Deep-fry the fish until it is golden and puffy. Remove and set aside.

Thoroughly combine all the ingredients for the mango sauce in a bowl.

Line a serving plate with the green leaf lettuce. Place the puffy fish on top of the lettuce and serve the mango sauce on the side.

SERVES 4

PUFFY CATFISH WITH MANGO SAUCE

The South

PLA MUK YANG

ปลาหมึกย่าง

Charcoaled Squid

The aroma of charcoal broiling squid to perfection attracts customers to the street stalls of many of the cities and small towns in this region. The flavor would be enhanced by any number of dipping sauces.

1 whole squid, about 1 lb (500 g)
2 tablespoons fish sauce (*nam pla*)
1 tablespoon soy sauce

SAUCE

6 garlic cloves (*kratiem*), minced
1 tablespoon chopped cilantro/coriander leaves (*bai pak chee*)
1 tablespoon chopped onion
3 tablespoons fish sauce (*nam pla*)
3 tablespoons lime juice
1 tablespoon palm sugar (*nam taan peep*)

▨ Cut open the squid and remove the entrails, leaving the tentacles intact. Remove the skin carefully.
▨ Place on a rack and charcoal-broil for 2 minutes on each side. Brush with the combined fish sauce and soy sauce during broiling to add color and more flavor.
▨ Mix together the sauce ingredients and pour into a bowl.
▨ Cut open the squid and remove the entrails, leaving the tentacles intact. Remove the skin carefully.

SERVES 4

Bangkok and the Central Plains

KANOM PANG NAA GOONG

ขนมปังหน้ากุ้ง

Shrimp Toast

Wonderful as an appetizer with your favorite sauce or dip, this recipe is also a delicious snack.

TOPPING

8 oz (250 g) minced shrimp/prawn meat
8 oz (250 g) ground/minced pork
4 egg yolks
1 tablespoon cornstarch/cornflour
4 garlic cloves (*kratiem*), minced
¼ teaspoon white pepper
1 tablespoon minced cilantro/coriander leaves (*bai pak chee*)

8 slices white bread, crust removed, and sliced in
   half diagonally
4 cups (1 qt/1 l) oil, for deep-frying

▨ Mix together all the topping ingredients. Spread one-eighth of the topping on each bread piece in an even layer.
▨ Heat the oil to 350°F (180°C) and deep-fry the bread until the topping is cooked and the bread is light golden brown, turning as required.

SERVES 4

NOODLES IN FISH CURRY SAUCE (LEFT, RECIPE PAGE 66),
SHRIMP TOAST (TOP) AND CHARCOALED SQUID (RIGHT)

PAN-STEAMED MUSSELS

Bangkok and the Central Plains

HOI MA-LAENG POO OB

หอยแมลงภู่อบ

Pan-Steamed Mussels

Mussels are a favorite shellfish of Thai cuisine. In this dish the flavor of lemon grass adds a fresh tang to the mussels.

4 lb (2 kg) mussels, cleaned and debearded
3 stalks lemon grass/citronella *(ta-krai)*, chopped
5 shallots, chopped
1 cup sweet basil leaves *(bai horapa)*
4 green jalapeño peppers *(prik chee fa)*, sliced
2 tablespoons fish sauce *(nam pla)*
2 tablespoons lime juice

Place all the ingredients in a large skillet and stir thoroughly. Then cover and steam for 5 minutes or until the mussels open and are hot. Remove to a serving plate and serve.

SERVES 4

Bangkok and the Central Plains

KANOM JEEN NAM YAA

ขนมจีนน้ำยา

Noodles in Fish Curry Sauce

Nam yaa is a medicinal soup using herbs such as lemon grass, lesser ginger, galangal and garlic. This recipe uses all of these ingredients and is considered a very healthy dish.

1 lb (500 g) thin wheat noodles

FISH CURRY SAUCE

2 lb (1 kg) fish or 1 lb (500 g) canned tuna
6 cups (1½ qt/1.5 l) water
6 tablespoons lesser ginger *(krachai)*, chopped
8 garlic cloves *(kratiem)*, chopped
2 tablespoons shrimp paste *(gapi)*
8 shallots, chopped
6 thin slices galangal *(kha)*, chopped
3 tablespoons chopped lemon grass/citronella *(ta-krai)*

8 dried jalapeño peppers (*prik chee fa haeng*), soaked in water until soft
4 cups (1 qt/1 l) coconut milk
½ cup (4 fl oz/125 ml) fish sauce (*nam pla*)

VEGETABLES

string beans
basil stems, with leaves (*bai horapa*)
bean sprouts
swamp cabbage or spinach
Chinese mustard pickles

▨ Heat a large pot of water to boiling and cook the noodles until just soft. Rinse and drain the noodles and arrange in eight small bundles on a large plate.
▨ If using fresh fish cut it into 2-in (5-cm) chunks. Heat the water to boiling and cook the fish for 10 minutes. Remove the fish and debone, retaining the shredded meat.
▨ Place the lesser ginger, garlic, shrimp paste, shallots, galangal, lemon grass and peppers in a mortar and blend with the pestle until smoothly mashed.
▨ In a large saucepan, heat the coconut milk, fish sauce and blended ingredients to boiling. Add the fish meat, boil again and cook for 5 minutes. Pour the entire mixture over the noodle bundles and arrange the raw vegetables and pickles around the plate.

SERVES 8   *Photograph pages 64–65*

Bangkok and the Central Plains

TAUD MAN PLA

ทอดมันปลา

Fish Cakes

Taud man pla *are eaten in many areas of Thailand, made with whatever fish is available. On the streets of Bangkok there are stands where these fish cakes are freshly made and cooked while you wait.*

8 oz (250 g) white fish fillets, minced
3 tablespoons red curry paste (*nam prik gaeng ped*) (see page 236)
2 tablespoons fish sauce (*nam pla*)
2 eggs, beaten
3 tablespoons cornstarch/cornflour
¼ teaspoon baking soda/bicarbonate of soda
6 kaffir lime leaves (*bai ma-grood*) or sweet basil leaves (*bai horapa*), very thinly sliced
3 cups (24 fl oz/750 ml) oil, for deep-frying

▨ Combine the fish with the next five ingredients in a food processor or mix thoroughly by hand. After the mixture is combined, continue to blend, adding the lime leaves. If using your hands, keep wetting them as you mix.
▨ Shape the mixture into 1-in (2.5-cm) thick patties about 2 in (5 cm) in diameter. Set aside on a tray until ready to fry.
▨ Heat the oil to 325°F (160°C) and deep-fry the fish cakes until light golden brown.
▨ Serve with cucumber salad (*tam taeng*), on page 176.

SERVES 4

STEAMED BLOODY CLAMS WITH DIPPING SAUCE
(LEFT, RECIPE PAGE 68) AND FISH CAKES (RIGHT)

Bangkok and the Central Plains

HOI KRAENG LUAK

หอยแครงลวก

Steamed Bloody Clams with Dipping Sauce

The flavor of the clams is balanced by the sweet and sour taste of the tamarind dip.

SAUCE

½ cup (4 fl oz/125 ml) tamarind juice (*ma-kaam piag*) (see glossary)
⅓ cup (3 fl oz/90 ml) fish sauce (*nam pla*)
¼ cup (2 oz/60 g) sugar
½ cup (4 oz/125 g) ground roasted peanuts
¼ cup minced green Thai chili peppers (*prik khee noo*)
½ cup cilantro/coriander leaves (*bai pak chee*), chopped

2 lb (1 kg) bloody clams in the shell (see glossary)
2 cups (16 fl oz/500 ml) water

▨ Place all the sauce ingredients in a small saucepan. Heat to boiling then simmer until the sauce is reduced by a quarter and is thick.
▨ Place the clams in a large pot with the water and heat to boiling. Continue to cook until the clams open. Remove to a serving platter, and serve with the dip in a bowl alongside.

SERVES 4   *Photograph page 67*

Bangkok and the Central Plains

KHAO MAN GAI

ข้าวมันไก่

Chicken Rice

Rice dishes like this are very popular as "lunch box" meals in Thailand. Although usually served as part of a complete meal, this is an ideal dish to be served for luncheon or a quick meal.

6 cups (1½ qt/1.5 l) water
1 chicken, about 3 lb (1.5 kg)
1 teaspoon salt
3 cups (1 lb 6 oz/700 g) jasmine rice
8 garlic cloves (*kratiem*), minced
½ teaspoon white pepper
¼ cup slivered ginger
1 teaspoon salt

SAUCE

¼ cup (2 fl oz/60 ml) yellow bean sauce (*tao jeow*)
¼ cup (2 fl oz/60 ml) lime juice
¼ cup minced garlic (*kratiem*)
¼ cup minced ginger
5 green Thai chili peppers (*prik khee noo*), chopped
¼ cup (2 fl oz/60 ml) light soy sauce
¼ cup (2 oz/60 g) sugar

1 cup cucumber slices
1 cup cilantro/coriander leaves (*bai pak chee*)

▨ Heat the water to boiling in a large steamer. Rub the chicken with salt and steam the chicken for about 45 minutes or until done. Reserving the liquid, remove the chicken and slice the meat. Set aside.

▨ Rinse the rice and drain. Measure 4 cups (1 qt/1 l) of the chicken stock and add to the rice in a medium saucepan. Heat the rice to boiling on high heat and boil for 2 minutes. Add the garlic, pepper, ginger and salt and stir into the rice. Cover and simmer for 10 minutes. More chicken stock may be added as needed if all the liquid is absorbed before the rice is cooked. Stir the rice after it is cooked.
▨ Thoroughly combine all the sauce ingredients. Arrange the slices of chicken with the rice on the side, garnished with the cucumber slices and cilantro leaves. Serve the sauce as a dip in a separate dish.

SERVES 6–8   *Photograph page 70*

The South

GAENG LUENG

แกงเหลือง

Light Yellow Curry

In the South, in the coastal regions, a great many fish dishes are served. Mackerel is found in quite a few of these recipes.

1 mackerel, or a number of smaller fish, about 1 lb (500 g), cleaned and sliced into 1-in (2.5-cm) steaks
6 cups (1½ qt/1.5 l) water
5 shallots
3 garlic cloves (*kratiem*)
1 teaspoon turmeric
1 tablespoon shrimp paste (*gapi*)
1 teaspoon salt
25 green Thai chili peppers (*prik khee noo*)
5 tablespoons (2½ fl oz/75 ml) fish sauce (*nam pla*)
2 tablespoons coconut sugar
⅓ cup (3 fl oz/90 ml) tamarind juice (*ma-kaam piag*) (see glossary) or lime juice
½ cup chopped string beans, in 1-in (2.5-cm) pieces
½ cup sliced bamboo shoots (see glossary), 1 in x 1 in x ⅛ in (2.5 cm x 2.5 cm x 0.3 cm) thick

▨ Dry the mackerel steaks with paper towels and set aside.
▨ In a blender place 1 cup (8 fl oz/250 ml) of the water, the shallots, garlic, turmeric, shrimp paste, salt and chilies. Blend until smooth.
▨ Pour this mixture into a large saucepan and add the remaining water. Heat to boiling and add the mackerel steaks, fish sauce, sugar, tamarind juice and the vegetables. Heat to boiling and reduce to medium heat. Continue cooking for 5 minutes, or until fish is cooked through. Serve hot with steamed jasmine rice (*khao suay*), on page 98.

SERVES 4

The South

PHLA HOI

พล่าหอย

Clam Salad

A popular appetizer with the people of the South, this recipe is served in many restaurants in the major cities of Thailand.

2 lb (1 kg) clams or mussels
¼ cup sliced lemon grass/citronella (*ta-krai*)
6 tablespoons sliced shallots

CLAM SALAD (TOP) AND LIGHT YELLOW CURRY (RIGHT)

1 tablespoon sliced kaffir lime leaves (*bai ma-grood*)
½ cup mint leaves
2 tablespoons chopped cilantro/coriander leaves (*bai pak chee*)
¼ cup chopped green onions/scallions/spring onions
5 green jalapeño peppers (*prik chee fa*), chopped
3 tablespoons fish sauce (*nam pla*)
3 tablespoons lime juice
1 bunch green leaf lettuce/Chinese lettuce

▓ Heat a large pot of water to boiling. Add the clams and cook for 2 minutes. Rinse them in cold water and remove the shells. Discard the shells.
▓ Place the clams in a bowl and add all the remaining ingredients except the green leaf lettuce. Toss to combine all ingredients.
▓ Serve on a platter lined with green leaf lettuce.

SERVES 4

The North

PEAK GAI YANG

ปีกไก่ย่าง

Barbecued Chicken Wings

This is a favorite barbecue recipe. The enticing aroma of the sizzling meat on the grill makes it very popular with the street vendors' clientele.

MARINADE

1 teaspoon salt
¼ cup chopped lemon grass/citronella *(ta-krai)*
8 garlic cloves *(kratiem)*, chopped
½ teaspoon white pepper
¼ cup minced cilantro/coriander root *(raak pak chee)*
1 teaspoon turmeric

1½ lb (750 g) chicken wings

▓ Combine all the marinade ingredients and marinate the chicken wings overnight. Barbecue the wings over medium coals for 5–7 minutes on each side until they are cooked through and golden brown.
▓ Serve with steamed sticky rice *(khao neow)*, on page 98.

SERVES 4

The North

NUEA SAWAN

เนื้อสวรรค์

Heavenly Beef

In this recipe the beef is first sautéed to dry it out and then deep-fried to give a crispy effect. The flavor is delicious.

MARINADE

3 tablespoons fish sauce *(nam pla)*
1 tablespoon soy sauce
1 teaspoon cilantro/coriander powder *(pak chee pon)*
  (see glossary)
3 tablespoons sugar

1 lb (500 g) sirloin or tenderloin/fillet beef, thinly sliced
2 cups (16 fl oz/500 ml) oil, for deep-frying

▓ Mix together the marinade ingredients and marinate the beef for about 10 minutes.
▓ Heat a skillet and cover with a thin coating of oil. Pan-fry the meat and marinade until the marinade is reduced.
▓ Heat the rest of the oil in another pan and deep-fry the beef on medium heat in small batches until the pieces float to the top. Serve with steamed sticky rice *(khao neow)*, on page 98.

SERVES 4

The North

KHAO NEOW NUEA

ข้าวเหนียวเนื้อ

Sticky Rice with Beef

The beef is sun-dried and then deep-fried. It is especially tasty served with the sticky rice of the North.

STICKY RICE WITH BEEF (TOP) AND HEAVENLY BEEF (BOTTOM)

½ cup (4 fl oz/125 ml) fish sauce *(nam pla)*
3 tablespoons sugar
2 tablespoons cilantro/coriander powder *(pak chee pon)*
  (see glossary)
2 lb (1 kg) tender beef, sliced into thin 4-in x 4-in
  (10-cm x 10-cm) squares
3 cups (24 fl oz/750 ml) oil, for deep-frying
4 cups steamed sticky rice *(khao neow)* (see page 98)

▓ Mix together the fish sauce, sugar and cilantro powder, and add the beef. Marinate for 20 minutes. Arrange the pieces of beef on a rack and allow to dry in the hot sun for half a day. Turn the pieces over and sun-dry for another half a day. Alternatively, bake the beef strips at 325°F (165°C) for 25 minutes.
▓ Heat the oil to 350°F (180°C). Deep-fry the beef for 2–3 minutes. Serve with the sticky rice.

SERVES 6–8

Bangkok and the Central Plains

NUEA SATAY

เนื้อสะเต๊ะ

Satay Beef

Satays are one of Thailand's most popular appetizers.

MARINADE

⅓ cup (3 fl oz/90 ml) coconut milk
2 tablespoons fresh cilantro/coriander leaves *(bai pak chee)*
3 tablespoons sugar
1 tablespoon yellow curry powder
⅓ cup (3 fl oz/90 ml) fish sauce *(nam pla)*
1 tablespoon oil

8 oz (250 g) sirloin or flank steak, cut in long narrow
   strips 1 in (2.5 cm) wide and 3 in (7.5 cm) long

In a large bowl mix together all the ingredients for the marinade. Dip each piece of meat in the sauce and set aside. Cover and leave in refrigerator for 15 minutes.

Weave each strip of meat onto an 8-in (20-cm) skewer lengthwise.

Broil/grill for 5 minutes on each side or pan-fry. To pan-fry, brush a large non-stick pan with coconut milk or leftover marinade and pan-fry meat for 2–3 minutes on each side. Brush the meat with the sauce as it is turned.

Serve with peanut sauce *(nam jim satay)*, on page 238.

SERVES 4

Bangkok and the Central Plains

GUAY TEOW NUEA SAB

ก๋วยเตี๋ยวเนื้อสับ

Noodles with Ground Beef

This easy and delicious appetizer can also be served as a light meal.

1 lb (500 g) wide rice noodles *(sen yai)*, cooked
2 tablespoons sweet soy sauce
3 tablespoons oil
1 lb (500 g) ground/minced beef
8 garlic cloves *(kratiem)*, minced
¼ cup minced cilantro/coriander leaves *(bai pak chee)*
½ teaspoon white pepper
1 tomato, cut into wedges
½ cup sliced onions
¼ cup (2 fl oz/60 ml) fish sauce *(nam pla)*
2 tablespoons oyster sauce
1 tablespoon Maggi seasoning
3 tablespoons sugar
2 tablespoons cornstarch/cornflour, dissolved in ¼ cup
   (2 fl oz/60 ml) water
1 bunch green leaf lettuce/Chinese lettuce

Rub the noodles with the sweet soy sauce. Heat a large skillet with 2 tablespoons of the oil and stir the noodles continually until they are hot. Set the noodles aside.

Heat the rest of the oil in the same skillet and stir-fry the beef with the garlic until the beef is cooked. Add the next eight ingredients and heat to boiling.

Stir constantly, adding the cornstarch mixture to thicken.

Cover the base of a serving platter with green leaf lettuce. Arrange the noodles on top and pour the beef mixture over the noodles and serve.

SERVES 6–8

NOODLES WITH GROUND BEEF (TOP) AND SATAY BEEF (BOTTOM)

FRESH SAUSAGE (TOP) AND TAPIOCA PORK (BOTTOM)

The North

NAEM SOD

แหนมสด

Fresh Sausage

This sausage mixture is not served in a casing in the traditional manner. The ground mixture can be served with a side salad of fresh vegetables or with green lettuce leaves to use as wrappers.

4 cups (1qt/1 l) water
8 oz (250 g) pork skin/pork rind
8 oz (250 g) ground/minced pork
4 garlic cloves (*kratiem*), sliced
¼ cup slivered ginger
½ cup (2½ oz/75 g) whole roasted peanuts
¼ cup fried dried Thai chili peppers
   (*prik khee noo haeng*)
¼ cup (2 fl oz/60 ml) fish sauce (*nam pla*)
¼ cup (2 fl oz/60 ml) lime juice
¼ cup chopped green onions/scallions/spring onions
¼ cup chopped cilantro/coriander leaves (*bai pak chee*)

◪ Heat the water to boiling in a medium saucepan and add the pork skin. Reheat to boiling then simmer for about 40 minutes or until the pork skin is tender.
◪ Remove the pork skin from the water, allow to cool, then slice into very thin 2-in x ¼-in (5-cm x 6-mm) strips.
◪ In a medium skillet on medium-high heat, cook the ground pork for about 4 minutes or until it is done, stirring to break up the meat.
◪ Combine the pork skin strips, ground pork and remaining ingredients except the green onion and cilantro. Place the mixture on a serving dish and sprinkle the green onion and cilantro on top.
◪ Serve with lettuce leaves and garnish if desired.

SERVES 4–6

Bangkok and the Central Plains

SA-KOO SAI MOO

สาคูไส้หมู

Tapioca Pork

Enjoy this as a snack or as a first course for four to six people.

2 tablespoons oil
½ cup garlic cloves (*kratiem*), minced
1 lb (500 g) ground/minced pork
3 tablespoons fish sauce (*nam pla*)
¼ cup (2 oz/60 g) sugar
¼ cup chopped salted turnip
1 cup (8 oz/250 g) ground roasted peanuts
8 oz (250 g) small pearl tapioca
½ cup (2 oz/60g) cornstarch/cornflour

ACCOMPANIMENTS

green leaf lettuce/Chinese lettuce
chopped green Thai chili peppers (*prik khee noo*)
cilantro/coriander leaves (*bai pak chee*)

◪ Heat the oil in a medium skillet, then add the garlic. Fry for 30 seconds, then remove half the garlic and reserve.
◪ Add the pork to the remaining garlic and oil and stir-fry until cooked. Add the fish sauce, sugar, turnip and peanuts. Mix well to combine, then reduce heat and stir until the sauce is absorbed. Remove from heat and allow to cool.
◪ Cover the tapioca pearls with warm water and soak for about 30 minutes, or until swollen. Drain. Add the cornstarch and mix with hands to form a soft dough.
◪ With wet hands pinch off about 1 tablespoonful of dough and shape into a 2-in (5-cm) diameter circle. Center 1 teaspoonful of the pork mixture on the circle then seal by wrapping the dough around the filling. Continue until all the dough is used.
◪ Heat some water to boiling in a large pot, then add the tapioca balls. Cook for 3–4 minutes, or until the dough is translucent, on high heat. Drain.
◪ Serve the tapioca balls on the lettuce, with the chilies, cilantro and reserved cooked garlic. The diners sprinkle these on each tapioca ball, which is wrapped inside a lettuce leaf.

MAKES 24 BALLS

The North

KAEP MOO

แคบหมู

Fried Pork Skin

Beautifully crisp pork skin's flavor is enhanced by a tasty dip.

4 cups (1 qt/1 l) water
1 lb (500 g) pork skin/pork rind, cut in 2-in x 2-in
   (5-cm x 5-cm) squares
1 teaspoon salt
4 cups (1 qt/1 l) oil, for deep-frying

◪ Heat the water to boiling in a large saucepan. Add the pork skin and return to the boil. Reduce heat and simmer for 40 minutes or until the pork skin is soft and tender. Drain. Rub with the salt.
◪ Place the cooked pork skin on a rack in a 350°F (180°C) oven and bake for 30 minutes or until it is dry.
◪ Heat the oil to 375°F (190°C) and deep-fry the pork skin until crisp. Serve with your favorite dipping sauce.

SERVES 4

FRIED PORK SKIN (LEFT), CHARCOAL-BROILED
PORK NECK (TOP, RECIPE PAGE 76) AND FRIED
NORTHEAST SAUSAGE (BOTTOM, RECIPE PAGE 76)

The Northeast

SAI GROG TAUD

ไส้กรอกทอด

Fried Northeast Sausage

This northeastern sausage specialty is most often fried to bring out the flavor of the meat, retaining the juices within the casing. It is often served with vegetables, which perfectly complement the spiciness of the sausage.

1 cup (8 fl oz/250 ml) oil
1 lb (500 g) northeast sausages *(sai grog Esan)* (see page 140)

ACCOMPANIMENTS

⅓ cup (2 oz/60 g) roasted peanuts
¼ cup sliced ginger
¼ cup sliced shallots
¼ cup sliced lemon grass/citronella *(ta-krai)*
¼ cup sliced green Thai chili peppers *(prik khee noo)*

▩ Heat a large skillet and add the oil. Use medium-high heat to bring the oil to approximately 350°F (180°C).
▩ Place half the sausages in the skillet and slowly fry for 6 minutes, turning the sausages to cook evenly. Remove and set aside. Cook the other sausages in the same manner.
▩ Slice the sausages and place on a serving plate. Combine the accompaniments and arrange beside the sausages.

SERVES 6   *Photograph page 75*

The Northeast

KAW MOO YANG

คอหมูย่าง

Charcoal-Broiled Pork Neck

In the Northeast not much food is wasted and every part of an animal is used. This is an easy recipe, with a dip that enhances the flavor of the broiled meat.

1 pork neck, 1 lb (500 g)

MARINADE

6 garlic cloves *(kratiem)*, minced
3 tablespoons minced cilantro/coriander root *(raak pak chee)*
1 teaspoon white pepper
2 tablespoons sugar
2 tablespoons soy sauce
2 tablespoons fish sauce *(nam pla)*

DIPPING SAUCE

2 tablespoons fish sauce *(nam pla)*
1 tablespoon sliced green Thai chili pepper *(prik khee noo)*
1 tablespoon sliced garlic *(kratiem)*
2 tablespoons lime juice
1 tablespoon sliced shallot
1 tablespoon chopped cilantro/coriander leaves *(bai pak chee)*
1 tablespoon chopped green onion/scallion/spring onion

▩ Place the pork neck in a dish with the combined marinade ingredients. Let stand for 15 minutes.
▩ Charcoal-broil for 10 minutes on each side or bake at 350°F (180°C) for 30 minutes. While this is cooking combine the dipping sauce ingredients.
▩ Slice the meat and place on a platter; serve with the dipping sauce.

SERVES 4   *Photograph page 75*

Bangkok and the Central Plains

KHAO MOO DAENG

ข้าวหมูแดง

Barbecued Pork with Rice

A delicious accompaniment to any noodle dish as well as being an appetizer, this recipe is easy to prepare.

2 lb (1 kg) pork, cut into 2-in x 6-in (5-cm x 15-cm) strips

MARINADE

6 garlic cloves *(kratiem)*, minced
½ teaspoon white pepper
1 cup (8 fl oz/ 250 ml) soy sauce
½ cup (3 oz/90 g) brown sugar
1 teaspoon red food coloring

GRAVY

2 tablespoons oil
¼ cup minced garlic cloves (*kratiem*)
½ teaspoon salt
½ cup (4 oz/125 g) ground roasted peanuts
½–1 cup (4–8 oz/125–250 ml) pan juices from pork
2 tablespoons cornstarch/cornflour dissolved in
  3 tablespoons water

4 cups steamed jasmine rice (*khao suay*) (see page 98)
1 cup cucumber slices
6–8 green onions/scallions/spring onions
½ cup cilantro/coriander leaves (*bai pak chee*)
½ cup (4 fl oz/125 ml) chili in vinegar (*prik dong*)
  (see page 241)

▩ Combine the pork strips with the combined marinade ingredients and marinate for 30 minutes. Place the strips on a rack in a baking pan and bake at 350°F (180°C) for 45 minutes. Reserve

all the pan juices for making the gravy, but skim off some of the fat. If the pan juices from the pork are too diluted reduce the sauce to achieve a greater concentration of flavor.

▩ To prepare the gravy, heat a small skillet and add the oil. Fry the garlic until golden brown. Add the remaining ingredients, stirring in the cornstarch and water mixture. Heat to boiling. Set aside.

▩ Slice the pork. Place a portion of cooked rice on each plate. Arrange slices of pork around the rice and pour some gravy over the pork. Garnish with cucumber slices, green onion and cilantro leaves. Serve with the chili in vinegar. If the pork and gravy are served on a platter with the garnish the rice must be served separately.

SERVES 6–8

BARBECUED PORK WITH RICE

CHIANG MAI SAUSAGE (LEFT) AND EGG NOODLES
WITH BARBECUED PORK (RIGHT)

The North

SAI OUA

ไส้อั่ว

Chiang Mai Sausage

The North is famous for the many varieties of sausages made there.

1 lb (500 g) ground/minced pork
1 teaspoon salt
¼ cup minced garlic cloves (*kratiem*)
¼ cup chopped cilantro/coriander leaves (*bai pak chee*)
¼ teaspoon canned peppercorns
¼ cup (2 fl oz/60 ml) lime juice
1 tablespoon chopped lemon grass/citronella (*ta-krai*)
½ teaspoon galangal powder (*kha pon*)
1 tablespoon chopped shallot
1 tablespoon shrimp paste (*gapi*)
1 teaspoon finely chopped green Thai chili pepper (*prik khee noo*)
1 sausage casing for 1 lb (500 g) meat

▓ Combine the ground pork with the other ingredients. Push the filling into the sausage casing, being careful not to stuff it too firmly. Tie the sausage into 4-in (10-cm) lengths and leave in the refrigerator overnight to allow the flavors to blend.
▓ The sausages can be fried or broiled for 4–5 minutes on each side until done. Serve with sticky rice (*khao neow*), on page 98.

SERVES 6–8

Bangkok and the Central Plains

BA-MEE MOO DAENG

บะหมี่หมูแดง

Egg Noodles with Barbecued Pork

The pork topping is also good on its own, served with hot mustard.

STOCK

2 lb (1 kg) pork bones
8 cups (2 qt/2 l) salted water

MARINADE

4 garlic cloves (*kratiem*), minced
½ teaspoon white pepper
¼ cup cilantro/coriander leaves (*bai pak chee*), minced
1 cup (8 fl oz/250 ml) soy sauce
½ cup (4 oz/125 g) sugar
1 teaspoon red food coloring

2 lb (1 kg) pork tenderloin, cut into thin strips
8 bunches (1 lb/500 g) fresh egg noodles (*ba mee*)
1 lb (500 g) bok choy, sliced and blanched
1 cup bean sprouts, blanched
½ cup (4 fl oz/125 ml) fish sauce (*nam pla*)

▓ Simmer the pork bones in the salty water for 15 minutes. Strain, and skim off the fat, leaving a clear soup stock.
▓ Combine the marinade ingredients with the pork, leave for 1 hour. Bake at 350°F (180°C) for 45 minutes. Cool, slice.
▓ Boil the egg noodles quickly, then drain. Divide the noodles, bok choy and bean sprouts between eight serving bowls.
▓ Place 1 tablespoon of fish sauce in each bowl. Divide the sliced pork between the bowls and pour 1 cup (8 fl oz/250 ml) of soup stock over each bowl before serving.

SERVES 8

SAUSAGE IN BANANA LEAF

Bangkok and the Central Plains

KHAO KA MOO

ข้าวขาหมู

Pork Leg with Rice

The delicious sauce used to flavor the pork during the cooking process is also suitable for other types of meat.

SAUCE

4 cups (1 qt/1 l) water
1 cup (8 fl oz/250 ml) light soy sauce
½ cup (4 fl oz/125 ml) sweet soy sauce
¼ cup (2 fl oz/60 ml) Maggi seasoning
¼ cup (1½ oz/45 g) brown sugar
1 teaspoon salt
6 garlic cloves *(kratiem)*, minced
1 teaspoon white pepper
¼ cup cilantro/coriander leaves *(bai pak chee)*
⅛ teaspoon cardamon powder
⅛ teaspoon cinnamon
4 clusters of star anise

1 leg of pork, about 2 lb (1 kg), from the chump end
4 cups cooked jasmine rice *(khao suay)* (see page 98)
½ cup cilantro/coriander leaves *(bai pak chee)*

❊ Combine all the sauce ingredients in a large saucepan. Heat the sauce to boiling and add the leg of pork.
❊ Simmer on low heat for 1 hour or until the pork is tender.
❊ When the leg is cooked remove it from the saucepan and slice into thin pieces to serve.
❊ Divide the cooked rice onto individual plates then add some slices of pork to each one. Ladle some sauce over the rice and pork. Garnish with the cilantro leaves.

SERVES 6-8

The North

NAEM

แหนม

Sausage in Banana Leaf

Throughout the markets of Bangkok there are vending carts selling these individually wrapped sausages. They are usually sold in neatly wrapped bundles, to be unwrapped and eaten with vegetables and sticky rice.

FILLING

1 lb (500 g) pork skin/pork rind
¼ cup whole green Thai chili peppers *(prik khee noo)*
¼ cup (2 fl oz/60 ml) lime juice
¼ teaspoon baking soda/bicarbonate of soda or saltpeter/sodium
   nitrite (as a curing agent)
8 garlic cloves *(kratiem)*, minced
¼ teaspoon salt
¼ cup steamed sticky rice *(khao neow)* (see page 98)

8 oz (250 g) banana leaves

ACCOMPANIMENTS

¼ cup lime slices
¼ cup sliced green onions/scallions/spring onions
¼ cup sliced red jalapeño peppers *(prik chee fa daeng)*
¼ cup mint leaves
¼ cup (1¼ oz/40 g) roasted peanuts

❊ Boil the pork skin in water for 20 minutes to soften, then slice into small thin pieces.
❊ Mix with the rest of the filling ingredients and allow to stand for 30 minutes.
❊ Meanwhile, cut the banana leaves into eight 6-in (15-cm) square sections.
❊ Roll the meat filling into eight 1-in x 4-in (2.5-cm x 10-cm) sausage shapes.
❊ Place each sausage on a piece of banana leaf and roll up tightly. Roll with the grain of the banana leaf, making sure the rolls are very tight, to prevent air from getting in. Then tie both ends with plastic twine or strips of banana leaf.
❊ Allow to hang in a cool place, or store in a refrigerator, for 5–7 days.
❊ Serve using banana leaves to make small containers for each unwrapped sausage and some of each accompaniment, or present everything on a serving plate lined with green leaf lettuce/Chinese lettuce.

SERVES 4-6

PORK LEG WITH RICE

The North

KANOM JEEN NAM NGEOW

ขนมจีนน้ำเงี้ยว

Noodle Rib Curry

Noodles are second only to rice as a favorite staple and the great variety of noodles provides many taste delights. Curry noodles make a very satisfying meal.

3 tablespoons oil
8 garlic cloves (*kratiem*), chopped
¼ cup (2 fl oz/60 ml) red curry paste (*nam prik gaeng ped*)
   (see page 236)
2 lb (1 kg) pork ribs, cut into 1-in x 1-in
   (2.5-cm x 2.5-cm) pieces
2 tablespoons yellow bean sauce (*tao jeow*)
1 cup diced tomatoes
¼ teaspoon turmeric
⅓ cup (3 fl oz/90 ml) fish sauce (*nam pla*)
4 cups (1 qt/1 l) water
8 oz (250 g) egg noodles (*ba mee*), cooked
1 green onion/scallion/spring onion, chopped
¼ cup cilantro/coriander leaves (*bai pak chee*)

CONDIMENTS

1 cup bean sprouts
1 cup string beans, cut in 2-in (5-cm) pieces
½ cup chopped vegetable pickles

▩ Heat a small skillet, add 2 tablespoons of the oil and brown the garlic, then remove and set aside.
▩ Heat a large saucepan, add the rest of the oil and fry the curry paste for 3 minutes on medium heat. Add the pork ribs and bean sauce and continue to brown for 3 more minutes.
▩ Add the tomatoes, turmeric, fish sauce and water. Continue to cook for 15 minutes on medium-high heat.
▩ Separate the noodles into individual bowls, and spoon some of the soup mixture over them. Top with the green onion, cilantro leaves and all the condiments and carefully pour more soup on top before serving.
▩ Serve the browned garlic separately, to be added as desired for extra flavor.

SERVES 4–6

Bangkok and the Central Plains

KHAO PAD MOO BAI GA-PROW

ข้าวผัดหมูใบกะเพรา

Pork Fried Rice with Basil Leaf

Fried rice is a favorite food of Thailand. This version has a delicate aroma imparted by the flavor of the basil leaf.

3 tablespoons oil
4 oz (125 g) pork loin, thinly sliced
3 garlic cloves (*kratiem*), minced
½ cup sliced green jalapeño peppers (*prik chee fa*)
¼ cup sliced onions
4 cups cooked rice
⅓ cup (3 fl oz/90 ml) fish sauce (*nam pla*)
2 tablespoons sugar

1 tablespoon sweet soy sauce
¼ teaspoon white pepper
1 cup hot basil leaves (*bai ga-prow*)
1 small tomato, cut into wedges
½ cup sliced cucumber
4 green onions/scallions/spring onions, cut in 4-in
   (20-cm) lengths
1 carrot, thinly sliced

NOODLE RIB CURRY (LEFT) AND PORK
FRIED RICE WITH BASIL LEAF (RIGHT)

▓ Heat a large skillet until hot and add the oil. Add the pork,
garlic, peppers and onions and cook for 30 seconds. Add the
rice, fish sauce, sugar, soy sauce and pepper and continue to
cook until the rice is hot.

▓ Toss in the basil leaves and stir to combine. Remove to a serving
plate and garnish with tomato, cucumber, carrot and green onions.

SERVES 4

83

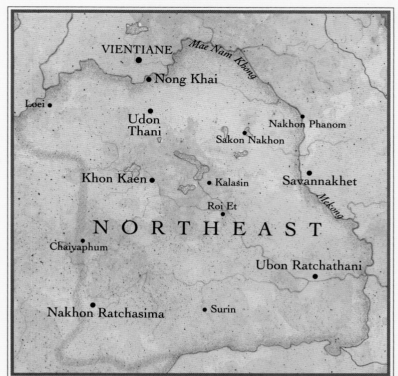

THE NORTHEAST

IN THE SUMMER of 1966 a young American student, the son of a former U.S. ambassador, happened to pass through an obscure hamlet called Ban Chiang in the northeastern province of Udon Thani. A road was being constructed in the area, and among the debris piled up along it the student noticed a large number of unusual pottery shards: buff-colored and adorned with bold, swirling red designs. He collected a few and brought them back to an art-collecting Thai princess with whom he was staying in Bangkok; she in turn showed them to a representative of an American museum, who thought they should be sent to the United States for precise dating.

Thus, quite accidentally, began one of the most exciting chapters in contemporary archeology. Later excavations by the Thai Fine Arts Department and the University of Pennsylvania revealed that an extraordinary prehistoric culture had flourished on Thailand's northeastern plateau, going back to nearly 4000 B.C. and numbering among its achievements the use of sophisticated bronze metallurgy as well as rice cultivation, fine pottery, and possibly even textiles. Indeed, some archeologists who worked on the site have become convinced that the so-called Ban Chiang culture ranks among humankind's first "cradles of civilization", thus challenging the traditional assumption of a gradual spread from the Middle East to Asia.

The findings are still incomplete, and many tantalizing mysteries remain about the people of Ban Chiang: where

ELEPHANTS AT THE ANNUAL SURIN ROUND-UP

PREVIOUS PAGES: PRASAT MUANG THAM, IN BURIRAM PROVINCE, BUILT BY THE KHMERS ONE THOUSAND YEARS AGO

JOHN HAY

THE FRIENDLY SMILE OF A FARMER BUSY AT WORK IN THE FIELDS

they came from, where they went, and why, with all their accomplishments, they never apparently developed an urban society. Enough is known, however, to dispel the old theory that Southeast Asia was a "cultural backwater", as a French historian once described it, and also to add a much-needed flavor of romance to the region the Thais call Esan.

For most of the present century, Esan, or the Northeast, has been known as Thailand's chronic problem region, in spite of the fact that it is almost a third of the country's total area and includes seven of the most populous provinces plus the second-largest Thai city, Khon Kaen. In many parts the soil is poor and yields only a subsistence livelihood for those who work it. Prolonged droughts are frequent; and when rain does come it often results in disastrous floods, especially along the Mekong River which serves as a border with Laos. Temperatures can also be extreme, ranging from some of the coldest in Thailand in provinces such as Loei, where it can drop to almost freezing, to some of the hottest, at more than 110 degrees Fahrenheit (over 43 degrees Celsius) recorded at Udon Thani. Despite considerable progress in recent years, real hardship is still more prevalent in the Northeast than in most other parts of Thailand, and many of its people are still forced to seek temporary employment in Bangkok, where they form the great majority of low-income construction laborers, taxi drivers, and domestic servants.

This was not always true. At the time of the Ban Chiang culture and probably for some time afterward, the Northeast was thickly forested and rich in animal life. In historical times, between the ninth and fourteenth centuries, it was an important center of Khmer culture, the remains of which constitute one of its principal tourist attractions today. The

great temple of Phimai, for instance, not far from the provincial capital of Nakhon Ratchasima, was linked by a direct road to Angkor and is artistically regarded as one of the finest examples of classical Khmer architecture. The recently restored Prasat Phanom Rung, near the Dongrek Mountains along the frontier of Cambodia, is another imposing ruin which has splendid stone figures and friezes; one of these, stolen in the 1960s, was retrieved from an American museum after a much-publicized protest a few years ago. Altogether there are more than thirty such sites scattered around the Northeast, and until Cambodia itself becomes accessible again they offer the best opportunity to view Khmer artistry outside a museum.

Following the decline of Khmer power in the fourteenth century, Thai kingdoms rose, ruling first from Sukhothai and then, for much longer, from Ayutthaya. Though the Northeast was theoretically under the control of both, and though armies sometimes marched through it to do battle in Laos and Cambodia, the region was actually as isolated as the far North and remained so even after Bangkok became the capital, its forests gradually diminishing and the life of its people growing steadily harder.

Immigrants filtered across the borders from both Laos and Cambodia, bringing various elements of those cultures; indeed, until recent years at least, ethnic Lao comprised the major part of the population in several large northeastern provinces, and there has long been an active trade across the Mekong River. Later Vietnamese refugees came in a series of waves, as well as hill tribes and other minority groups fleeing the turmoil in Indochina. Like elsewhere in Thailand, sizeable numbers of Chinese settled in the cities, where they opened businesses, became middlemen for the region's farmers, and added their own flavor to the ethnic mixture.

Though a railway line was built to link Bangkok with Nakhon Ratchasima in 1900 and extended eastwards to Ubon Ratchathani in 1926, and though an airmail service was started in the region in 1922—the first airmail service in all of Southeast Asia—travel in most of the Northeast remained difficult until relatively recent years. There were almost no paved roads as late as the early 1960s, only rutted tracks that became impassable during the rainy season, and few people from the capital ever went to the more distant

GLASS BRACELETS AND BEAD NECKLACES FROM THE BAN CHIANG PRE-HISTORIC CULTURE, SHOWN AT THE SUAN PAKAAD PALACE MUSEUM

LUCA INVERNIZZI TETTONI/PHOTOBANK

THE TEMPLE OF PRASAT HIN PHIMAI, NEAR KORAT, BUILT BY THE KHMERS IN THE LATE ELEVENTH AND EARLY TWELFTH CENTURIES

AN OPEN-AIR DUCK FARM, WHERE POULTRY IS RAISED
FOR MEAT RATHER THAN EGGS

provinces. When King Bhumibol Adulyadej and Queen Sirikit made a three-week tour of the northeastern provinces in the mid-1950s, it was the first time a ruling monarch had ever been seen by most residents. It also marked the beginning of the determined efforts to improve rural life that have characterized King Bhumibol's long rule.

At least one reason for the previous lack of development was a perceptible prejudice against northeasterners, especially on the part of Bangkok people. Many of their popular foods, too, were regarded as "strange" by sophisticated city dwellers, and in Bangkok northeastern restaurants tended to be very modest establishments tucked away on obscure side-streets, patronized mainly by immigrants from the region. When William Klausner, an American anthropologist, announced in 1955 that he was going to do ethnographic research in a northeastern village, he was strongly advised against it by several government officials who warned that "the area was remote, the food unpalatable, the women not very attractive". And the most telling criticism: "It wouldn't be sanuk", meaning it wouldn't be fun.

All these factors have powerfully influenced northeastern life and culture as it exists today. Having usually worked on their own land, however infertile it might be, typically northeasterners have a strong sense of independence which they are willing to assert; it is no accident that many of Thailand's most outspoken writers and politicians in modern times have come from Esan backgrounds. They are also resourceful, able to derive a livelihood (and also a distinctive cuisine) from meager resources. Not surprisingly, they have a fatalistic bent that helps them accept the natural disasters that

so often afflict them, but they are by no means gloomy or brooding. Like Thais everywhere, they have devised numerous local forms of amusement, from building huge rockets to fire in a ceremony believed to bring rain, to staging impromptu battles between two of the giant horned beetles native to the region. Despite the recent growth of several large northeastern cities, they are more than likely to live in a small village and to leave it only when forced by dire economic need; even after years of driving a Bangkok taxi or loading ships at the capital's port, northeasterners still think of the village as the home to be returned to one day.

Many northeasterners from the provinces along the Mekong River speak Lao as fluently as they do Thai, and those in the southern part speak Khmer. Northeastern food reflects the influence of both cultures as well, particularly the former, just as it reflects a past when staples were often unavailable. "Esan people eat anything," Bangkok residents often remark, and so it may seem to a finicky outsider invited for a meal in one of the more distant hamlets, for this is a region where little is wasted, however unusual. Fried grub worms or grasshoppers are likely to be offered as a snack, or perhaps grilled lizard, ant eggs, snail curry, or a dried semi-decayed fish of exceptional pungency (and also, to its many admirers, of exceptional flavor).

William Klausner, contrary to official warnings, managed to settle down quite happily in the northeastern village of his choice and ultimately to marry one of the local girls. He did, however, have certain problems with food at first. "I developed my own cooked variations of such staples as ... raw fermented fish and the cold salad of unripe papaya, raw

90

fermented fish, peppers, tomatoes, and onions. I soon became accustomed to glutinous rice but remained wary of cooked silkworms, frogs, crickets and red ants. It is often said that the way to a villager's heart is through speaking the village dialect and eating such favorite village staples as uncooked fermented fish. After sampling the latter, I decided to stress my linguistic ability," he wrote.

But such exotica is actually the exception rather than the rule, especially in larger communities where better supplies are available. Indeed, more and more frequently, one hears connoisseurs of Thai cuisine proclaiming that northeastern fare is the best in all the country. Typical Esan dishes can now be found on the menus of the smartest Thai restaurants in Bangkok, and many of those humble side-street food shops are crowded with well-dressed diners as well as taxi drivers. As in Laos (and also in northern Thailand) glutinous rice is the staple, eaten either as a base for other dishes or as a sweet when steamed in a hollow piece of bamboo with coconut milk and black beans. Typical Laotian herbs such as dill (called *pak chee Lao*, or Lao cilantro or coriander, by Thais) also often turn up as seasonings. Another popular dish of Lao origin is *khanom buang*, a thin crispy crepe stuffed with dried shrimp, bean sprouts, and other assorted ingredients, which requires considerable skill to prepare properly and is thus usually served only on special occasions.

Laab, spicy minced meat or chicken, is a specialty of the region—the methods of preparation varying from province to province—along with *som tam* (green papaya salad), barbecued chicken, *hor mok* (fish with curry paste and steamed in

BRIGHTLY COLORED UMBRELLAS SHADE MELONS FROM
THE SUN ON A ROADSIDE STALL

banana leaf), catfish curry, and entrails cooked in numerous ways. Since meat is often scarce in villages, freshwater fish and shrimps are the principal sources of protein, either in the fermented form that William Klausner found difficult to appreciate or cooked with herbs and spices. One of the great regional delicacies for those who live along the Mekong is a giant catfish called *pla buk*, which can reach 10 feet (3 meters) in length and weigh more than 550 pounds (250 kilograms). Perhaps in a sort of culinary reaction to their difficult lives, or perhaps merely because some of the traditional ingredients

A BOY FROM THE NORTHEAST TENDING HIS FAMILY'S BUFFALOES
AT THE END OF THE DAY

MICHAEL FREEMAN

JOHN HAY

A COLLECTION OF FRESHLY MADE SAUSAGES LOOPED
OVER A POLE FOR DISPLAY AT THE MARKET

needed strong seasoning to make them more palatable, northeasterners like their food not just spicy but very hot, and chili peppers are used with a greater abandon than almost anywhere else.

Certain foods are reserved for festivals and ceremonial days, among them a noodle dish called *khaw pun* made from non-glutinous rice flour. The noodles take a long time to prepare, and the long thin strands are said to resemble the sacred thread used in Brahmanical blessing ceremonies, giving them a special symbolic quality not regarded as proper for ordinary meals.

Cut off from the outside world, northeastern villagers in the past made most of the items needed in their daily life, from cooking pots and rice baskets to fish traps and textiles. Silk is probably the most noted regional handicraft, especially a subtly colored traditional form of tie-and-dye ikat known as *mudmee* which has been popularized in recent years by Queen Sirikit. (Pierre Balmain, who often designed for the Queen, once did an entire fashion collection based on *mudmee*.) Weaving and sericulture continued to be important home industries in this region long after they had declined in areas more exposed to Western culture, and to a large extent northeastern skills were responsible for the great Thai silk revival that took place shortly after the Second World War. One especially active weaving center was in a village called Pakthongchai just outside Nakhon Ratchasima, and it was here that Jim Thompson, the American who led the revival, supervised most of the dazzling silks produced for the original Broadway production of *The King and I*, a breakthrough exposure that brought international fame to the fabric. At that time, in the late 1940s, it took Thompson an exhausting eleven hours to reach his weavers by train and local bus from Bangkok; today it takes less than two hours. The company that Thompson founded maintains the largest hand-weaving silk facility in the world at Pakthongchai.

A number of factors were responsible for finally opening the Northeast to the outside world. One of the most important of these was a military and political leader named Field Marshal Sarit Thanarat, who came from the region himself—like many northeasterners, he also had close relatives across the border in Laos—and was determined to bring development to it when he came to power toward the end of the 1950s. Among his achievements was the construction of

the Friendship Highway, a joint Thai-American undertaking that linked Saraburi, just north of Bangkok, with Nakhon Ratchasima and thereby made travel to the Korat Plateau by car relatively easy for the first time. Sarit also launched many other projects to raise the standard of living in the Northeast, including rural electrification, much-needed reservoirs and expanded irrigation.

The Indochina War accelerated the building of more all-weather roads to move military equipment to sensitive areas along the Cambodian and Laotian borders. Several large American military bases were built during the conflict, pumping money into the region and virtually overnight turning once-sleepy provincial capitals like Ubon Ratchathani and Udon Thani into boomtowns. Though the Americans (and much of the money) disappeared in due course once the war had ended, some of the innovations they brought profoundly altered local ways of life.

Communist insurgents, too, played a role in awakening Bangkok authorities to northeastern needs. Esan's poverty made it a natural target for those trying to destabilize the government and for a time in the mid-1970s the area probably contained more openly discontented people than any other in the country. This problem was met by a number of enlightened military commanders—among them the future Prime Minister, General Prem Tinsulanonda—who recognized that greater prosperity was the key to winning the support of the people and who launched a massive campaign of development that continues today.

King Bhumibol Adulyadej, as already mentioned, became aware of northeastern problems early in his reign, and hundreds of royally initiated projects have resulted throughout the region. The royal family now maintains a residence at Sakon Nakhon which is used as a base when overseeing regional activities and when making regular visits to remote hamlets. Another, newer palace is located in mountainous Phetchabun at the western extremity of the Northeast, once a notorious center for insurgents but now a peaceful scenic area of farms and fruit orchards being promoted by local travel writers as "the Switzerland of Thailand".

Among the other signs of a renewed sense of purpose in the Northeast was the opening of a university in Khon Kaen, the first to be established outside the capital. Modern highways now connect every major provincial town, and there is regular air service within the region as well. An extensive reafforestation program, known as "Green Esan", is underway, and farmers are beginning to learn that while rice may have been the traditional crop of their forefathers, it is not necessarily the right one for a region where the rains often fail. Other crops may be better suited to local conditions—soya beans, vegetables, and fruit, for example—and may also bring a better income. Many of Thailand's avocados, a relatively recent introduction to local markets, are being grown on the Korat Plateau.

Tourism still ranks low on the list of income-earners, but an increasing number of outsiders are discovering that their preconception of the Northeast as a barren wasteland devoid of cultural or scenic interest is untrue. Though much of the region's original forest cover has been destroyed, some tracts still remain, particularly in a number of splendid national forests in the more mountainous areas. The best known, thanks to its easy accessibility to Bangkok, is Khao Yai, which covers more than 770 square miles (2,000 square

SILK WEAVING IS A HOME INDUSTRY IN THE NORTHEAST, THE BEST
KNOWN BEING THE TIE-AND-DYE IKAT KNOWN AS MUDMEE

kilometers) in four provinces and accounts for about a tenth of Thailand's total area of national parks and game preserves. Khao Yai offers usually cool fresh air, impressive scenery with evergreen tropical trees, native orchids, and waterfalls, and a chance to glimpse nearly all of the two hundred species of protected wildlife in Thailand, including elephants, tigers, deer, and a wide assortment of birds. In 1987 a herd of more than fifty wild elephants was spotted in the park, delighting conservationists who had doubted that such large numbers of the species still existed in Thailand.

Another extensive park is Phu Kadung in Loei province, centered on a mountain topped by a plateau of 23 square miles (60 square kilometers) of exceptional natural beauty. Though there is no road to the plateau and the ascent involves a strenuous four-hour climb, it is becoming a popular holiday destination for nature-loving (and athletic) student groups from Bangkok and elsewhere.

Others are coming to see the archeological sites, not only the great Khmer ruins mentioned previously but newer discoveries such as Ban Chiang, which now has an excellent museum displaying relics which were found in the excavations. A famous mountaintop Khmer temple called Khao Phra Vihar was awarded to Cambodia in a controversial decision by the World Court during the 1950s and remains inaccessible from the Thai side; if the political situation improves and visitors are once more allowed, this will undoubtedly be another major attraction.

The Tourism Authority of Thailand, which is actively promoting the Northeast, has helped to publicize a number of traditional festivals in the region. One is the Elephant Roundup, held every November in Surin province, when nearly two hundred of the huge animals take part in a four-hour show enjoyed by thousands of spectators. Surin people have long been noted for their skill at training elephants, which in former days they captured in the forests of Cambodia; that source, obviously, is no longer available, but Surin elephants and their enterprising mahouts appear in many parts of the country, including the streets of Bangkok, to earn a little money from performances.

Boon Bang Fais, or rocket festivals, are held in several northeastern provinces, though the most famous is undoubtedly the one in Yasothon province in May, just before rice is planted. Enormous rockets almost 30 feet (9 meters) long are fired at the peak of the lively celebrations, the purpose being to ensure a plentiful supply of rain as well as to provide an opportunity for villagers to enjoy themselves.

A more solemn occasion is *Khao Phansa* in July, marking the start of the three-month Buddhist Lent, or "Rains Retreat", when the monks are supposed to remain in their temples. This is of course observed throughout Thailand, but Ubon Ratchathani, in the heart of the Northeast, has become especially renowned for the huge imaginative candles carved by local people and paraded proudly through the streets in a two-day festival.

No longer isolated, no longer ignored by authorities in the capital, the Northeast is now a center of purposeful activity—"the region of the future", as one government official recently described it in a discussion of the role it will play when peace and economic stability return to the countries that share its borders. Already, in the space of just a few decades, its distinctive customs and cuisine are better known and more appreciated than ever before, and the time when "Esan" was a term heavily weighted with pejorative connotations may finally be drawing to an end.

SORTING CHILIES AT A MARKET IN BANGKOK

CURRIES AND MAIN COURSES

A TEEMING, NOISY SEA OF DUCKS AT ONE OF THE
FARMS THAT SUPPLY BANGKOK'S NUMEROUS MARKETS

THERE IS A SAYING that there are two seasons in Thailand: hot and hotter. What better way to thrive in the tropical warmth of this country than with a cuisine whose spicy heat helps to cool down the body.

The intensity of many curries owes itself to Thai chili peppers (*prik khee noo*).

Prik khee noo are found in Thailand's famous green curry (*gaeng keow wan gai*), whose cool, lime green color deceives the unwary diner tasting this most incendiary of Thai curries. Take a bite of green curry, and it bites back. But it can become habit-forming, and make you want to return for more. The green color comes from the fresh green jalapeño peppers and the smaller *prik khee noo*.

The perfect complement to the searing assault of chilies is rice, which is usually served at every meal. Thai jasmine rice, a long-grained rice, is the best choice of rice, possessing a faint fragrance like jasmine.

For those who favor milder curries, the choices are many. Red curry uses long red chili peppers and lemon grass, with an array of other spices and herbs. Equally flavorful, but less fiery, are some curries from central Thailand like Panaeng curry (*panaeng nuea*) and Massaman curry (*massaman nuea*).

All curry-making begins with the curry paste. In days past, when the lifestyle was more relaxed, time allowed the making of curry paste by each household from the freshest ingredients available, using a stone mortar and

PREVIOUS PAGES: BARBECUED CHICKEN (RIGHT, RECIPE PAGE 124), GREEN CURRY WITH CHICKEN AND THAI EGGPLANT (TOP LEFT, RECIPE PAGE 124) AND RED CURRY CHICKEN (LEFT, RECIPE PAGE 124)

pestle. Because each family devised its own recipe for the paste, the balance of ingredients was based upon personal taste, giving rise to subtle differences in the recipes, even though curries employ a common ingredient, chili peppers. Homemade curry paste is always the best because all the ingredients are fresh. But for those living in cities with their unrelenting schedules, prepared curry paste can be purchased at most markets.

In the making of fresh, traditional Thai curry paste, one first pounds the dried spices such as cumin and peppercorns in a mortar with a pestle. A visitor to a Thai village can hear the rhythmic pounding that accompanies this most time-consuming step in the curry-making process. The other ingredients, such as fresh or dried chilies, lemon grass, garlic and shallots, are incorporated to yield a smooth paste.

Most Thai curries, unlike Indian curries, are very easy to make because the cooking stage only requires a short time. Massaman curry *(massaman nuea)* is one of the few exceptions to this rule. Indian curries are usually simmered for many hours.

Curries, like other main courses, draw upon a rich variety of seafood, vegetables and meats.

Thailand's coastal regions yield an abundance of fresh fish, crab, shrimp, clams and mussels. The harvest from the land is similarly bountiful. In rural areas, villagers in long, narrow boats glide along shallow canals, selling a variety of produce at the floating marketplace. It is also a time to share the latest news of the day and is an important part of the people's social life.

For seafood and meat dishes, barbecuing is one of the most preferred cooking styles. Simple dips or sauces can be served on the side. Other cooking methods include frying and steaming. Seafood is also sun-dried: a visitor to a dried-fish stall can find anything from squid to prawns, all neatly laid out on platters.

The liquid essence of Thai cuisine is fish sauce *(nam pla)*, made by fermenting fish with salt. *Nam pla* is found in many Thai recipes, heightening the flavor of any meat, seafood or vegetable dish. Another key flavoring is shrimp paste *(gapi)*.

In a typical Thai dinner, at least four or five different dishes are served together, each having equal importance in the enjoyment of the meal. A nicely balanced meal would include a soup, a curry, a vegetable or salad dish, a seafood dish, perhaps a meat dish, and, of course, rice.

ROADSIDE FOOD STALLS IN BANGKOK OFFER THE PASSERBY
A SELECTION OF DELICIOUS CURRIES TO SAMPLE

JENNY MILLS

STEAMED JASMINE RICE

Bangkok and the Central Plains

KHAO SUAY

ข้าวสวย

Steamed Jasmine Rice

The wonderful aroma and subtle flavor of jasmine rice complement every dish perfectly. Thais cook rice almost instinctively—it is their staple food.

3 cups (1 lb/500 g) jasmine rice
3 cups (24 fl oz/750 ml) water

❊ Place the rice in a large saucepan. Rinse twice to clean the rice, draining thoroughly. Add the water to the rice.
❊ Cover the saucepan and heat to boiling. Allow to boil on high heat for 1 minute. Turn the temperature to low and steam for 10 minutes. Reduce the heat to the lowest setting and allow to steam for 10 minutes more.

SERVES 4

The North

KHAO NEOW

ข้าวเหนียว

Steamed Sticky Rice

Sticky rice is a glutinous rice eaten by the people of the North and Northeast. The rice is sometimes referred to as sweet rice because it has a sweet flavor. It is often used to make rice wine and vinegar.

4 cups (2 lb/1 kg) sticky rice

❊ Place the rice in a saucepan or bowl and add enough water to cover. Rub the rice between your hands several times and drain off the milky water. Add clean water and repeat the process until the water runs clear.
❊ Soak the rice overnight in enough water to cover or, to save time, the rice can be soaked in hot water for 3 hours before steaming, rather than overnight.
❊ Drain the rice and place in a cloth-lined steamer or in a steaming basket. Place the basket over a pot of boiling water, making sure that the basket does not touch the water. Cover the steamer and steam for approximately 30 minutes.

SERVES 4

Bangkok and the Central Plains

KAI LOOK-KUEY

ไข่ลูกเขย

Eggs with Tamarind Sauce

Whether just fried, used as toppings, or as an essential component of many desserts, eggs are a favorite food in Thailand. In this dish, deep-frying boiled eggs gives them a different texture while their flavor is enhanced by the accompanying sauce.

STEAMED STICKY RICE (TOP)
AND EGGS WITH TAMARIND SAUCE (BOTTOM)

4 cups (1 qt/1 l) water
6 eggs
2 cups (16 fl oz/500 ml) oil, for deep-frying
½ cup chopped shallots

TAMARIND SAUCE

½ cup (4 fl oz/125 ml) tamarind juice (*ma-kaam piag*)
  (see glossary)
½ cup (4 fl oz/125 ml) fish sauce (*nam pla*)
¼ cup (2 oz/60 g) sugar

※ Pour the water into a large pot and boil the eggs for 5 minutes.

※ Remove from the heat and plunge the eggs into cold water. Peel the eggs and set aside.

※ In a large saucepan heat the oil to 325°F (165°C). Dry the eggs and deep-fry them until they are golden brown. Remove and set aside. With the same oil, deep-fry the shallots until golden brown. Drain and set aside.

※ Combine all the ingredients for the sauce. Heat to boiling and simmer for 5 minutes.

※ To serve, cut the eggs in half, lengthwise. Pour the sauce over the eggs and sprinkle with the fried shallots.

SERVES 4

99

Bangkok and the Central Plains

GAENG KUA SAPPAROD

แกงคั่วสับปะรด

Pineapple Curry

The delicate sweet and sour flavor of this curry sauce comes from the pineapple. It is also delicious with mussels or smoked salmon instead of shrimp.

2 cups (16 fl oz/500 ml) coconut milk
1 cup crushed fresh pineapple
2 tablespoons red curry paste *(nam prik gaeng ped)* (see page 236)
¼ cup (2 fl oz/60 ml) fish sauce *(nam pla)*
1½ tablespoons sugar
8 oz (250 g) shrimp/prawns, shelled and deveined

▓ Combine all the ingredients except the shrimp in a large saucepan and heat to boiling.
▓ Add the shrimp, reheat to boiling and cook for about 3 minutes or until done.
▓ Serve with steamed jasmine rice *(khao suay)*, on page 98.

SERVES 4

The South

POO NEUNG

ปูนึ่ง

Steamed Crab with Hot Sauce

As soon as the fishing boats return to harbor in the South the locals want to taste the sweetness of the fresh crabs. Simple cooking methods allow the natural taste of these crabs to be enjoyed.

1 crab, about 2 lb (1 kg), cleaned

HOT SAUCE

8 garlic cloves *(kratiem)*, minced
10 green Thai chili peppers *(prik khee noo)*, minced
2 tablespoons finely chopped cilantro/coriander root *(raak pak chee)* and leaves *(bai pak chee)*
¼ cup (2 fl oz/60 ml) fish sauce *(nam pla)*
¼ cup (2 fl oz/60 ml) lime juice
2 tablespoons sugar

▓ Leaving the shell intact, place the crab in a large steamer and steam for 10 minutes on high heat. After the crab is cooked, remove and set aside.
▓ Prepare the hot sauce by combining all the ingredients in a small bowl. Use as a dipping sauce. Crack the crab and dip into the sauce before eating.

SERVES 4

STEAMED CRAB WITH HOT SAUCE (LEFT),
PINEAPPLE CURRY (TOP RIGHT) AND CLAMS WITH
CHILI SAUCE (BOTTOM RIGHT, RECIPE PAGE 102)

Bangkok and the Central Plains

HOI PAD NAM PRIK POW

หอยผัดน้ำพริกเผา

Clams with Chili Sauce

An easy cooking method gives delicious results. Mussels or other shellfish can be used as an alternative to clams or as an added extra.

2 tablespoons oil
1 teaspoon red curry paste (*nam prik gaeng ped*) (see page 236)
2 lb (1 kg) clams in their shells
2 tablespoons fish sauce (*nam pla*)
2 teaspoons sugar
¼ cup sliced green bell pepper/capsicum
¼ cup sliced red bell pepper/capsicum
1 tablespoon slivered fresh ginger
¼ cup sweet basil leaves (*bai horapa*)

❀ Heat a large skillet, add the oil and the curry paste and sauté the clams for 1 minute.
❀ Add the fish sauce, sugar, peppers, ginger and basil, stir thoroughly then cover the pan and cook for 6 minutes on medium heat.

SERVES 4   *Photograph pages 100–101*

Bangkok and the Central Plains

HAW MOK

ห่อหมก

Steamed Fish in Banana Leaf

While these folded packets are a delight to serve in small numbers, for a larger group the leaves can be folded into a large boat shape and the mixture steamed in larger portions with an extended cooking time.

1 lb (500 g) white fish fillets, cut into chunks

SAUCE

½ cup (4 fl oz/125 ml) red curry paste (*nam prik gaeng ped*)
   (see page 236)
2 cups (16 fl oz/500 ml) coconut milk
4 egg yolks (reserve whites for topping)
2 tablespoons fish sauce (*nam pla*)
2 tablespoons cornstarch/cornflour

TOPPING

1 cup (8 fl oz/250 ml) coconut cream
4 egg whites

1 large banana leaf, cut into 4 pieces, each 8 in x 8 in
   (20 cm x 20 cm)
1 cup shredded lettuce, blanched
1 cup sliced zucchini/courgette, blanched
1 cup sweet basil leaves (*bai horapa*)
2 green jalapeño peppers (*prik chee fa*), sliced
¼ cup cilantro/coriander leaves (*bai pak chee*)

❀ Marinate the fish chunks with the combined sauce ingredients and place in the refrigerator to chill for about 15 minutes.
❀ Beat the topping ingredients together with a fork.
❀ Wipe each piece of banana leaf with a damp cloth before use. Place a quarter of each of the blanched vegetables and of the fish in the center of each piece of banana leaf. Spoon on a quarter of the topping. Top with a scattering of basil leaves, pepper slices and cilantro leaves.
❀ Bring the sides of each square together and fold in the ends. Secure with a small piece of wood or a toothpick.

❀ Arrange the packets in a steamer and steam for 15 minutes or until done. Alternatively, the packets can be baked in the oven at 350°F (180°C) for 20 minutes.

SERVES 4

Bangkok and the Central Plains

PLA NEUNG KIAMBOUY

ปลานึ่งเกี้ยมบ๊วย

Steamed Whole Fish with Plum Pickles

Different methods of preparation are used to give variety to the abundance of fresh fish in Thailand. This recipe uses the popular method of steaming, and the saltiness of the plum pickles adds a unique flavor.

1 rock cod or other white-fleshed fish, about 1–1½ lb
   (500–750 g)
½ teaspoon salt
½ teaspoon ground white pepper
1 tablespoon fish sauce (*nam pla*)
1 tablespoon white wine
3 whole pickled plums, cut into small pieces
2 tablespoons slivered fresh ginger
2 green jalapeño peppers (*prik chee fa*), sliced
2 tablespoons lime juice

❀ Clean the fish, retaining the head, and make three slashes to the backbone on each side of the fish.
❀ Rub the fish with the salt and pepper and place on a steaming plate. Add all the other ingredients. Place in the steamer, cover, and steam for 30 minutes until the fish is cooked.

SERVES 4

The Northeast

GAENG NAW MAI

แกงหน่อไม้

Bamboo Shoot Curry

A delicious curry supplemented with fresh fish and enhanced with the flavor of pickled fish. More sauce can be added for a wetter curry.

CURRY PASTE

6 garlic cloves (*kratiem*), chopped
8 shallots, sliced
½ cup sliced green jalapeño peppers (*prik chee fa*)
1 stalk lemon grass/citronella (*ta-krai*), chopped
1 tablespoon chopped galangal (*kha*)

1 lb (500 g) pickled fish
2 cups (16 fl oz/500 ml) water
1 lb (500 g) freshwater fish fillets, cut into 2-in (5-cm) slices
1 cup sliced tender bamboo shoots (see glossary)
2 tablespoons fish sauce (*nam pla*)
3 tablespoons tamarind juice (*ma-kaam piag*) (see glossary)

❀ Prepare the curry paste by mashing the ingredients in a mortar with a pestle, or by combining in a blender, until a paste is formed. Set aside.
❀ Boil the pickled fish in the water for 10 minutes and strain to retain the juice. Discard the pickled fish. Add the curry paste to the fish stock and heat to boiling. Add all the other ingredients and reheat to boiling. Remove to a serving bowl.

SERVES 4

102   BAMBOO SHOOT CURRY (LEFT), STEAMED WHOLE FISH WITH PLUM
      PICKLES (FRONT) AND STEAMED FISH IN BANANA LEAF (TOP RIGHT)

Bangkok and the Central Plains

PLA KAPONG KEEMOW

ปลากะพงขี้เมา

Whole Fish with Garlic Sauce

Cooking a fish whole ensures that the flesh remains juicy, and the skin is crisp. The blending of the garlic with the flavors of the peppers provides a dish worthy for any celebration.

1 whole fish, about 1 lb (500 g), cleaned, head retained
½ cup (2 oz/60 g) all-purpose/plain flour
4 cups (1 qt/1 l) oil, for deep-frying

SAUCE

8 garlic cloves *(kratiem)*
¼ cup chopped green jalapeño pepper *(prik chee fa)*
¼ cup chopped red jalapeño pepper *(prik chee fa daeng)*
¼ cup chopped green onions/scallions/spring onions
¼ cup chopped cilantro/coriander root *(raak pak chee)*

3 tablespoons oil
⅓ cup (3 fl oz/90 ml) fish sauce *(nam pla)*
3 tablespoons sugar
3 tablespoons lime juice
¼ teaspoon white pepper
6 kaffir lime leaves *(bai ma-grood)*, torn in half
¼ cup sweet basil leaves *(bai horapa)*

Cut three slashes to the bone on both sides of the fish, then coat with flour on both sides. This will prevent it from sticking to the skillet and will also make the skin crisp.

Heat the oil in a wok or large skillet to 350°F (180°C). Carefully lay the fish in the oil and deep-fry for approx-imately 5 minutes. Turn the fish with the aid of a large spatula and deep-fry the other side for 5 minutes. Remove from the oil and set on a large plate.

Heat a medium skillet on medium-high heat, then add the oil and the blended sauce ingredients. Stir and cook for 3 minutes.

Add the fish sauce, sugar, lime juice and pepper and cook for a further 2 minutes. Stir in the lime leaves and the basil.

Pour the sauce over the fish and serve.

SERVES 4

WHOLE FISH WITH GARLIC SAUCE

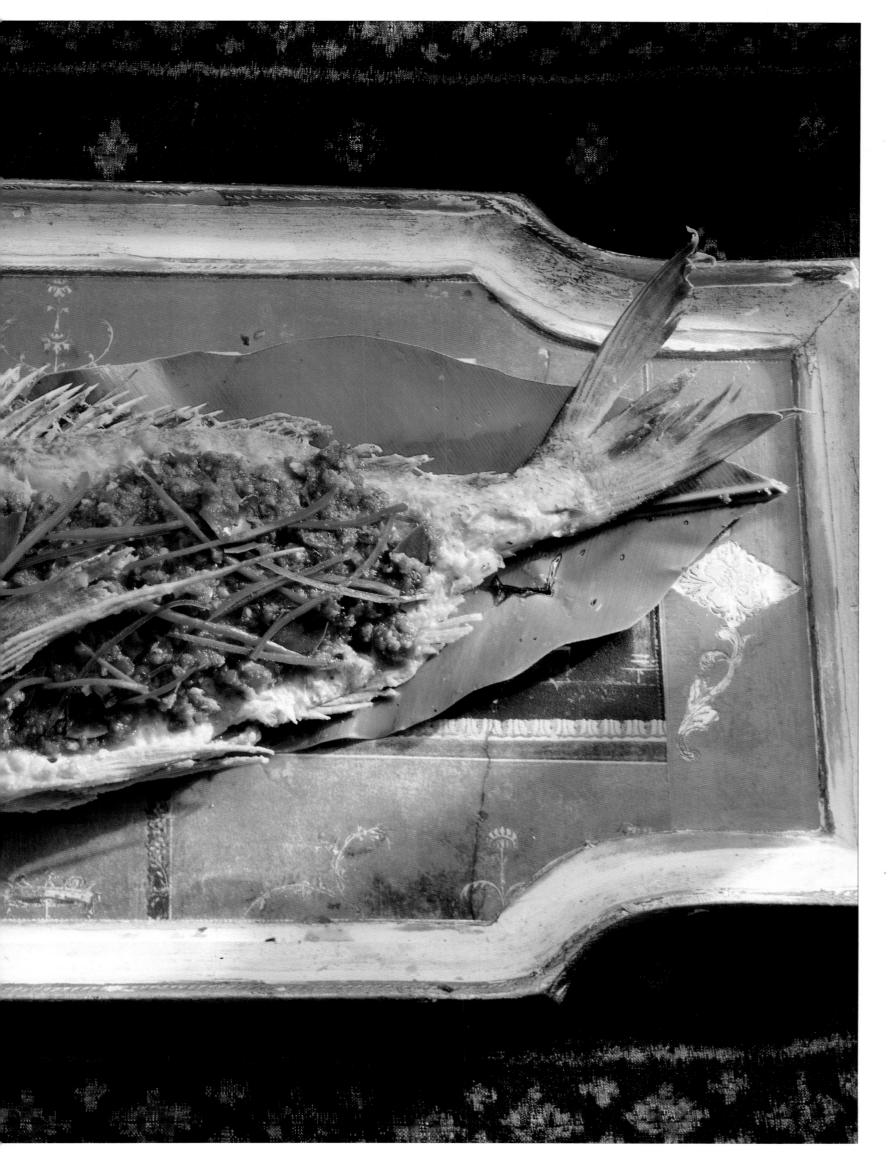

CRAB WITH LEEKS

Bangkok and the Central Plains

Poo Pad Ton Kratiem

ปูผัดต้นกระเทียม

Crab with Leeks

This simple cooking method nevertheless results in a delicious dish, in which the richness of crab is lightened by the fresh flavor of leeks.

1 crab, about 2 lb (1 kg)
3 tablespoons Oriental sesame oil
4 garlic cloves (*kratiem*), minced
1 cup sliced leeks
2 tablespoons fish sauce (*nam pla*)
2 tablespoons sugar
½ cup sliced onions
1 egg

Remove the crab's body shell, discard the internal gills and clean the cavity. Cut the crab in half. Separate the legs and claws and crack gently, and remove tips from legs. Rinse all the pieces.
Heat a large skillet and add the sesame oil and garlic. Add the crab and stir-fry for 30 seconds to blend the flavors.
Add all the remaining ingredients except the egg and stir-fry for 30 seconds, then cover the skillet and allow to steam for 3 minutes.
Remove the lid, crack in the egg and stir until the egg is blended and cooked. Remove to a serving platter.

SERVES 4

Bangkok and the Central Plains

Pae-Sa Banrai

แป๊ะซะบ้านไร่

Steamed Fish Country Style

Steaming seafood makes sure that the moistness of the flesh is retained, and that the flavor of herbs and spices permeates through.

1 red fin, snapper or rock cod, about 1½ lb (750 g)
2 tablespoons rice wine
½ teaspoon salt
½ teaspoon white pepper
3 tablespoons fish sauce (*nam pla*)
¼ cup (2 fl oz/60 ml) lime juice
2 stalks lemon grass/citronella (*ta-krai*), crushed and cut into large pieces
¼ cup sliced onions
2 garlic cloves (*kratiem*), crushed
2 green onions/scallions/spring onions, sliced in halves and crushed
4 fresh or dried green Thai chili peppers (*prik khee noo*), crushed
¼ cup sweet basil leaves (*bai horapa*)
¼ cup slivered galangal (*kha*)

Slash the fish on both sides.
Place the fish on a steaming plate. Spread the remaining ingredients evenly over it.
Steam for 25 minutes. Serve with your favorite dipping sauce.

SERVES 4

BROILED RED SNAPPER (TOP, RECIPE PAGE 108)
AND STEAMED FISH COUNTRY STYLE (BOTTOM)

The South
PLA KAPONG POW

ปลากะพงเผา

Broiled Red Snapper

Fish cooked in this way is particularly flavorful, with the marinade enhancing the delicate taste of fresh fish. Fish fillets can be substituted for the whole fish.

1 whole red snapper, about 1 lb (500 g)

MARINADE

2 tablespoons red curry paste (*nam prik gaeng ped*) (see page 236)
1¾ cups (14 fl oz/440 ml) coconut milk
3 tablespoons fish sauce (*nam pla*)
2 tablespoons sugar
5 kaffir lime leaves (*bai ma-grood*)

banana leaf or foil for wrapping fish
green and red bell pepper/capsicum slices, for garnish
kaffir lime leaves (*bai ma-grood*), for garnish

🔲 Clean the fish and cut three slashes to the bone on both sides.
🔲 Combine the marinade ingredients in a large bowl. Marinate the fish for 20 minutes.
🔲 Wrap the fish in a banana leaf or in foil. Broil/grill or bake at 350°F (180°C) for 15 minutes per side or until done. Place on a serving dish and add the garnish.

SERVES 4   *Photograph page 107*

Bangkok and the Central Plains
GAAM POO OB WOON SEN

ก้ามปูอบวุ้นเส้น

Baked Crab Claws

A classic dish distinguished by the flavor of crab claws, which is usually served in the casserole it is cooked in.

3 tablespoons oil
2 lb (1 kg) crab claws, cracked
6 garlic cloves (*kratiem*), minced
1 teaspoon ground black peppercorns
2 tablespoons Maggi seasoning
3 tablespoons fish sauce (*nam pla*)
2 tablespoons sugar
2 oz (60 g) cellophane noodles (*woon sen*), soaked for 10 minutes
   in warm water.
2 stems cilantro/coriander (*pak chee*) including roots, chopped
2 green onions/scallions/spring onions, cut into 1-in
   (2.5-cm) pieces
cilantro/coriander leaves (*bai pak chee*), for garnish

🔲 Heat a large skillet, add the oil, crab claws, garlic and black pepper. Add the sauces, sugar and cellophane noodles. Stir to combine the flavors and cook for 1 minute.
🔲 Place the crab pieces in a metal or clay casserole dish then add the rest of the mixture.
🔲 Scatter the cilantro and green onions on top, cover the casserole and bake at 350°F (180°C) for 10–15 minutes, taking care not to let the liquid dry out.
🔲 Garnish with the cilantro leaves before serving.

SERVES 4

BAKED CRAB CLAWS (LEFT) AND CURRIED SHRIMP
(RIGHT, RECIPE PAGE 110)

The South

GOONG PAD PONG GAREE

กุ้งผัดผงกะหรี่

Curried Shrimp

The subtle flavor of the curry complements the fresh flavor of the shrimp very well in this quick and easy recipe.

2 tablespoons oil
3 garlic cloves (*kratiem*), minced
8 oz (250 g) shrimp/prawns, shelled and deveined
1 teaspoon curry powder
2 tablespoons fish sauce (*nam pla*)
1 tablespoon oyster sauce
1½ tablespoons sugar
¼ cup slivered green bell pepper/capsicum
¼ cup slivered red bell pepper/capsicum
¼ cup sweet basil leaves (*bai horapa*)
¼ cup sliced onions

▦ Heat a large skillet and add the oil, garlic and shrimp. Sauté for 1 minute. Add all the other ingredients and cook for 2 minutes.
▦ Serve with steamed jasmine rice (*khao suay*), on page 98.

SERVES 4   *Photograph pages 108–109*

Bangkok and the Central Plains

PLA RAD PRIK

ปลาราดพริก

Whole Crispy Fish with Chili Sauce

The presentation of a whole fish is always the highlight of a meal. The crispy outside surface contrasts with the juiciness of the flesh, the whole perfectly balanced with the sauce.

1 whole fish, 1 lb (500 g), cleaned
1 tablespoon white rice wine
½ cup (2 oz/60 g) all-purpose/plain flour
4 cups (1 qt/1 l) oil, for deep-frying

SAUCE

3 tablespoons oil
6 garlic cloves (*kratiem*), crushed
¼ cup sliced green bell pepper/capsicum
¼ cup sliced red bell pepper/capsicum
¼ cup sliced onions
⅛ cup cilantro/coriander leaves (*bai pak chee*)
¼ cup (2 fl oz/60 ml) fish sauce (*nam pla*)
2 tablespoons sugar
¼ cup sweet basil leaves (*bai horapa*)

▦ Cut three slashes to the bone on each side of the fish, then sprinkle it with rice wine. Flour the fish on all sides.
▦ Heat the oil to 350°F (180°C) and carefully immerse the fish in the hot oil.
▦ Deep-fry the fish until done (about 6 minutes on each side).
▦ While the fish is cooking, heat a medium skillet, add the oil and then all the sauce ingredients except the basil. Cook the mixture for 5 minutes on medium-high heat. Add the basil and mix.
▦ Place the fish on a serving dish and pour the sauce over the fish.
▦ Serve with fish sauce with chili (*nam pla prik*), on page 242.

SERVES 4

Bangkok and the Central Plains

PLA MUK PAD PED

ปลาหมึกผัดเผ็ด

Spicy Calamari

Squid is marinated in wine and fish sauce to both tenderize it and add flavor, and is then decorated with carved cucumber, carrot and tomato.

1 lb (500g) cleaned squid

MARINADE

5 garlic cloves (*kratiem*), minced
2 tablespoons white wine
⅛ teaspoon white pepper
1 tablespoon cornstarch/cornflour
2 tablespoons fish sauce (*nam pla*)
1 tablespoon soy sauce
1 tablespoon sugar

2 tablespoons oil

GARNISH

green leaf lettuce/Chinese lettuce
cucumber slices
tomato slices
carrot slices
cilantro/coriander leaves (*bai pak chee*)

▦ Slash the mantle/hood of the squid diagonally, then cut diagonal slashes in the opposite direction. Slice into 2-in (5-cm) pieces.
▦ Mix together all the marinade ingredients, then add the squid and marinate for 10 minutes.
▦ Heat a large skillet, add the oil and sauté the squid on medium-high heat until all the squid curls.
▦ Garnish with the ingredients listed above, or with any decoratively carved vegetables, and serve.

SERVES 2   *Photograph page 112*

Bangkok and the Central Plains

PAD PLA KAPONG KUNCHAI

ผัดปลากระพงขึ้นฉ่าย

Stir-Fried Snapper with Celery

Celery's pleasing taste gives extra flavor to this popular dish.

3 tablespoons oil
1 lb (500 g) snapper fillets, sliced into 2-in (5-cm) pieces
1 cup sliced celery
4 garlic cloves (*kratiem*), minced
½ teaspoon white pepper
½ cup chopped green onions/scallions/spring onions,
    in 1-in (2.5-cm) pieces
3 tablespoons fish sauce (*nam pla*)
1 tablespoon Maggi seasoning
mint leaves for garnish

▦ Heat a large saucepan, add the oil, then all the other ingredients except the mint.
▦ Stir-fry to mix then cover the saucepan and cook for 3 minutes.
▦ Serve with sprigs of mint leaves.

SERVES 4

WHOLE CRISPY FISH WITH CHILI SAUCE (TOP)
AND STIR-FRIED SNAPPER WITH CELERY (BOTTOM)

SPICY CALAMARI (LEFT, RECIPE PAGE 110) AND
BROILED LOBSTER WITH SWEET SAUCE (RIGHT)

Bangkok and the Central Plains
GOONG POW NAM PLA WAN

กุ้งเผา น้ำปลาหวาน

Broiled Lobster with Sweet Sauce

One of the best methods of cooking lobster is simply to broil it until just cooked. The tamarind sauce provides added flavor.

1 lobster, about 2 lb (1 kg), cleaned and left whole
2 tablespoons oil
6 shallots, sliced

SAUCE

½ cup (4 fl oz/125 ml) fish sauce (*nam pla*)
½ cup (4 fl oz/125 ml) tamarind juice (*ma-kaam piag*)
  (see glossary)
¼ cup (2 oz/60 g) sugar

▨ Broil/grill the lobster over charcoal for 5 minutes on each side or until done. After broiling cut the lobster in half lengthwise. Meanwhile heat a small skillet and add the oil. Stir-fry the shallots until golden brown; remove from the oil.
▨ Heat another small skillet and combine the fish sauce, tamarind juice and sugar. Cook the sauce for 3 minutes on high heat to reduce some of the liquid. Pour the sauce into a serving bowl and top with shallots. Use as a dip for the lobster.
▨ If desired crack the claws and legs and remove the meat from the body.

SERVES 4

Bangkok and the Central Plains
GOONG KRATIEM PRIK THAI

กุ้งกระเทียมพริกไทย

Garlic Shrimp

The garnish of tomato and cucumber slices adds freshness to this rich spicy dish, which should be served with plenty of fresh vegetables.

MARINADE

8 garlic cloves (*kratiem*), crushed
2 tablespoons minced cilantro/coriander root (*raak pak chee*)
1 teaspoon white pepper
½ teaspoon salt
2 tablespoons fish sauce (*nam pla*)
1½ tablespoons sugar

1 lb (500 g) shrimp/prawns, shelled, deveined and cleaned
3 tablespoons oil
1 tomato, cut into wedges
1 cucumber, sliced

▨ Thoroughly mix together all the marinade ingredients. Combine the shrimp with the marinade and set aside to marinate for 10 minutes.
▨ Heat a medium skillet, add the oil and sauté the marinated shrimp for 4 minutes.
▨ Remove to a serving plate and garnish with the tomato and cucumber.

SERVES 4

112

CRAB FRIED RICE (TOP LEFT, RECIPE PAGE 114), GARLIC
SHRIMP (TOP RIGHT) AND STIR-FRIED LOBSTER WITH
GINGER SAUCE (BOTTOM, RECIPE PAGE 114)

The South

Pad Goong Mang-Gorn

ผัดกุ้งมังกร

Stir-Fried Lobster with Ginger Sauce

The lobster in the southern part of Thailand is considered a large shrimp and is therefore called goong mang-gorn—*dragon shrimp.*

1 cooked lobster, about 1½ lb (750 g)
2 tablespoons oil
4 garlic cloves (*kratiem*), minced
6 slices (about 2 tablespoons) fresh ginger
¼ cup sliced green jalapeño peppers (*prik chee fa*)
½ cup green onions/scallions/spring onions, chopped
1 egg, beaten
1 teaspoon freshly ground peppercorns
2 tablespoons oyster sauce
1 tablespoon fish sauce (*nam pla*)
1 tablespoon sugar

▨ Scrub the lobster clean and separate into large 2-in (5-cm) pieces. Cut the tail into individual sections.
▨ Heat a large skillet on high and add the oil. Add all the remaining ingredients except the lobster and stir-fry for 30 seconds. Add the lobster pieces to the skillet, cover, and steam on medium-high heat for 2 more minutes. Remove to a platter and serve.

SERVES 4   *Photograph page 113*

Bangkok and the Central Plains

Khao Pad Poo

ข้าวผัดปู

Crab Fried Rice

A delicious accompaniment for any dish. Vary the number of chili peppers in the sauce according to personal taste.

2 tablespoons oil
1 garlic clove (*kratiem*), chopped
1 cup crab meat, cooked
2 eggs, beaten
3 cups cooked rice
2 tablespoons Maggi seasoning
2 tablespoons fish sauce (*nam pla*)
2 tablespoons sugar
1 green onion/scallion/spring onion, chopped

SAUCE

¼ cup (2 fl oz/60 ml) fish sauce (*nam pla*)
5 green Thai chili peppers (*prik khee noo*), finely chopped

GARNISH

1 tomato, sliced
½ cup sliced cucumber
cilantro/coriander leaves (*bai pak chee*)
4 lemons, cut in wedges

▨ Heat a large skillet and add the oil. Stir-fry the garlic, crab and eggs together until the egg is cooked.
▨ Add the rice, Maggi seasoning, fish sauce and sugar. Continue to stir-fry until the mixture is hot. Add the green onion.
▨ Mix together the sauce ingredients. Remove the rice to a serving dish, decorate with the garnish, and serve with the sauce on the side.

SERVES 4   *Photograph page 113*

Bangkok and the Central Plains

Pad Ped Pla Lai

ผัดเผ็ดปลาไหล

Eel Curry

Fresh eel cooked in this style is firm and juicy. Any seafood or firm-fleshed fish can be substituted.

3 tablespoons corn oil
1 eel, about 1 lb (500 g), skinned, cleaned, and cut into ½-in (1-cm) sections
2 tablespoons red curry paste (*nam prik gaeng ped*) (see page 236)
3 tablespoons fish sauce (*nam pla*)
½ cup sweet basil leaves (*bai horapa*)
¼ cup thinly sliced lesser ginger (*krachai*)
5 kaffir lime leaves (*bai ma-grood*), thinly sliced

▨ Heat a large saucepan, add the oil, eel slices and curry paste and stir-fry for 30 seconds. Add the remaining ingredients and continue cooking for 5 minutes more.

SERVES 4

EEL CURRY

CRISPY FISH WITH TAMARIND SAUCE

Bangkok and the Central Plains

GAENG SOM PAE-SA

แกงส้มแป๊ะซะ

Crispy Fish with Tamarind Sauce

With the crispy outer surface of the fish contrasting with its firm moist flesh, and the sourness of the tamarind sauce balancing the garlic and onion, this dish offers a variety of flavors and textures.

TAMARIND SAUCE

5 large dried jalapeño peppers (*prik chee fa haeng*)
1 cup (8 fl oz/250 ml) warm water
4 garlic cloves (*kratiem*)
1 cup sliced onions
1 teaspoon shrimp paste (*gapi*)
½ cup (4 fl oz/125 ml) tamarind juice (*ma-kaam piag*)
   (see glossary)
¼ cup (2 fl oz/60 ml) fish sauce (*nam pla*)
2 tablespoons sugar

1 whole fish, about 1–1½ lb (500–750 g), with head removed if preferred
1 teaspoon salt
4 cups (1 qt/1 l) oil, for deep-frying
5 sprigs of swamp cabbage or young spinach leaves, for garnish
green jalapeño peppers (*prik chee fa*), for garnish

🔲 Soak the dried peppers in the warm water for 10 minutes to soften.

🔲 Combine the soaked peppers with the water and all the remaining sauce ingredients in a blender. Process until the peppers, garlic and onions are coarsely chopped. Pour into a saucepan and heat to boiling. Cook for 1 minute.

🔲 Cut three slashes on each side of the fish and rub with salt. Heat the oil to 350°F (180°C) in a large skillet and deep-fry the fish for 10–15 minutes.

🔲 Remove the fish when it is fried to a golden brown and cooked through. Place on a serving dish, then pour the cooked sauce over the fish and garnish with the sprigs of swamp cabbage and green jalapeño peppers.

SERVES 4

115

Bangkok and the Central Plains

TOM SOM PLA TOO

ต้มส้มปลาทู

Mackerel in Tamarind Sauce·

Tamarind juice is used to add richness to this sauce, which beautifully complements the sweet flesh of the mackerel. This combination of flavors is a feature of Thai seafood cookery.

1 mackerel, about 2 lb (1 kg) or 2 lb (1 kg) smaller mackerel
3 cups (24 fl oz/750 ml) water
6 shallots, minced
¼ cup minced cilantro/coriander root (*raak pak chee*)
1 teaspoon white pepper
½ teaspoon salt
⅓ cup (3 fl oz/90 ml) fish sauce (*nam pla*)
⅓ cup (3 fl oz/90 ml) tamarind juice (*ma-kaam piag*)
   (see glossary)
3 tablespoons sugar
¼ cup sliced ginger
6 green onions/scallions/spring onions

▒ Clean the mackerel and remove the backbone. Cut into four serving pieces.
▒ Heat the water to boiling in a large saucepan and add the fish and all the other ingredients except the ginger and green onions. Simmer for 10 minutes, then add the ginger and four of the green onions, cut into 1-in (2.5-cm) pieces.
▒ Remove from the heat and allow to rest for 2 minutes. Place the fish pieces on a serving plate and drizzle with some of the sauce. Garnish with the extra green onions.

SERVES 4

Bangkok and the Central Plains

PLA CHON PAE-SA

ปลาช่อนแป๊ะซะ

Steamed Whole Fish

Although rock cod is a freshwater fish, snapper or sole can be substituted. In fact this is delicious with any saltwater fish.

1 rock cod, about 1–1½ lb (500–750 g)
1 teaspoon salt
½ teaspoon white pepper
2 garlic cloves (*kratiem*), minced
1 cup chopped celery
2 tablespoons white wine
1 tablespoon fish sauce (*nam pla*)
2 green jalapeño peppers (*prik chee fa*), sliced
1 cup chopped green onions/scallions/spring onions

▒ Clean the fish and slash to the bone three times on each side. Rub with salt and pepper. Place on a steaming plate and top with the remaining ingredients.
▒ Place in a steamer, cover and steam for 15 minutes on high heat. Remove and serve.

SERVES 4

STEAMED WHOLE FISH (FRONT) AND MACKEREL
IN TAMARIND SAUCE (TOP)

The South

GOONG NEUNG KRATIEM

กุ้งนึ่งกระเทียม

Steamed Garlic Shrimp

Steaming the shrimp with the shells intact keeps them very moist and juicy. With the addition of garlic and cilantro this is a favorite Thai style of cooking seafood.

1 lb (500 g) shrimp/prawns, with shells
2 tablespoons oil
1/2 teaspoon salt
1/2 teaspoon white pepper
1 tablespoon Maggi seasoning
8 garlic cloves (*kratiem*), minced
3 tablespoons chopped cilantro/coriander leaves (*bai pak chee*)

▒ Rinse the shrimp and drain thoroughly. Place on a plate that will fit in a steamer. Combine the remaining ingredients with the shrimp.
▒ Place the entire plate of shrimp with the sauce in a steamer. Heat the steamer to boiling then reduce the temperature to medium-high. Continue steaming for 10 minutes. Serve hot.

SERVES 4

The South

POO PAD PONG GAREE

ปูผัดผงกะหรี่

Stir-Fried Crab Curry

Cooking fresh crab in its shell retains the sweetness of the meat. Eating crab cooked in this manner is an informal affair, allowing enjoyment of the company and much conversation between friends.

1 whole crab, about 1 1/2 lb (750 g)
3 tablespoons oil
4 garlic cloves (*kratiem*), minced
1 small onion, sliced
1/4 cup (2 fl oz/60 ml) fish sauce (*nam pla*)
2 tablespoons sugar
2 tablespoons curry powder
1 tablespoon Oriental sesame oil
1/4 teaspoon white pepper
1 egg, beaten
1 tablespoon chopped cilantro/coriander leaves (*bai pak chee*)
2 green onions/shallots/spring onions, cut into 1-in (2.5-cm) lengths

▒ Clean the crab by removing the shell from the body only. Disjoint the legs and crack the shell of the legs with a mallet. Rinse to remove small pieces of shell, drain and set aside.
▒ Heat a wok or large skillet on medium-high heat. Add the oil, garlic and onion. Stir-fry for 30 seconds. Add the cracked crab pieces and stir-fry for 2 minutes.
▒ Add all remaining ingredients except the egg, cilantro and green onions. Cover the skillet and continue cooking on medium-high heat for another 3 minutes, or until the crab is cooked.
▒ Add the egg and stir to combine thoroughly.
▒ Remove to a serving dish and garnish with the cilantro and green onions.

SERVES 4

STIR-FRIED CRAB CURRY (FRONT) AND STEAMED GARLIC SHRIMP (TOP)

SPICY CATFISH (BOTTOM) AND JUNGLE CURRY WITH CATFISH (TOP, RECIPE PAGE 120)

Bangkok and the Central Plains

PAD PED PLA DOOK

ผัดเผ็ดปลาดุก

Spicy Catfish

The abundance of freshwater fish in Thailand has led to the development of many ways in which to cook them. This recipe is a favorite and catfish is a popular choice although other types of freshwater fish can also be used. Both whole fish and fillets are suitable.

2 tablespoons oil
1 lb (500 g) catfish, cleaned and cut into 1/2-in (1-cm) wide sections
1/2 cup Thai eggplant (*ma-khue puang*), cut into wedges
6 garlic cloves (*kratiem*), minced
2 stalks lemon grass/citronella (*ta-krai*), cut into 1-in (2.5-cm) pieces
1/4 cup thinly sliced lesser ginger (*krachai*)
1/2 cup sweet basil leaves (*bai horapa*)
1/4 cup (2 fl oz/60 ml) fish sauce (*nam pla*)
1 tablespoon sugar

▒ Heat a large skillet and add the oil. Wait for 1 minute for the oil to heat then add all the ingredients. Stir thoroughly then cover and cook for 3 minutes on high heat. Remove to a serving dish.

SERVES 4

Bangkok and the Central Plains

GAENG PAA PLA DOOK

แกงป่าปลาดุก

Jungle Curry with Catfish

In the days when travel through various parts of Thailand required journeying through areas of jungle, the people had to make do with what was available there. This recipe is so named because the ingredients and cooking method made it a suitable dish for the jungle. Best eaten in the presence of monkeys, tigers and snakes to keep it more authentic!

CURRY PASTE

2 tablespoons chopped lemon grass/citronella *(ta-krai)*
8 shallots
6 garlic cloves *(kratiem)*
¼ cup chopped lesser ginger *(krachai)*
8 dried jalapeño peppers *(prik chee fa haeng)*
1 teaspoon canned peppercorns
1 teaspoon shrimp paste *(gapi)*
½ teaspoon salt

2 tablespoons oil
1 whole catfish, 1½ lb (750 g), cut into 1-in (2.5-cm) slices
¼ cup (2 fl oz/60 ml) fish sauce *(nam pla)*
3 cups (24 fl oz/750 ml) water
½ cup Thai eggplant *(ma-khue puang)*
¼ cup sliced green jalapeño pepper *(prik chee fa)*
½ cup sweet basil leaves *(bai horapa)*
10 whole kaffir lime leaves *(bai ma-grood)*

▓ Combine all the ingredients for the curry paste, using a mortar and pestle or a blender.
▓ Heat a large saucepan and add the oil and curry paste. Stir-fry for 1 minute on medium-high heat.
▓ Add the fish, fish sauce, water and eggplant and heat to boiling. Cook, stirring, for 3 minutes. Add the remaining ingredients and remove from the heat. Serve.

SERVES 4   *Photograph page 119*

The South

PLA KEM

ปลาเค็ม

Sun-Dried Salty Fish

One day of bright hot sunlight is an essential part of this recipe. This method of food preservation is particularly suitable for fish of all types, although mackerel is a favorite.

1 mackerel, 2 lb (1 kg) or 2 lb (1 kg) smaller mackerel
3 tablespoons salt
½ cup (4 fl oz/125 ml) water

▓ Remove only the entrails and rinse the fish until clean. Dissolve the salt in the water and soak the fish overnight in the salt solution. The next day, hang the fish in bright sunlight and allow it to dry for at least one whole day. Alternatively, bake the fish at 325° F (165°C) for 45 minutes.
▓ Seafood dried by this method keeps indefinitely, and can be used in other recipes, such as fried sun-dried fish *(pla kem taud)*, on page 122.

SERVES 4

The South

PAD PO TAEK

ผัดโป๊ะแตก

Lemon Grass Seafood Combination

The flavor of fresh lemon grass balances the flavor of the seafood, serving the same purpose as the fresh lemon wedges served with seafood in other cuisines.

SUN-DRIED SALTY FISH (LEFT) AND LEMON
GRASS SEAFOOD COMBINATION (RIGHT)

2 tablespoons oil
4 oz (125 g) shrimp/prawns, shelled and deveined
4 oz (125 g) scallops
4 oz (125 g) fish fillets, sliced ½ in (1 cm) thick
4 oz (125 g) mussels, cleaned
¼ cup green curry paste (*nam prik gaeng keow wan*) (see page 236)
¼ cup (2 fl oz/60 ml) coconut milk
¼ cup (2 fl oz/60 ml) fish sauce (*nam pla*)
1 tablespoon sugar
⅛ cup slivered bamboo shoots

1 stalk lemon grass/citronella (*ta-krai*), in 1-in (2.5-cm) lengths
¼ cup sliced green bell pepper/capsicum
⅓ cup sweet basil leaves (*bai horapa*)

▓ Heat a large skillet and add the oil. Add all the seafood and sauté for 2 minutes on high heat.
▓ Add the remaining ingredients and gently combine. Cover the pan and continue cooking for about 3 minutes.
▓ Remove to a serving plate.

SERVES 4

121

FRIED SUN-DRIED FISH (BOTTOM) AND STEAMED FISH (TOP)

The Northeast

PLA NEUNG

ปลานึ่ง

Steamed Fish

Northeastern Thailand has many recipes for freshwater fish and one of the most popular cooking methods is steaming, which retains the flavor and moistness of the fish.

1 whole fish, about 1–1½ lb (500–750 g)
5 shallots, sliced
4 garlic cloves (*kratiem*), minced
4 green jalapeño peppers (*prik chee fa*)
½ teaspoon salt
¼ teaspoon white pepper
3 tablespoons fish sauce (*nam pla*)
3 tablespoons tamarind juice (*ma-kaam piag*) (see glossary)
2 tablespoons lime juice
4 thin slices galangal (*kha*)
2 kaffir lime leaves (*bai ma-grood*), thinly sliced
1 tablespoon oil

🔲 Clean the fish and then make three slashes on each side with a sharp knife.
🔲 Place on a steaming plate. Sprinkle the remaining ingredients over the fish.
🔲 Place in a steamer and steam on high heat for 20 minutes. Present on a serving dish or a banana leaf.

SERVES 4

Bangkok and the Central Plains

NAM PRIK PLA TOO

น้ำพริกปลาทู

Fried Mackerel with Shrimp Paste Sauce

Although mackerel is traditionally used, other favorite fish may be substituted. The sauce will still give the dish the authentic flavor.

4 small mackerel, 1–1½ lb (500–750 g) altogether
1 teaspoon salt
4 cups (1 qt/1 l) oil, for deep-frying

SHRIMP PASTE SAUCE

½ cup dried shrimp paste
6 garlic cloves (*kratiem*)
6 green Thai chili peppers (*prik khee noo*)
3 tablespoons shrimp paste (*gapi*)
¼ cup (2 fl oz/60 ml) fish sauce (*nam pla*)
⅓ cup (3 fl oz/90 g) lime juice
2 tablespoons palm sugar (*nam taan peep*)

2 Thai eggplants (*ma-khue puang*), thinly sliced
4 Thai eggplants, cut into 1-in (2.5-cm) slices
4 snake beans, cut into 4-in (10-cm) lengths
4 red and yellow jalapeño peppers (*prik chee fa daeng*)

🔲 Clean the mackerel and rub them with the salt. Steam for 20 minutes then heat the oil to 375°F (190°C) and deep-fry the mackerel until golden brown. Remove and set aside.
🔲 Place the dried shrimp paste, garlic, chilies and shrimp paste in a mortar and, with the pestle, press for 30 seconds. Then add the remaining ingredients for the shrimp paste sauce and mix together. Remove to a serving bowl and place the thinly sliced eggplant on top of the sauce.
🔲 Serve the fish with the dip and the assorted raw vegetables.

SERVES 4

The South

PLA KEM TAUD

ปลาเค็มทอด

Fried Sun-Dried Fish

The South is known for its abundance of seafood and supplies much of the seafood of Thailand. This is one of the many easy but delicious recipes for simply prepared fish. Sun-dried mackerel is available already prepared, but its flavor may be too strong for Western palates. Other fish may be substituted if desired.

4 steaks, 2 in (5 cm) thick, cut from sun-dried mackerel
  (*pla kem*) (see page 120)
3 tablespoons oil
2 shallots, thinly sliced
1 tablespoon chopped green Thai chili peppers (*prik khee noo*)
2 tablespoons fresh lime juice

🔲 Rinse the mackerel steaks and dry them thoroughly with paper towels, removing as much moisture as possible.
🔲 Heat the oil in a large skillet on medium-high heat. Carefully lay the mackerel steaks onto the oil and fry for 5 minutes on each side, or until the outside of the fish is golden brown and the inside is hot.
🔲 Remove the steaks to a serving dish and scatter the shallots and chili peppers on top. Drizzle with lime juice and serve immediately.

SERVES 4

Bangkok and the Central Plains

CHOO CHEE PLA

ฉู่ฉี่ปลา

Whole Fish with Curry Sauce

Steaming is one of the best methods of cooking fish. This fish is steamed in the pan with a curry sauce, offering simplicity with flavor.

1 whole snapper, about 1½ lb (750 g), or 2 smaller fish
2 tablespoons oil
2 tablespoons red curry paste (*nam prik gaeng ped*) (see page 236)

2 cups (16 fl oz/500 ml) coconut milk
¼ cup (2 fl oz/60 ml) fish sauce (*nam pla*)
3 tablespoons sugar
5 kaffir lime leaves (*bai ma-grood*), thinly sliced

▓ Clean the fish, retaining the head and tail. Make three slashes on each side of the fish.
▓ Heat a large skillet and add the oil and curry paste. Stir-fry for 1 minute and add the coconut milk, fish sauce, sugar and the whole fish.
▓ Cover and cook for 20 minutes, carefully turning the fish once.
▓ Remove to a serving dish and sprinkle with the lime leaves before serving.

SERVES 4

FRIED MACKEREL WITH SHRIMP PASTE SAUCE (TOP)
AND WHOLE FISH WITH CURRY SAUCE (BOTTOM)

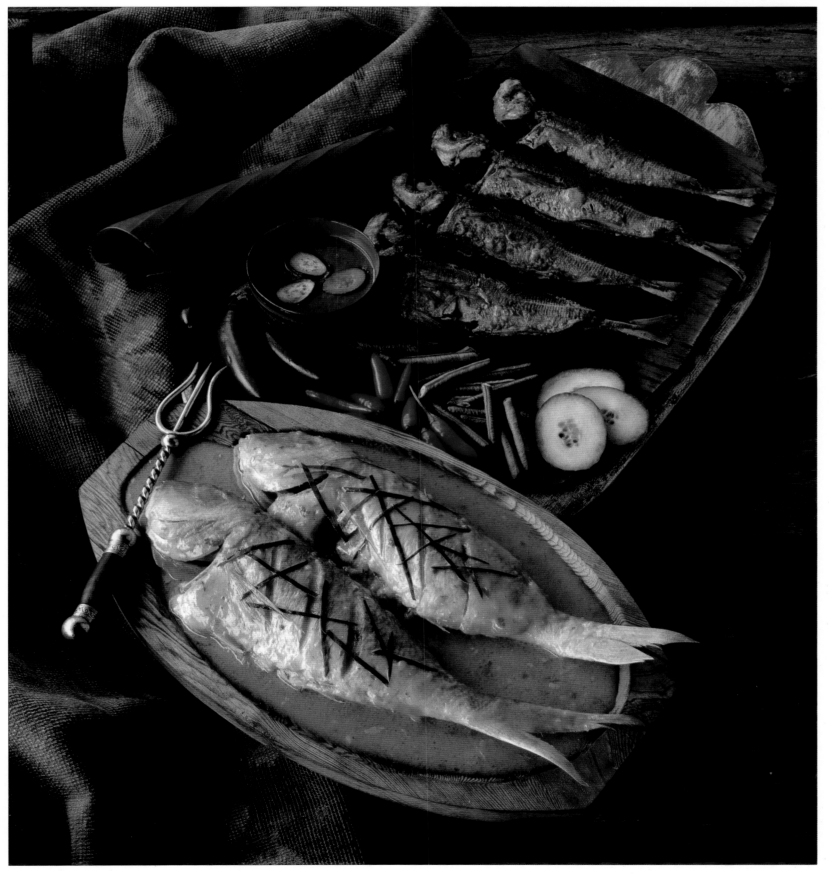

GREEN CURRY WITH CHICKEN AND THAI EGGPLANT (TOP) AND RED CURRY CHICKEN (BOTTOM)

The Northeast

GAI YANG ESAN

ไก่ย่างอีสาน

Northeast Barbecued Chicken

Barbecuing is a premier method of cooking marinated meats. Served with sticky jasmine rice, a staple of the northeastern part of Thailand, gai yang Esan *makes for a very memorable meal. The aroma and the golden brown color entice both the palate and the eye.*

1 chicken, about 2 lb (1 kg)
1 teaspoon salt
8 garlic cloves *(kratiem)*, minced
1 teaspoon white pepper
¼ cup chopped cilantro/coriander leaves *(bai pak chee)*
¼ cup chopped lemon grass/citronella *(ta-krai)*

Clean the chicken and split it in half lengthwise. Marinate the chicken in the remaining ingredients overnight.

Prepare charcoal 30 minutes in advance, so that the coals reach a stage of low heat. Barbecue the chicken over coals for 20 minutes on each side or until the chicken is golden brown and cooked through.

Serve this dish with spicy anchovy dip *(nam prik jaew)*, on page 243, and sticky rice *(khao neow)*, on page 98.

SERVES 4

Photograph pages 94–95

Bangkok and the Central Plains

GAENG PED GAI

แกงเผ็ดไก่

Red Curry Chicken

This curry is best eaten as soon as it is made and served with steamed jasmine rice (khao suay), *on page 98. The coconut flavor is enhanced by adding half the coconut milk towards the end of the cooking process.*

2 cups (16 fl oz/500 ml) coconut milk
2 tablespoons red curry paste *(nam prik gaeng ped)* (see page 236)
1 lb (500 g) chicken breast, cut into 1-in (2.5-cm) pieces
¼ cup (2 fl oz/60 ml) fish sauce *(nam pla)*
3 tablespoons sugar
½ cup canned bamboo shoots, in strips
¼ cup Thai eggplant *(ma-khue puang)*, cut into wedges
5 to 8 kaffir lime leaves *(bai ma-grood)*
¼ cup sweet basil leaves *(bai horapa)*

Heat half the coconut milk in a large saucepan and add the red curry paste. Heat to boiling and cook for 2 minutes.

Add the chicken and boil for 2 minutes. Add the fish sauce, sugar, canned bamboo shoot strips and eggplant, and reheat to boiling.

Add the remaining coconut milk, lime leaves and basil leaves and heat just to boiling. Remove from heat and serve.

SERVES 4

Bangkok and the Central Plains

GAENG KEOW WAN GAI

แกงเขียวหวานไก่

Green Curry with Chicken and Thai Eggplant

This curry is always hot, the heat being determined by the amount of green chilies that are used. To make the dish more flavorful, 1/2 cup of fresh green peppercorns can also be added to the curry mixture.

GREEN CURRY PASTE

2 stalks lemon grass/citronella *(ta-krai)*, cut into ½-in (1-cm) pieces
1 tablespoon sliced galangal *(kha)*
1 teaspoon cumin
½ cup chopped fresh cilantro/coriander root *(raak pak chee)*
8 garlic cloves *(kratiem)*
10 green Thai chili peppers *(prik khee noo)*
10 green jalapeño peppers *(prik chee fa)*
1 teaspoon shrimp paste *(gapi)*
1 tablespoon chopped shallot
¼ teaspoon minced kaffir lime skin *(piew ma-grood)*

2 cups (16 fl oz/500 ml) coconut milk
1 lb (500 g) boned chicken breast, sliced in 1/2-in x 2-in (1-cm x 2.5-cm) pieces
¼ cup (2 fl oz/60 ml) fish sauce *(nam pla)*
3 tablespoons sugar
1 cup Thai eggplant *(ma-khue puang)* or 1 cup canned bamboo shoots
½ cup (4 fl oz/125 ml) coconut cream
6 fresh kaffir lime leaves *(bai ma-grood)*
¼ cup sweet basil leaves *(bai horapa)*
red jalapeño pepper *(prik chee fa daeng)*, for garnish

Place all the green curry paste ingredients in an electric blender and process until the mixture is smooth, or pound in a pestle and mortar.

Pour the coconut milk and the green curry paste into a large saucepan. Heat to boiling and add the chicken, fish sauce and sugar. Cook for 5 minutes at a slow boil. Add the eggplant and reheat to boiling, simmering for 2 minutes. Add the coconut cream and stir to combine. Add the kaffir lime leaves and basil leaves. Remove the contents to a serving bowl, garnish with the red pepper and serve.

SERVES 4

Bangkok and the Central Plains

GAI PAD BAI GA-PROW

ไก่ผัดใบกะเพรา

Spicy Chicken with Basil

This is a quick and easy dish which is a favorite of the people of downtown Bangkok. Sometimes it is served over rice with a fried egg.

6 garlic cloves (*kratiem*), minced
4 shallots, minced
12 mixed green and red jalapeño peppers (*prik chee fa* and *prik chee fa daeng*), sliced
1 teaspoon canned green peppercorns
1 tablespoon oil
1 lb (500 g) ground/minced chicken
¼ cup (2 fl oz/60 ml) fish sauce (*nam pla*)
2 tablespoons sugar
1 cup hot basil leaves (*bai ga-prow*)

Place the garlic, shallots, peppers and peppercorns in a mortar and mash with a pestle until a paste is formed.

Heat a large sauté pan to medium-high heat and add the oil. Add the garlic paste and stir for 1 minute, then add the ground chicken, fish sauce and sugar. Continue to cook until the sauce is reduced. Toss in the basil leaves.

As a luncheon dish, serve over rice with a fried egg.

As a dinner dish, serve separately with rice and with an accompaniment such as hot and sour shrimp soup (*tom yam goong*), on page 47.

SERVES 4

Bangkok and the Central Plains

GAI PAD MED MA-MUANG HIMAPAN

ไก่ผัดเม็ดมะม่วงหิมพานต์

Cashew Chicken

Vegetables can be added while the chicken is cooking, if desired.

¼ cup (2 fl oz/60 ml) oil
4 garlic cloves (*kratiem*), minced
1 lb (500 g) boned chicken, thinly sliced

SAUCE

2 tablespoons fish sauce (*nam pla*)
2 tablespoons oyster sauce
2 tablespoons sugar
⅛ teaspoon white pepper
1 teaspoon cornstarch/cornflour dissolved in a little water, optional

½ cup (70 g/2½ oz) roasted cashew nuts
1 green onion/scallion/spring onion, chopped
¼ cup sliced red bell pepper/capsicum

Heat a large skillet then add the oil, garlic, chicken, the sauces, sugar and pepper.

Turn the heat to high and reduce the sauce until a glaze forms. If the sauce is not reduced and is thin, add enough of the cornstarch mixture to produce a thick sauce. Add the cornstarch and water mixture only if you prefer a richer looking sauce.

Mix in the roasted cashews and then turn the mixture onto a serving dish. Garnish with the green onion and bell pepper.

SERVES 4

CASHEW CHICKEN (LEFT) AND SPICY CHICKEN WITH BASIL (RIGHT)

STEAMED DUCK

PET PALO

เป็ดพะโล้

Steamed Duck

The flavors in this dish reflect the influence of Chinese cuisine on that of Thailand.

1 whole duck, 4 lb (2 kg)

SAUCE

6 cups (1½ qt/1.5 l) water
8 garlic cloves (*kratiem*)
¼ cup minced cilantro/coriander root (*raak pak chee*)
1 teaspoon white pepper
1 teaspoon salt
½ cup (4 fl oz/125 ml) Maggi seasoning
1 cup (8 fl oz/250 ml) mushroom soy sauce
1 cup (8 fl oz/250 ml) sweet soy sauce
½ cup (4 oz/125 g) sugar

Clean the duck and rinse it inside and out. Set aside.
Pour the water into a steamer large enough to enclose the duck. Add the remaining ingredients to the water in the steamer and place the duck in the steamer.
Cover and heat to boiling. Turn the heat to medium-high and steam for 45 minutes.
Allow the duck to cool then fillet out the meat from the bones, reserving the legs and wings. Arrange the meat, legs and wings on a large platter. Skim the fat from the sauce from the steamer and pour some of the sauce over the duck before serving.

SERVES 4

The North

GAI TAUD

ไก่ทอด

Chiang Mai Fried Chicken

Chicken cooked in this way makes a good picnic dish, as it can be eaten hot or cold.

1 chicken, about 3 lb (1.5 kg), cut into 12 pieces

MARINADE

1 tablespoon fish sauce (*nam pla*)
1 teaspoon salt
6 garlic cloves (*kratiem*), finely minced
1 teaspoon white pepper

3–4 cups (24–32 fl oz/750–1000 ml) oil, for deep-frying

Rinse the chicken and pat dry with paper towels. Mix the marinade ingredients together and then rub the mixture evenly over the pieces of chicken to coat them.
Allow to marinate for 30 minutes.
Heat the oil in a wok or deep-fryer to 350°F (180°C). Deep-fry the chicken for approximately 10 minutes until golden brown, turning the pieces often so as to achieve an even color.
Serve with hot or cold young tamarind paste (*nam prik ma-kaam*), on page 244.

SERVES 4

The North

GAENG GAI BAMA

แกงไก่พม่า

Burmese Chicken Curry

This recipe, with its rich tastes, shows a definite Burmese influence.

4 tablespoons (2 oz/60 g) butter
8 shallots, thinly sliced
2 tablespoons red curry paste (*nam prik gaeng ped*) (see page 236)
2 tablespoons yellow curry powder
1 chicken, about 3 lb (1.5 kg), cut into 12 pieces
6 cups (1½ qt/1.5 l) water
⅓ cup (3 fl oz/90 ml) fish sauce (*nam pla*)
3 tablespoons sugar
1 cup (8 fl oz/250 ml) milk
1 cup tomato wedges

Heat a large pan and add three-quarters of the butter and the shallot slices. Stir and cook until the shallots are golden brown. Remove the shallots and set aside.
Heat the same pan and add the rest of the butter. Add the curry paste and curry powder, stir, and cook for 2 minutes. Add the chicken and continue to cook on high heat for 5 more minutes. Add the water and all the remaining ingredients except the fried shallots and reheat to boiling. Cook for 30 minutes.
Remove to a serving bowl and sprinkle with the fried shallots.

SERVES 4

CHIANG MAI FRIED CHICKEN (TOP LEFT) AND
BURMESE CHICKEN CURRY (RIGHT)

The North

GAENG HOH

แกงโฮะ

Mixed Curry

This dish is a rich blend of many flavors and textures.

2 tablespoons oil
2 garlic cloves (*kratiem*), minced
4 oz (125 g) pork, cut into 1-in (2.5-cm) cubes
4 oz (125 g) chicken, cut into ½-in x 2-in (1-cm x 5-cm) slices
2 tablespoons red curry paste (*nam prik gaeng ped*) (see page 236)
1 tablespoon yellow bean sauce (*tao jeow*)
1 oz (30 g) cellophane noodles (*woon sen*), soaked in warm
    water for 15 minutes, until soft, then drained and set aside
½ teaspoon turmeric
1 teaspoon curry powder
¼ cup (2 fl oz/60 ml) fish sauce (*nam pla*)
3 tablespoons coconut sugar or brown sugar
½ cup Thai eggplant (*ma-khue puang*)
½ cup slivered bamboo shoots
½ cup chopped string beans, in 1-in (2.5-cm) pieces
½ cup straw mushrooms
½ cup sliced Chinese mustard pickles
1 tomato, cut into ¼-in (6-mm) dice

Heat a large saucepan then add the oil, garlic, pork and chicken. Stir-fry for 4 minutes to cook the meat. Add the curry paste and yellow bean sauce and stir to combine.

Mix in the drained noodles, turmeric, curry powder, fish sauce and sugar. Stir-fry for 4 minutes.

Add the remaining vegetables and continue cooking for a further 2 minutes or serve the vegetables separately.

SERVES 4

Bangkok and the Central Plains

GAENG GAREE GAI

แกงกะหรี่ไก่

Yellow Curry Chicken

Thai curries are usually quickly and easily prepared. This one is especially popular with families with busy lifestyles.

2 tablespoons oil
¼ cup onion, chopped
¼ cup garlic (*kratiem*), chopped
3 cups (24 fl oz/750 ml) coconut milk
1 lb (500 g) boned chicken, sliced
3 tablespoons yellow curry powder
¼ cup (2 fl oz/60 ml) fish sauce (*nam pla*)
2 tablespoons sugar

Heat a large saucepan then add the oil, onion and garlic. Stir-fry the onion and garlic until almost golden brown, then remove and set aside.

Pour the coconut milk into the pan, heat to boiling and add the chicken. Reheat to boiling and cook for 3 minutes.

Add the remaining ingredients, including the fried onion and garlic, and simmer for 1 minute. Place the mixture in a serving bowl and serve with steamed rice.

SERVES 4

YELLOW CURRY CHICKEN (LEFT) AND MIXED CURRY (TOP AND RIGHT)

BAKED RICE WITH PINEAPPLE

Bangkok and the Central Plains

KHAO OB SAPPAROD

ข้าวอบสับปะรด

Baked Rice with Pineapple

The pineapple in this recipe serves dual purposes: first to enhance the flavor, and second to provide an attractive presentation.

1 pineapple
3 tablespoons oil
8 oz (250 g) boned chicken, diced

SEASONINGS

¼ cup (2 fl oz/60 ml) fish sauce (*nam pla*)
1 tablespoon Maggi seasoning
¼ cup (2 oz/60 g) sugar
2 cups coconut milk
¼ teaspoon white pepper
¼ cup cilantro/coriander leaves (*bai pak chee*), chopped

½ cup toasted cashew nuts
½ cup (3 oz/90 g) raisins
1 tablespoon chopped cilantro/coriander leaves (*bai pak chee*)
4 cups steamed jasmine rice (*khao suay*) (see page 98)

❊ Cut the pineapple in half lengthwise and remove the fruit so both pineapple shells can be used as containers. Place ½ cup of the fruit in a blender and process until finely chopped. Set aside. The rest of the fruit is not needed for this dish.

❊ Heat a large skillet and add the oil. Sauté the chicken until done. Add all the seasonings and allow the mixture to cook until it foams.

❊ Add the cashews, pineapple, raisins, cilantro and rice. Remove from the heat and mix thoroughly.

❊ Stuff the rice mixture into pineapple halves and bake in a 350°F (180°C) oven until hot, about 15 minutes, or microwave for 5 minutes. Cover the pineapple leaves with foil before baking so that they are not burned.

❊ If fresh pineapple is unavailable, the rice mixture could also be wrapped in banana leaves and baked at 350°F (180°C) for 15 minutes or until hot.

SERVES 4

SURAT BAKED CHICKEN (TOP LEFT) AND STIR-FRIED CHICKEN WITH BASIL AND GREEN CURRY (BOTTOM)

Bangkok and the Central Plains

PAD BAI GA-PROW
KEOW WAN GAI

ผัดใบกะเพราเขียวหวานไก่

Stir-Fried Chicken with Basil and Green Curry

The strong flavors in this dish make it a good partner for steamed rice.

3 tablespoons oil
3 tablespoons green curry paste (*nam prik gaeng keow wan*) (see page 236)
1 lb (500 g) boned chicken, sliced
½ cup bamboo shoots (see glossary)
½ cup sliced green and red jalapeño peppers (*prik chee fa* and *prik chee fa daeng*)
¼ cup (2 fl oz/60 ml) coconut milk
3 tablespoons fish sauce (*nam pla*)
3 tablespoons sugar
1 cup hot basil leaves (*bai ga-prow*)
3 tablespoons coconut cream

⁂ Heat a large skillet and add the oil and green curry paste. Add the chicken and stir-fry for 3 minutes, then add all but the last two ingredients. Cook on high heat for 4 minutes.
⁂ Toss in the basil leaves and pour the coconut cream on top. Remove to a serving plate.

SERVES 4

The South

GAI OB SURAT

ไก่อบสุราษฎร์

Surat Baked Chicken

Southern Thailand style baked chicken is usually served in large portions and is a very good single main course.

MARINADE

3 garlic cloves (*kratiem*), minced
⅛ teaspoon white pepper
¼ cup (2 fl oz/60 ml) fish sauce (*nam pla*)
2 tablespoons cognac or whiskey or wine
2 tablespoons chopped lemon grass/citronella (*ta-krai*)
3 tablespoons coconut milk
1 tablespoon red curry paste (*nam prik gaeng ped*) (see page 236)
1 teaspoon salt

1 whole chicken, 3 lb (1.5 kg)

⁂ Mix together the ingredients for the marinade. Thoroughly coat the chicken with the marinade and set aside for 15 minutes.
⁂ Bake the chicken for 1 hour, or until done, at 325°F (165°C).
⁂ Present the chicken whole, or carve into portions of legs, thighs, breast, and serve with a dipping sauce.

SERVES 4

Bangkok and the Central Plains

GAI YANG

ไก่ย่าง

Barbecued Chicken

Barbecued meats are sold by street vendors and restaurants throughout Thailand. This is a popular recipe for chicken, which is a favorite meat. A good picnic recipe.

1 whole chicken, about 3 lb (1.5 kg), cut in half

MARINADE

1 teaspoon salt
4 garlic cloves (*kratiem*), chopped
1 teaspoon white pepper
1 tablespoon minced cilantro/coriander leaves (*bai pak chee*) and root (*raak pak chee*)
2 tablespoons cognac or whiskey or rice wine
2 tablespoons coconut milk
1 tablespoon fish sauce (*nam pla*)
1 teaspoon chopped fresh ginger
2 tablespoons soy sauce

sliced raw vegetables for garnish

⁂ Rub the entire chicken with the combined marinade ingredients. Allow to marinate for 15 minutes.
⁂ Bake at 350°F (180°C) for 45 minutes and then broil/grill for 10 minutes or until done.
⁂ Cut into serving-sized pieces and garnish before serving. Serve with any chili sauce dip.

SERVES 4

BARBECUED CHICKEN

Bangkok and the Central Plains

PAD TAP GAI

ผัดตับไก่

Chicken Liver with Onion

Liver is a good source of iron and is quite a popular meat. This recipe uses one of the most common methods of cooking liver, although broiling and barbecuing are also used.

3 tablespoons oil
1 small onion, sliced
6 garlic cloves (*kratiem*), minced
1 lb (500 g) chicken livers, thinly sliced
2 tablespoons Maggi seasoning
2 tablespoons fish sauce (*nam pla*)
2 tablespoons sugar
2 tablespoons red wine or whiskey
2 green onions/scallions/spring onions, cut into 1-in (2.5-cm) pieces

❀ Heat a large skillet, add the oil, onion and garlic and stir for 30 seconds. Add the chicken livers and turn the heat to high.
❀ Add the remaining ingredients and cook for 3 more minutes or until the livers are just cooked through. Remove to a serving dish.

SERVES 4

Bangkok and the Central Plains

NUEA PAD KANAA

เนื้อผัดคะน้า

Beef with Chinese Broccoli

This combination of fresh broccoli and meat is delicious. However, this recipe is very easy to vary with different fresh vegetables in season.

MARINADE

4 garlic cloves (*kratiem*), minced
1 egg
2 tablespoons sugar
¼ teaspoon white pepper
1 teaspoon Oriental sesame oil
2 tablespoons rice wine
1 tablespoon cornstarch/cornflour
2 tablespoons fish sauce (*nam pla*)

8 oz (250 g) tender beef, thinly sliced
1 lb (500 g) Chinese broccoli or broccoli
2 tablespoons oil
¼ cup straw mushrooms
3 tablespoons oyster sauce

❀ Combine the marinade ingredients, then add the beef pieces and marinate for 5 minutes.
❀ Wash the broccoli and cut it into 3-in (7.5-cm) pieces and set aside.
❀ Heat a large skillet and add the oil. Sauté the beef until almost cooked.
❀ Add the broccoli and the other ingredients and continue to cook for another 3 minutes.

SERVES 4

GINGER CHICKEN (BOTTOM) AND CHICKEN LIVER WITH ONION (TOP)

Bangkok and the Central Plains

GAI PAD KHING

ไก่ผัดขิง

Ginger Chicken

A quick and easy recipe for a healthy meal, this is one of the most popular dishes in Thai restaurants. However, it is equally suitable for home kitchen preparation.

2 tablespoons oil
8 oz (250 g) boned chicken breast, thinly sliced
2 garlic cloves (*kratiem*), minced
2 tablespoons fish sauce (*nam pla*)
1 tablespoon oyster sauce
1 tablespoon sugar
pinch white pepper
⅛ cup slivered ginger
⅛ cup sliced green bell pepper/capsicum
⅛ cup sliced red bell pepper/capsicum
⅛ cup sliced mushrooms
⅛ cup sliced onion
cilantro/coriander leaves (*bai pak chee*), for garnish (optional)

❀ Heat a large skillet, add the oil, chicken and garlic. Cook for 2 minutes.
❀ Add the remaining ingredients and stir-fry for another 3 minutes. Transfer to an attractive serving dish and garnish with cilantro if desired.

SERVES 1–2

PEPPER STEAK (TOP LEFT, RECIPE PAGE 134) AND
BEEF WITH CHINESE BROCCOLI (BOTTOM RIGHT)

CHARCOAL BEEF

Bangkok and the Central Plains

NUEA PAD PRIK

เนื้อผัดพริก

Pepper Steak

A delicious dish usually served over steamed jasmine rice (khao suay), on page 98, with a garnish of fried egg as a variation.

MARINADE

1 teaspoon fish sauce (nam pla)
1 tablespoon cornstarch/cornflour
1/4 teaspoon white pepper

1 lb (500 g) tender beef, sliced
2 tablespoons oil
4 garlic cloves (kratiem), minced
1/4 cup sliced onion
1/4 cup sliced green bell pepper/capsicum
1/4 cup sliced red bell pepper/capsicum
3 tablespoons fish sauce (nam pla)
1 tablespoon Maggi seasoning
2 tablespoons sugar
1 tablespoon Oriental sesame oil

▦ Mix the marinade ingredients together, then combine with the beef and set aside for 10 minutes.
▦ Heat a large skillet, add the oil and sauté the beef with the garlic, onion and bell peppers for 3 minutes. Add the remaining ingredients and continue cooking for 2 minutes.

SERVES 4   *Photograph page 132*

The Northeast

NUEA YANG

เนื้อย่าง

Charcoal Beef

This recipe is served with a side dish of fresh local vegetables as well as its fiery dipping sauce.

1 lb (500 g) beef sirloin, cut into 1-in x 1-in x 6-in (2.5-cm x 2.5-cm x 15-cm) strips
3 tablespoons fish sauce (nam pla)

DIPPING SAUCE

1/4 cup (2 fl oz/60 ml) fish sauce (nam pla)
5 tablespoons (2½ fl oz/75 ml) lime juice
1 teaspoon ground chili pepper (prik khee noo pon)
1 tablespoon chopped green onion/scallion/spring onion
1 teaspoon chopped cilantro/coriander leaves (bai pak chee)

VEGETABLES

cucumber slices
swamp cabbage or spinach
sweet basil stems with leaves (bai horapa)
mint stems with leaves
green onions/scallions/spring onions

▦ Place the beef strips in a bowl and rub the fish sauce into the meat. Allow to marinate for 5 minutes. Then charcoal-broil/grill the strips for approximately 3 minutes on each side. Remove.
▦ Combine all the dipping sauce ingredients in a small bowl and serve with the beef slices and a selection of the raw vegetables for dipping.

SERVES 4

Bangkok and the Central Plains

PAD PED NUEA

ผัดเผ็ดเนื้อ

Stir-Fried Curry Beef with Long Beans

Other meats can be substituted for the ground beef to vary the flavor of this quick and easy recipe. The addition of hot peppers will give a spicier taste if that is preferred.

2 tablespoons oil
1 garlic clove (kratiem), minced
8 oz (250 g) lean ground/minced beef
2 cups chopped snake beans or string beans, in 1-in (2.5-cm) pieces
3 tablespoons fish sauce (nam pla)
1 teaspoon red curry paste (nam prik gaeng ped) (see page 236)
1 tablespoon sugar
1/4 cup sliced green bell pepper/capsicum
1/4 cup sliced red bell pepper/capsicum
1/4 teaspoon white pepper
5–8 green Thai chili peppers (prik khee noo), sliced (optional)

▦ Heat a large skillet and add the oil and garlic. Add the ground beef and sauté on medium-high heat until done.
▦ Add the beans and all the other ingredients, including the chilies if desired, and continue to cook for about 30 seconds or until the beans are tender.

SERVES 4

STIR-FRIED CURRY BEEF WITH LONG BEANS (TOP LEFT)
AND CHIANG MAI CURRY (TOP RIGHT)

The North

GAENG HANG LAY

แกงฮังเล

Chiang Mai Curry

Because the meat is simmered in coconut milk to tenderize it, less expensive cuts can be used. A popular variation involves the substitution of side pork/pork flap for the beef.

1 lb (500 g) beef, cut into ½-in (1-cm) slices
2 cups (16 fl oz/500 ml) coconut milk
¼ cup chopped lemon grass/citronella (*ta-krai*)
1 teaspoon shrimp paste (*gapi*)

5 dried green jalapeño peppers (*prik chee fa haeng*)
2 tablespoons yellow bean sauce (*tao jeow*)
6 garlic cloves (*kratiem*), chopped
1 tablespoon chopped ginger
3 tablespoons palm sugar (*nam taan peep*)
2 shallots
¼ cup (2 fl oz/60 ml) tamarind juice (*ma-kaam piag*) (see glossary)
2 tablespoons curry powder

Simmer the beef slices in the coconut milk for 30 minutes in a large covered saucepan.
Blend together the remaining ingredients to make a paste, add to the beef and continue to simmer, covered, for another 10 minutes.

SERVES 4

WATERFALL BEEF (LEFT) AND MASSAMAN STEAK (RIGHT)

The Northeast

NUEA YANG NAM TOK

เนื้อย่างน้ำตก

Waterfall Beef

The rhythmic sound of the dripping juices from the steak as it cooks over a charcoal grill gives this dish its poetic name.

1 lb (500 g) beef sirloin steak
⅓ cup (3 fl oz/90 ml) fish sauce (*nam pla*)
¼ cup (2 fl oz/60 ml) lime juice
2 tablespoons chopped green onion/scallion/spring onion
2 tablespoons chopped cilantro/coriander leaves (*bai pak chee*)
¼ cup mint leaves
1½ tablespoons ground roasted sticky rice (see glossary)
1 tablespoon toasted sesame seeds
½ teaspoon ground chili pepper (*prik khee noo pon*)

▨ Place the steak in a dish and rub both sides with 1 tablespoon of the fish sauce and marinate for 5 minutes. Charcoal-broil/grill the steak for 3 minutes on each side, or until the steak is medium rare. Remove the steak from the broiler and slice into ⅛-in (3-mm) thin pieces which are about 1 in x 2 in (2.5 cm x 5 cm).
▨ Place the strips in a medium saucepan and add the remaining fish sauce and the lime juice. Stir on medium-high heat for 1 minute. Remove from heat, and add the green onion, cilantro, mint, ground roasted rice, sesame seeds and chili pepper. Combine the entire mixture thoroughly.
▨ Place the beef on a serving plate with a selection of raw or blanched vegetables.

SERVES 4

Bangkok and the Central Plains

MASSAMAN NUEA

มัสมั่นเนื้อ

Massaman Steak

This popular recipe, like many from Bangkok, shows a Muslim influence.

1 lb (500 g) round steak, cut into 1-in (2.5-cm) cubes
3 ½ cups (28 fl oz/880 ml) coconut milk
2 tablespoons oil
⅓ cup (2 oz/60 g) peeled peanuts
¼ cup sliced onion
¼ cup minced garlic (*kratiem*)
6 large dried red jalapeño peppers (*prik chee fa daeng haeng*)
3 tablespoons massaman curry paste (*nam prik gaeng massaman*) (see page 241)
¼ cup (2 fl oz/60 ml) fish sauce (*nam pla*)
3 tablespoons sugar

▨ Combine the beef with half the coconut milk in a medium saucepan and simmer for 45 minutes to tenderize the meat.
▨ Heat a skillet, add the oil and fry the peanuts until golden brown. Remove the peanuts and set aside.
▨ Using the same oil, fry the onion, garlic and peppers.
▨ Place the fried onion, garlic and chili peppers in a blender and process until a smooth paste forms.
▨ Combine in a large saucepan the remaining coconut milk, massaman curry paste, fish sauce and sugar. Add the beef mixture, blended mixture and fried peanuts. Heat to boiling and cook for 5 minutes.

SERVES 4

The Northeast

TAP WAAN

ตับหวาน

Sweet Liver

Make sure the liver is not overcooked, so that the flavorful sauce ingredients can be better absorbed.

1 lb (500 g) beef liver, thinly sliced
¼ cup (2 fl oz/60 ml) fish sauce (nam pla)
¼ cup (2 fl oz/60 ml) lime juice
½ teaspoon ground chili pepper (prik khee noo pon)
1 tablespoon ground roasted sticky rice (see glossary)
4 shallots, thinly sliced
¼ cup lemon grass/citronella (ta-krai), thinly sliced
¼ cup mint leaves
selection of raw vegetables

▨ Heat a large saucepan of water to boiling. Blanch the liver slices in the boiling water for 30 seconds or until they are almost cooked. Drain and set aside.
▨ Place the liver slices in a large skillet, add the fish sauce and lime juice and cook on medium-high heat for 1 minute. Remove from heat and add the chili, rice, shallots and lemon grass. Stir to combine. Sprinkle with the mint leaves and remove the contents of skillet to a serving plate.
▨ Arrange the vegetables around the liver slices.

SERVES 4

Bangkok and the Central Plains

PANAENG NUEA

พะแนงเนื้อ

Stir-Fried Beef Curry

Its rich thick sauce helps to make this a very popular dish. Try replacing the beef with chicken for an interesting variation.

SAUCE

3 fl oz (90 ml) coconut milk
2 tablespoons fish sauce (nam pla)
2 tablespoons sugar
6 kaffir lime leaves (bai ma-grood)

1 tablespoon oil
2 tablespoons Panaeng curry paste (nam prik panaeng)
   (see page 241)
8 oz (250 g) tender beef, sliced
⅛ cup sliced green bell pepper/capsicum
⅛ cup sliced red bell pepper/capsicum
¼ cup sliced onions
2 tablespoons ground roasted peanuts
1 tablespoon coconut cream
1 kaffir lime leaf (bai ma-grood), very thinly sliced

▨ Mix together the ingredients for the sauce and set aside.
▨ Heat a large skillet and add the oil and curry paste. Cook for 1 minute on low heat. Return the temperature to high and sauté the beef, adding the sauce. Cook until the sauce is thick.
▨ Add the sliced peppers, onions and ground peanuts. Cook for 2 minutes, then pour the mixture into a serving bowl. Top with the coconut cream and lime leaf strips.

SERVES 4

STIR-FRIED BEEF CURRY (BOTTOM) AND SWEET LIVER (TOP RIGHT)

The Northeast
Sai Grog Esan

ไส้กรอกอีสาน

Northeast Sausage

This is a specialty of the Northeast and is always made with cooked sticky jasmine rice. The rice gives the sausage a firm yet delicate texture.

FILLING

1 lb (500 g) ground/minced pork
¼ cup chopped garlic cloves *(kratiem)*
½ cup steamed sticky rice *(khao neow)* (see page 98)
1 teaspoon white pepper
1 teaspoon salt
¼ cup (2 fl oz/60 ml) lime juice
2 tablespoons fish sauce *(nam pla)*

1 sausage casing for 1 lb (500 g) of ground/minced pork,
   2 ft (60 cm) long

▦ Combine all the filling ingredients thoroughly. Fill the sausage casing. Allow the flavors to combine overnight.
▦ On the next day the sausage can be steamed for 30 minutes or hung outside to be dried in the sun.
▦ Fry the sausage or broil/grill before using in other recipes, such as fried northeast sausage *(sai grog taud)*, on page 76.

MAKES 12 SAUSAGES

The South
Kua Haeng Moo Paa

คั่วแห้งหมูป่า

Wild Pig Curry (Dry Style)

This recipe was designed to use the meat from wild pigs but it tastes just as good with pork from domestic sources.

3 tablespoons oil
1 lb (500 g) side pork/pork flap with skin, cut in ½-in
   (1-cm) cubes
2 tablespoons red curry paste *(nam prik gaeng ped)* (see page 236)
3 tablespoons fish sauce *(nam pla)*
2 tablespoons sugar

▦ Heat a large skillet and add the oil and the other ingredients.
▦ Cook on medium-high heat until the sauce is reduced and the pork is cooked, about 10 minutes.
▦ Serve with light yellow curry *(gaeng lueng)*, on page 68.

SERVES 4

Bangkok and the Central Plains
Moo Pad Woon Sen

หมูผัดวุ้นเส้น

Stir-Fried Glass Noodles with Pork

These noodles become clear when soaked and so have been given the name cellophane or glass noodles. They are frequently used in soups and stir-fried dishes.

PORK CURRY

2 oz (60 g) cellophane noodles *(woon sen)*
2 tablespoons oil
8 oz (250 g) ground/minced pork
2 eggs
4 garlic cloves *(kratiem)*, minced
½ cup sliced cabbage
½ cup chopped green onions/scallions/spring onions, in 1-in
   (2.5-cm) pieces
3 tablespoons fish sauce *(nam pla)*
1 tablespoon Maggi seasoning
2 tablespoons sugar

▦ Soak the noodles in warm water for 10 minutes.
▦ Heat a large skillet and add the oil, pork, eggs and garlic. Stir-fry for 2 minutes, then add the remaining ingredients, and continue to cook (on lower heat if necessary) until the noodles are tender and the sauce has reduced. Remove to a serving platter.

SERVES 4

Bangkok and the Central Plains
Gaeng Moo Tay Po

แกงหมูเทโพ

Pork Curry

Most of the curries in Thailand are made with chicken, beef or seafood. When pork curry is made, this is always used as a base.

3 cups (24 fl oz/750 ml) coconut milk
3 tablespoons red curry paste *(nam prik gaeng ped)* (see page 236)
1 lb (500 g) pork, cut into ½-in (1-cm) cubes
¼ cup (2 fl oz/60 ml) fish sauce *(nam pla)*
2 tablespoons sugar
¼ cup (2 fl oz/60 ml) tamarind juice *(ma-kaam piag)*
   (see glossary)
8 whole kaffir lime leaves *(bai ma-grood)*
4 cups swamp cabbage or spinach, cut into 1-in
   (2.5-cm) sections

▦ Combine one-third of the coconut milk with the curry paste in a large saucepan and cook for 1 minute.
▦ Add the pork and continue to cook until tender. Add all the remaining ingredients and bring to a slow boil. Remove from heat and serve.

SERVES 4

NORTHEAST SAUSAGE (TOP LEFT), STIR-FRIED GLASS NOODLES
WITH PORK (BOTTOM) AND WILD PIG CURRY (DRY STYLE) (RIGHT)

Bangkok and the Central Plains

Pad Prik Khing Moo

ผัดพริกขิงหมู

Stir-Fried Crispy Pork with Swamp Cabbage

In olden times, side pork was used to render fat to be used for cooking. The resulting crispy pork was then used in other recipes.

3 tablespoons oil
1 lb (500 g) side pork/pork flap, thinly sliced
2 tablespoons oil
3 tablespoons curry paste
¼ cup (2 fl oz/60 ml) fish sauce (*nam pla*)
2 tablespoons sugar
1 cup chopped swamp cabbage or spinach, in 2-in (5-cm) sections
5 kaffir lime leaves (*bai ma-grood*), sliced very thinly

▨ Heat a large skillet and add 1 tablespoon of the oil and the pork. Stir-fry for 7 minutes or until the pork is crispy, then remove from the pan and set aside.

▨ Pour out the excess fat and add the rest of the oil. Add the curry paste and cook for a few seconds. Add all the other ingredients except the kaffir lime leaves, heat to boiling, then stir in the crispy pork.

▨ Remove to a serving bowl and garnish with the kaffir lime leaves.

SERVES 2–4

Bangkok and the Central Plains

Khao Pad Moo

ข้าวผัดหมู

Pork Fried Rice

With the addition of more meat or vegetables on the side, this easy dish is a complete meal in itself.

2 tablespoons oil
2 garlic cloves (*kratiem*), minced
8 oz (250 g) sliced pork
2 eggs, beaten
4 cups cooked white rice
¼ cup (2 fl oz/60 ml) fish sauce (*nam pla*)
1 tablespoon sweet soy sauce
2 tablespoons sugar
¼ teaspoon white pepper
½ cup sliced onion
½ cup tomato chunks
1 green onion/scallion/spring onion, chopped
⅛ cup cilantro/coriander leaves (*bai pak chee*)
¼ cup cucumber slices

▨ Heat a large skillet and add the oil. Stir-fry the garlic and pork until cooked.

▨ Add the eggs and scramble until cooked. Add the rice, sauces, sugar and white pepper. Continue cooking until the rice is hot, reducing the temperature if necessary. Add the onion, tomato chunks and green onion. Garnish with the cilantro and cucumber slices. Serve with fish sauce with chili (*nam pla prik*), on page 242.

SERVES 4

PORK FRIED RICE (LEFT), STIR-FRIED CRISPY PORK WITH
SWAMP CABBAGE (FRONT) AND FIVE SPICE PORK SPARE RIBS
(TOP RIGHT, RECIPE PAGE 144)

Bangkok and the Central Plains

SEE-KRONG MOO OB

ซี่โครงหมูอบ

Five Spice Pork Spare Ribs

Baking the ribs in the oven is the modern-day approach to this recipe—barbecuing over charcoal is the traditional method. Here the best of both worlds is used, with flavor added by a spell on the barbecue while the oven gives the convenience of controlled heat for the rest of the cooking time.

MARINADE

½ cup (4 fl oz/125 ml) soy sauce
¼ cup (2 fl oz/60 ml) fish sauce (*nam pla*)
1 teaspoon five spice powder
1 tablespoon Oriental sesame oil
½ cup (4 oz/125 g) sugar
6 garlic cloves (*kratiem*), minced
¼ cup coriander/cilantro leaves (*bai pak chee*), minced
2 tablespoons rice wine or cognac

4 lbs (2 kg) pork spare ribs, cut into 1-in (2.5-cm) pieces
1 tablespoon oil

Mix together the marinade ingredients, then rub the mixture into the ribs thoroughly and marinate for about 10 minutes.
Brush barbecue grill with the oil. Place the ribs on the grill and barbecue for 10 minutes. Remove from the barbecue and bake at 350°F (180°C) for 30 minutes.
Serve with fresh cucumber slices and whole green onions/scallions/spring onions.

SERVES 4   *Photograph pages 142–143*

STIR-FRIED PORK STOMACH WITH LIVER

Heat a large skillet then add the oil, garlic, liver, stomach, black mushrooms, light soy sauce and fish sauce. Continue to cook for 2 minutes. Add the prepared cornstarch mixture to the skillet. Cook for 2 minutes then add the green onions. Remove and serve.

SERVES 4

Bangkok and the Central Plains

PAD KREUNG NAI MOO

ผัดเครื่องในหมู

Stir-Fried Pork Stomach with Liver

Many organ meats are cooked in this way, giving them a texture which is a favorite among Thai people.

8 oz (250 g) pork stomach
8 oz (250 g) pork liver
4 black mushrooms/Chinese mushrooms
4 cups (1 qt/1 l) water
3 tablespoons oil
4 garlic cloves (*kratiem*), minced
2 tablespoons light soy sauce
1 tablespoon fish sauce (*nam pla*)
1 tablespoon cornstarch/cornflour, dissolved in
   2 tablespoons water
2 green onions/scallions/spring onions, cut into 1-in
   (2.5-cm) pieces

Scrub the pork stomach well and remove any fat attached to it. Rinse the liver. Slice the stomach and liver into ½-in (1-cm) wide slices.
Soak the black mushrooms in very hot water for about 10 minutes or until soft. Drain carefully, then slice into ½-in (1-cm) thick slices.
Heat the water to boiling in a large pot. Put the stomach in the water and cook for 10 minutes on high heat. Add the liver and cook for 1 minute. Remove from water, drain and set aside.

Bangkok and the Central Plains

MOO YANG TA-KRAI

หมูย่างตะไคร้

Lemon Grass Pork Chops

Broiling over charcoal is a common Thai cooking method which gives meat a distinctive flavor. Boneless pieces of pork threaded onto skewers can be substituted for the chops in a delicious variation of this recipe.

MARINADE

2 garlic cloves (*kratiem*), minced
½ teaspoon white pepper
2 tablespoons sugar
2 tablespoons fish sauce (*nam pla*)
2 tablespoons soy sauce
1 tablespoon Oriental sesame oil
1 tablespoon cognac or whiskey or wine
2 tablespoons chopped lemon grass/citronella (*ta-krai*)
1 tablespoon finely chopped green onion/scallion/spring onion
2 tablespoons coconut milk

4 pork chops, about 1 lb (500 g) altogether

Mix together the marinade ingredients then thoroughly combine with the pork chops. Allow to sit for 10 minutes.
Broil/grill the meat over charcoal for about 8 minutes on each side, or until done.
Serve with sweet and sour sauce or other dip of your choice.

SERVES 4

Bangkok and the Central Plains

Moo Tom Kem Palo

หมูต้มเค็มพะโล้

Steamed Five Spice Pork

This dish can be prepared a day in advance and left to marinate, giving a richer flavor to the pork.

1 tablespoon oil
4 garlic cloves (*kratiem*), minced
1 lb (500 g) side pork/pork flap, cut in 1-in (2.5-cm) cubes
8 oz (250 g) fried tofu (see glossary)
1 teaspoon five spice powder
¼ cup coriander root (*raak pak chee*), minced
½ teaspoon white pepper
¼ cup (2 fl oz/60 ml) sweet soy sauce
2 tablespoons light soy sauce
¼ cup (2 fl oz/60 ml) fish sauce (*nam pla*)
3 tablespoons sugar or brown sugar
2 cups (16 fl oz/500 ml) water
6 hard-cooked (hard-boiled) eggs

Heat a large saucepan and add the oil and garlic. Add the pork and stir, then add all the remaining ingredients, leaving the eggs whole.

Cover and simmer for 15 minutes until the pork is tender. Remove to a serving bowl and serve with rice.

SERVES 4

Bangkok and the Central Plains

Kai Jeow Moo Sab

ไข่เจียวหมูสับ

Thai Pork Omelet

Egg dishes are among the favorites on Thai menus. This one is delicious for lunch or as an accompaniment to a curry.

2 eggs
2 tablespoons fish sauce (*nam pla*)
1 teaspoon Maggi seasoning
¼ cup chopped green onions/scallions/spring onions
8 oz (250 g) ground/minced pork
½ cup (4 fl oz/125 ml) oil

Combine the eggs with the fish sauce, Maggi seasoning and green onions. Beat the mixture well and add the ground pork. Continue to stir until the ground pork is evenly dispersed.

Heat an 8-in (20-cm) skillet and add a quarter of the oil. Wait for the pan to get hot, then pour in a quarter of the egg mixture. Turn down the temperature to medium-high and fry the mixture for 2 minutes or until cooked.

Turn the omelet on to a plate and continue to cook the remaining mixture in the extra oil until all four omelets are cooked. Serve with a choice of dips.

MAKES 4 OMELETS

THAI PORK OMELET (TOP) AND STEAMED FIVE SPICE PORK (FRONT)

STIR-FRIED SQUASH

Bangkok and the Central Plains

PAD FAK THONG

ผัดฟักทอง

Stir-Fried Squash

This is one of the many ways of cooking winter squash. It is easy, and does not take as long as baking large pieces.

3 tablespoons oil
6 garlic cloves (*kratiem*), minced
8 oz (250 g) pork, sliced into ½-in x 2-in (1-cm x 2.5-cm) thick pieces
1 lb (500 g) winter squash/pumpkin, peeled and cut into ½-in x 2-in (1-cm x 2.5-cm) slices
¼ cup (2 oz/60 g) fish sauce (*nam pla*)
2 tablespoons sugar
3 eggs, beaten

Heat a large skillet, add the oil, garlic and pork and stir-fry for 1 minute.

Add the squash, fish sauce and sugar. Cover and cook on medium heat for 6 minutes or until the squash is tender and the sauce is reduced. Add the eggs and mix with the ingredients in the skillet. Continue to cook until the eggs are cooked. Remove to a serving bowl.

SERVES 4

Bangkok and the Central Plains

PAD TAP MOO

ผัดตับหมู

Sautéed Pork Liver

Liver, a good source of iron, is often paired with chives or onions. Sometimes it is included in noodle soups and other dishes.

4 cups (1 qt/1 l) water
1 lb (500 g) pork liver, thinly sliced
2 tablespoons oil
6 garlic cloves (*kratiem*), chopped
1 cup sliced onions
1 tablespoon canned peppercorns
¼ cup (2 fl oz/60 ml) fish sauce (*nam pla*)
2 tablespoons sugar
¼ cup julienned carrot strips, for garnish
¼ cup chopped chives, in 1-in (2.5-cm) sections, for garnish

Heat the water to boiling in a large saucepan. Blanch the liver for 1 minute and drain.

Heat a large skillet on medium-high heat, then add the oil, liver, garlic, onion, peppercorns, fish sauce and sugar.

Cook for 3 minutes then remove to a serving dish and garnish with the carrot and chives.

SERVES 4

SAUTÉED PORK LIVER (TOP) AND SWEET PORK
(BOTTOM, RECIPE PAGE 150)

The South

MOO WAN

หมูหวาน

Sweet Pork

To achieve a glazed effect, reduce the sauce further.

1 lb (500 g) pork belly, cut into 1-in (2.5-cm) strips
¼ cup (2 fl oz/60 ml) cooking oil
2 tablespoons sweet soy sauce
⅓ cup (3 fl oz/90 ml) fish sauce *(nam pla)*
¼ cup (1¼ oz/40 g) brown sugar or coconut sugar

☒ Heat a medium skillet and add the oil. Add the pork and all the other ingredients. Heat to boiling, reduce heat and cover the skillet. Simmer for 15 minutes, until the pork is tender.

SERVES 4   *Photograph page 149*

Bangkok and the Central Plains

KAI YAD SAI

ไข่ยัดไส้

Square Thai Omelets

Usually a luncheon dish, these omelets can also be served for breakfast.

4 oz (125 g) pork
4 oz (125 g) shrimp/prawns, shelled and deveined
3 tablespoons oil
1 garlic clove *(kratiem)*, minced
2 tablespoons fish sauce *(nam pla)*
1 tablespoon Maggi seasoning
2 tablespoons sugar
¼ teaspoon white pepper
1 small tomato, chopped
1 small onion, chopped
2 tablespoons chopped sugar peas/snow peas or green peas
⅛ cup chopped carrots
6 eggs, beaten
chopped cilantro/coriander leaves *(bai pak chee)*, for garnish
green onions/scallions/spring onions, for garnish

☒ Mince the pork and shrimp together. Heat a 10-in (25-cm) skillet and add 1 tablespoon of the oil, with the garlic. Add the pork and shrimp mixture and stir-fry for about 2 minutes over medium-high heat or until cooked. Add the fish sauce, Maggi seasoning, sugar and pepper. Continue to cook for about 1 minute until the sauce is reduced. Add the vegetables and stir to combine. Remove the mixture from the skillet, drain off excess juice, and set aside.
☒ Warm a medium skillet over medium heat and coat with a thin layer of oil. Add a quarter of the beaten eggs and roll to coat the skillet surface evenly. Place a quarter of the filling mixture in the center of the egg surface and allow the omelet to cook over low heat until set.
☒ Fold the omelet Thai-style by bringing the lower portion of the cooked egg sheet up to cover the filling mixture. Bring in the sides to overlap each other and then fold down the top portion to cover the entire top of the omelet, so that it forms a square. Invert the omelet by placing a plate over the skillet and turning the skillet upside-down. Keep warm.
☒ Make three more omelets, move to a serving plate and garnish with the cilantro leaves and green onions.

SERVES 4

150

SPICY WILD PIG (TOP LEFT, RECIPE PAGE 152)
AND SQUARE THAI OMELETS (RIGHT)

Bangkok and the Central Plains

PAD PED MOO PAA

ผัดเผ็ดหมูป่า

Spicy Wild Pig

Originally prepared using the very lean meat of the wild pig, this dish tastes just as good with the pork available today.

3 tablespoons oil
1 tablespoon red curry paste (*nam prik gaeng ped*) (see page 236)
1 lb (500 g) pork, thinly sliced (¼ in x 2 in x 1 in)
   (6 mm x 5 cm x 2.5 cm)
¼ cup canned green peppercorns
5 green jalapeño peppers (*prik chee fa*), sliced
3 tablespoons fish sauce (*nam pla*)
2 tablespoons sugar
¼ cup (2 fl oz/60 ml) coconut cream

▨ Heat a large skillet then add the oil and red curry paste and cook for 1 minute.
▨ Add the slices of pork, peppercorns, peppers, fish sauce and sugar. Cook on medium-high heat for 3 minutes.
▨ Remove from pan to a serving plate and top with the coconut cream.

SERVES 4   *Photograph pages 150–151*

The North

MOO YANG

หมูย่าง

Chiang Mai Barbecued Pork

Sweet and juicy skewered pork combines well with steamed sticky rice, and the addition of a spicy chili sauce as a dip would further enhance this dish. It can also be served as a cold meat.

1 lb (500 g) pork loin, sliced into ½-in x 1-in (1-cm x 2.5-cm) thin strips

MARINADE

1 cup (8 fl oz/250 ml) coconut milk
¼ cup (2 fl oz/60 ml) fish sauce (*nam pla*)
6 garlic cloves (*kratiem*), finely minced
6 cilantro/coriander roots (*raak pak chee*), finely chopped
2 tablespoons soy sauce
3 tablespoons sugar
1 teaspoon white pepper
1 tablespoon ground cilantro/coriander seed (*pak chee pon*)

▨ Skewer each piece of pork onto a bamboo skewer, making sure that the meat is flat and skewered in the center. Mix the marinade ingredients together and marinate the pork skewers in the mixture for 15 minutes.
▨ Barbecue the pork skewers, or cook on a pre-heated broiler/griller, for 4 minutes on each side, or until the meat is cooked through.
▨ Serve with steamed sticky rice (*khao neow*), on page 98.

SERVES 4

The South

PAD SA-TAW

ผัดสะตอ

Beans with Shrimp Paste

Southern beans grow only in the South and have a slightly bitter taste, similar to that of raw peanuts. Ordinary green beans can be substituted for these beans, but the flavor will be different.

8 oz (250 g) southern beans (*sa-taw*) or snake beans
10 green Thai chili peppers (*prik khee noo*)
8 garlic cloves (*kratiem*), finely minced
1 tablespoon shrimp paste (*gapi*)
3 tablespoons fish sauce (*nam pla*)
3 tablespoons lime juice
2 tablespoons coconut sugar or brown sugar
3 tablespoons oil
8 oz (250 g) ground/minced pork
8 oz (250 g) shrimp/prawns, peeled and deveined

▨ Remove the southern beans from their pods. Set aside.
▨ Using a pestle and mortar, pound together the chili peppers, garlic and shrimp paste until the mixture is well mashed. Stir in the fish sauce, lime juice and sugar. Set aside.
▨ Heat a large skillet and add the oil. When the oil is hot, add the pork.
▨ Stir-fry for 2 minutes and then add the shrimp, beans and shrimp paste mixture. Continue cooking for approximately 3 minutes on medium-high heat, then serve.

SERVES 4

Bangkok and the Central Plains

Gaeng Om Mara

แกงอ่อมมะระ

Bitter Melon Curry

The bitter melon which gives this curry a bitter flavor is an acquired taste. There is nothing else which has the same flavor.

2 tablespoons oil
2 tablespoons red curry paste (*nam prik gaeng ped*) (see page 236)

8 oz (250 g) pork, sliced
1 lb (500 g) bitter melon, cut into ½-in (1-cm) thick
    lengthwise slices
2 cups (16 fl oz/500 ml) coconut milk
¼ cup (2 fl oz/60 ml) fish sauce (*nam pla*)
2 tablespoons sugar

▓ Heat a large skillet and add the oil. Add the curry paste and pork and stir-fry for 1 minute. Then add the bitter melon slices.

▓ Stir-fry for 3 minutes and add the remaining ingredients. Heat to boiling and serve.

SERVES 4

BITTER MELON CURRY

BANGKOK AND THE CENTRAL PLAINS

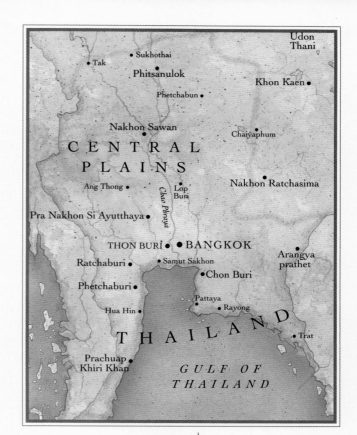

BANGKOK AND THE CENTRAL PLAINS

THE CENTRAL PLAINS region is a vast, flat, extremely fertile basin, regularly watered and enriched by the winding Chao Phraya River. It is the kingdom's geographical, cultural, and economic heart, the source of its agricultural strength and the stage where nearly all the major events in Thai history have been enacted.

On either side of the river, as far as the eye can see, extends a complex jigsaw puzzle of irrigation canals and rice fields, seas of acid green at the start of the rainy season, turning pale gold by harvest time. There are miles, too, of neat vegetable gardens, lush orchards of mangoes, durians, rambutans and citrus fruits, and canals and ponds that teem with a readily available supply of fish and shrimp. Not far from where the river empties into the gulf, rising out of the low-lying level earth like a sudden improbable dream, is the City—the only city, really—sprawling and splendid, chaotic and alluring. And then more fields, gardens, and orchards, wrapping around both sides of the sea.

The Thais were by no means the first to discover this wonderfully productive region, guarded by mountains on three sides, and to leave monuments scattered throughout it. There were the Mons, who established a distinctive Buddhist culture known as Dvaravati and built cities along the fringes of the Central Plains. There were the Khmers, who settled mostly in the Northeast

THE PLOUGHING CEREMONY IS HELD EVERY APRIL AT SANAM LUANG IN BANGKOK

PREVIOUS PAGES: THE TEMPLE OF DAWN, WAT ARUN

THE DUSIT MAHAPRASAT, THE OLDEST BUILDING
IN THE ROYAL PALACE, HOUSES A THRONE THAT IS
STILL USED FOR STATE CEREMONIES

but whose power extended over nearly all of the Chao Phraya basin during the eleventh and twelfth centuries. But it was the Thais who ultimately predominated and used the immense natural wealth of the Central Plains to create their own distinctive culture.

Their rise began at Sukhothai, near the ridge of the northern mountains and just above the point where three lesser rivers meet to form the Chao Phraya. Groups of Thais had been filtering down into the area for some time, drawn by a desire for better land and greater freedom, and by the early thirteenth century they probably outnumbered the Khmers who were theoretically in control. In 1238 two Thai chieftains combined forces and after overthrowing the local Khmer commander established an independent kingdom of their own.

Sukhothai's cultural and political achievements were considerable, exerting an influence still felt today in such key institutions as Buddhism and the monarchy. Its real power, however, lasted just a little more than a century before succumbing to another Thai state, Ayutthaya, which had risen on the Chao Phraya in the very heart of the river valley. Here over a period of four hundred years Thai culture was consolidated, absorbing a wide variety of outside influences that affected not only art and architecture but also cuisine and social life, yet maintaining a uniquely Thai identity.

The Chao Phraya remained the focal point of regional development, annually revitalizing the fields with deposits of silt from the northern highlands and serving as the gateway to contact with the outside world. When Ayutthaya

was destroyed by the Burmese in 1767 a new capital was built further downriver at Thonburi; in 1782 King Rama I, founder of the present Chakri dynasty, decided that the opposite bank offered better protection against future invasions and moved his palace to a small trading port known as Bangkok, literally "the village of the wild hog plum".

Although it appears on most foreign maps, Bangkok is not in fact the proper name of the Thai capital. When it was elevated to that high status a more imposing title was required, and King Rama I bestowed one so filled with honorifics that according to the Guinness Book of Records it ranks as the world's longest city name. The Thais shorten it to Krung Thep, "City of Angels", while outsiders have generally continued to use the older village appellation.

Whatever name is used, it would be difficult to overestimate the importance of the role played by the city in Thailand's modern development. King Rama I's aim—a highly ambitious one in view of the country's war-ravaged condition and the dearth of foreign trade at the time—was nothing less than a re-creation of magnificent Ayutthaya, then a moldering but still vividly remembered expanse of ruins. To this end he built a fortified city on an artificial island achieved by digging a canal at a point where the river curved. Its core was the Grand Palace, a dazzling collection of classic Thai structures covering nearly a square mile and containing, besides the royal residences and audience halls, a magnificent temple to house the sacred Emerald Buddha. Outside the walls but still adjacent to the river was a

STATUES OF KINNARI, A MYTHICAL BIRD-LIKE CREATURE,
STAND IN THE GRAND PALACE COMPOUND

A LACQUER PANEL FROM AYUTTHAYA, NOW IN THE SUAN PAKAAD PALACE IN BANGKOK, SHOWING WOMEN PREPARING NOODLES

thriving community of Chinese merchants who had originally occupied the palace site and been relocated.

Ayutthaya had been known as the "Venice of the East" by European visitors, and Bangkok soon acquired the same sobriquet, for water also dominated its early life: the Chao Phraya served as the main highway, lined with double and sometimes triple rows of steep-roofed floating houses, while an intricate network of *klongs*, or canals, led off like streets into the countryside on either bank. Endless processions of huge hump-backed teak barges moved up and down the river loaded with rice and other produce from outlying provinces, and every household had a small dugout canoe for daily commuting. "Boats are the universal means of conveyance and communication," wrote Sir John Bowring in 1855. "Except about the palaces of the Kings, horses or carriages are rarely seen, and the sedan of the Chinese appears unknown in Siam."

But change was in the air even at the time of Bowring's visit to negotiate a historic treaty with King Rama IV. Almost from the beginning, as the threat of foreign invasion receded, Bangkok had prospered. Chinese junks sailed up the river in steadily increasing numbers, eager to buy high-quality Thai rice, which then, as now, was regarded as among the best in the world. They were soon joined by ships from more distant countries, and the Thai capital became a major Asian port of call. Immigrants came to seek their fortunes in the new capital, mainly Chinese but also Laotians, Indians, Cambodians, Malays, and *farangs*, or Westerners. Only a few years

THE TRADITIONAL PROCESSION OF ROYAL BARGES NOW ONLY TAKES PLACE ON EXCEPTIONAL OCCASIONS, SUCH AS THE KING'S SIXTIETH BIRTHDAY

after Bowring's mission, the first proper road was constructed running parallel to the river for most of its length; according to some accounts, it was built as a result of European complaints to the king that their health was suffering for lack of a place to take an evening carriage ride. Bangkok's riverine character would remain intact for some time afterward—actually until the early years of the twentieth century—but its future as a Western-style city was already beginning to be clear.

Today, with an officially estimated population of about six million (though the true figure is probably closer to seven or eight million) and covering an area of some 2,311 square miles (5,986 square kilometers) on both sides of the Chao Phraya, Bangkok is sixty times the size of Khon Kaen, Thailand's second largest city. It dominates the country in more than just size, however. The king's permanent residence, all the government ministries, and most of the leading educational, medical, sporting, and cultural facilities are located in the capital, as well as the great majority of the biggest Thai and foreign business firms. It is the hub of air, rail, and bus transportation to all parts of the kingdom. Industry, until recent years at least, has been largely concentrated in the city or in nearby provinces, thus serving as a magnet for provincial Thais in search of work, and nearly all the country's exports and imports pass through its facilities. Its wealth is reflected not only in a relatively recent skyline of towering residential and office blocks, hotels, and shopping centers but also in notorious traffic jams arising from the fact that 90 percent of the motor vehicles in Thailand are registered there.

Bangkok's urban problems are manifest: squalid slums that house migrant workers, periodic floods caused partly by inadequate drainage and partly by indiscriminate pumping of underground water, alarming air pollution, traffic congestion that appears to defy solution. Yet in spite of these, it is vibrantly alive, a city of incredible diversity and serendipitous surprises, a city where one may be frustrated, perhaps bewildered, but never for an instant bored.

Nowhere is Bangkok's variety more apparent than in the culinary opportunities it offers. As an introduction, go to any of the city's great public markets and view the produce of the countryside piled in artful pyramids, spilling colorfully out of bamboo baskets, or arranged on trays in patterns like a display of rare jewels.

Spices are there in abundance, of course, essential for achieving the subtle gradations of flavor that characterize all Thai cooking. Some will be familiar to a visitor from the West: chili peppers both fresh and dried, in dozens of different varieties and sizes, from large and relatively mild to the deceptively tiny *prik khee noo* which is the hottest of all; cilantro (coriander), the fresh leaf sprinkled on almost everything and the root and seed used to flavor many meat dishes; basil of several kinds; black and white peppercorns; garlic; mint; dill; ginger root; and cardamon. Others may seem more exotic: sword-shaped pandanus leaves, which impart a delicate fragrance to anything cooked in them; lemon grass, a basic for several of the best known soups and salads; bumpy-skinned kaffir limes and their leaves; cinnamon-colored tamarind pods, from which a sharp-tasting liquid is extracted for many

LUCA INVERNIZZI TETTONI/PHOTOBANK

THE LAYOUT OF THE ANCIENT THAI CITY OF SUKHOTHAI REFLECTS THE COSMOLOGICAL AND URBAN CONCEPTS OF THE EARLIER KHMER CIVILIZATION

THE TOWERING OFFICE BLOCKS OF BANGKOK

LUCA INVERNIZZI TETTONI/PHOTOBANK

THE KLONGS AROUND BANGKOK ARE
CROWDED WITH SMALL CRAFT

JOHN HAY

dishes; tiny eggplants called *ma-khue puang*, with a distinctive bitter flavor; and galangal, a rhizome sometimes called Siamese ginger. In addition to such fresh or dried ingredients, there is also a wide selection of prepared seasonings found in every Thai kitchen, the most important of which are shrimp paste, fish sauce, and chili sauce in various degrees of potency.

Vegetables, which the Thais eat in large quantities, are imaginatively presented, too, and the choice is far more varied today than it was in the past: not only such traditional staples as cabbages, mushrooms, morning glory, bitter gourds, bamboo shoots, cucumber, celery, and tomatoes, but also newer ones such as asparagus, broccoli, lettuce, and tender baby corn. Elsewhere in the market there are displays of fresh beef and pork, chicken and duck, small game birds and, above all, fish, the main source of protein in the Thai diet, which is offered fresh, dried, and salted, and appears in some form at all meals.

Fresh fruits constitute one of Thailand's greatest treats. Thanks to improved methods of growing, many are now available throughout the year: oranges, limes, and huge succulent pomeloes which look like grapefruits but have a very different taste; some of the sweetest pineapples in the world, mostly grown along the western coast of the gulf; crispy cool guavas; mangosteens, the ruby-red shells encasing juicy white pearls; hairy rambutans; some twenty-eight different kinds of banana, from large to finger-sized; nutty-tasting sapodillas; papayas, or pawpaws, eaten both green and ripe; young coconuts with tender meat; custard apples, watermelons, cantaloupes, honeydews, and sweet grapes in varieties especially hybridized for tropical cultivation.

A number are seasonal, eagerly sought during the few months when the best specimens appear on the market. Perhaps the most controversial, at least among foreigners, is the celebrated durian: the size of a football, covered with lethal-looking spines, and, in the view of one early European traveler, smelling "like exceedingly defective sanitation". Thais, like many other Asians, think differently and would agree with the famous naturalist Alfred Russel Wallace, who was introduced to durian on the island of Borneo and later wrote, "The more you eat of it the less you feel inclined to stop." To them the durian is nothing less than the king of fruits, a treat well worth the high prices commanded by prized hybrids bearing such names as "Golden Pillow", "Long Stem", and "Gibbon". Each kind of durian has a special name, some of them useful to buyers. "Deception", for instance, is so-called because from the outside it looks as if it contains a large quantity of golden flesh but doesn't. "Transvestite", on the other hand, is quite meaty but the seeds won't germinate.

Another favorite is the mango, which in Thailand is a very different fruit from the large red or orange-fleshed varieties familiar to most Westerners. Here it is smaller and pale yellow, sweet but tempered with a slight hint of tartness, an altogether more subtle and delicate flavor. Thais eat mangoes fresh, often accompanied by sweetened glutinous rice, but the fruit is equally popular green, when it is used in salads or as a snack with sugar and salt.

As suggested by the abundance of its markets, eating is a major pastime in Bangkok and a highly visible one, too, since almost every street contains at least one sidewalk restaurant—usually several of them—along with countless itinerant vendors offering everything from tasty grilled baby squid and noodle soup to chunks of chilled fruit and brightly colored sweets. Until quite recently the most authentic Thai cooking was to be found principally in private homes, especially those of the wealthier class, where there were adequate servants and family members to take care of all the requisite chopping, mincing, and grinding; when they went out, city Thais preferred to eat Chinese food which even then was plentifully available, or occasionally at a Western restaurant. New lifestyles have changed that: today there are numerous elegantly decorated places specializing in properly prepared Thai dishes from all the country's regions as well as one style often described as "Royal" or "Palace" cooking, with a more refined taste and exquisite presentation, unique to the capital.

Ayutthaya was noted for its cosmopolitan atmosphere, and in this regard King Rama I's aspirations were amply fulfilled; for Bangkok, too, is a cultural melting pot composed of many flavors. Among the foreign influences, the most pervasive is Chinese, though thanks to long and successful assimilation it may now be more accurate to use the term Sino-Thai. Indians have established a prominent economic presence, especially in the past decade or so, and there are significant communities of Japanese, Malays, Laotians, and Burmese. The diversity of Westerners living in the capital is reflected in the fact that diners with a taste for *farang* food have a choice of French, British, German, Italian, Swiss, Spanish, Greek, and Mexican restaurants, not to mention American fast-food outlets and at least one place offering Louisiana Cajun cuisine.

But Bangkok, despite its power and glamor, is only one aspect of life in the Central Plains region. Beyond the urban sprawl lie the endless rice fields, and there, in villages consisting of a few dozen simple wooden houses and a local *wat*, or Buddhist temple, other Thais follow patterns and precepts that have remained remarkably unchanged and reveal the country's true culture far more accurately than those of the worldly city.

Village society is at once democratic—the head, or *phu-yai-ban*, is popularly elected—and highly organized, reflecting the Thai belief that social harmony is more important than individual freedom. Buddhist concepts, symbolized by the *wat* which serves as a social center for most community activities, are instilled in children almost from birth, and are prevalent at every level. William Klausner was writing of a northeastern village in the 1950s but his comments on ideal behavior apply equally to those in the Central Plains region today: "Being gentle is a highly valued character trait. One often hears the compliment 'he acts in a gentle way' as well as the criticism 'he did not speak or act in a gentle manner.' Gentle behavior flows from a 'cool heart' with avoidance of expressions of anger, hatred, and annoyance. Harmonious personal relationships must be preserved."

Families tend to be large, including not only parents and children but also grandparents and perhaps a few other relatives, all living under the same roof or in the same compound, a communal lifestyle that naturally

TRADITIONAL HOUSES ON STILTS ARE STILL A COMMON SIGHT ON THE CANALS AROUND AYUTTHAYA AND SINGHBURI

BUNCHES OF ROSES, THEIR BUDS STILL TIGHTLY CLOSED, AT BANGKOK'S WHOLESALE MARKET AT PAKLONG TALAT

calls for compromise and tact. Respect for elders is another important Thai value that begins in the family, extending from the youngest child up to the oldest grandparent and formulated through a complex system of words and gestures; this conditioning later determines behavior outside the immediate family, whether in village society or in the business and government offices of cosmopolitan life.

Life revolves around the seasonal cycles of planting and harvesting. Rice planting in the Central Plains usually begins in April or May, just before the arrival of the monsoon rains, and is a co-operative undertaking, with families joining to plough the fields, repair dikes, release water from nearby canals and irrigation ditches, and plant the young rice seedlings. Though many farmers now grow other crops—fruits, vegetables, or, especially in the eastern area, tapioca—rice remains the mainstay of Thai agriculture, with a significance that is not merely economic but almost mystical. *Kin khao* is the Thai expression for "to eat"; literally translated it means "to eat rice", reflecting the belief that any meal without the staple is incomplete. Central Thais prefer polished rice—the unhusked form is associated with poverty or with such unfortunate groups as prisoners and military conscripts—and usually steam it, though it is also fried in the Chinese manner or boiled for the traditional breakfast dish known as *khao tom*.

Phansa, the three-month Buddhist "Rains Retreat", commences after the rice plants are established. During this period monks are required to remain in their monasteries, meditating and studying the scriptures, and many young village men enter the monkhood for spiritual training. Such an experience is regarded as one of the essential steps in every male Thai's life, bringing merit to his family and also certifying his emergence as a mature adult. In many parts of the country a man who has not been ordained is called a *khon dip*, an "unripe person", and thus avoided by marriageable girls of the community.

By the end of the rains, usually in late November, Central Plains rice is ready for harvest, another co-operative effort that occupies most able-bodied villagers from early morning until late at night. Afterward, many farmers plant a second crop, sometimes more rice and sometimes vegetables, to supplement their incomes.

And so the cycle continues, as timeless as the great river that makes it possible: not an easy life (no farmer's is), though a far more profitable one in the fertile Central Plains region than elsewhere in the country. At the same time, the Thai penchant for *sanuk*, or pleasure, ensures that it is not a monotonous routine. Ordinations, marriages, auspicious birthdays, Buddhist holy days, all offer a welcome opportunity for villagers to get together and enjoy special foods, folk dancing, perhaps a demonstration of Thai-style boxing or a performance by an itinerant theater troupe, relaxing the natural conservatism that ordinarily prevails.

Widespread industrial development has come to the eastern part of the Central Plains region, thanks to offshore discoveries of oil and natural gas in the gulf; under the huge Eastern Seaboard Project, which will eventually extend into three provinces, gas separation plants and a petrochemical complex have already been

EVERY YOUNG THAI MAN HAS TO SPEND SOME TIME IN A MONASTERY. HERE A NOVICE IS BEING SHAVED BEFORE THE INITIATION CEREMONY

constructed and more facilities are scheduled over the coming decade. Tourism, too, has had an impact through such seaside resorts as Pattaya, once a quiet fishing community and now an internationally famous recreation center which stretches for miles along the coast.

Despite these changes, traditional village life continues in the area, though occupations may differ from those of the rice-oriented Chao Phraya valley. Both Chanthaburi and Rayong provinces, for example, are noted for their fruit orchards, producing some of the country's best pomeloes, rambutans, jackfruit, and durian. Rayong, not far from the bright lights of Pattaya, is also one of the best known sources of *nam pla*, the clear, amber-colored fish sauce that appears as a seasoning on every Thai dinner table, as well as of pungent shrimp paste. From countless ports on either side of the gulf, trawlers go out daily to bring back catches of seafood—the much-prized pomfret (*pla jaramet*), snapper (*pla gapong*), cotton fish (*pla samlii*), grouper (*pla karang*), squid, and an abundance of shellfish. A large number of residents have also taken up the profitable, relatively new career of raising large freshwater prawns, a delicacy popular locally and abroad.

Thailand's dynamic present is more apparent in the Central Plains region than in any other part of the country; at the same time, as the traditional heartland, its countryside probably offers some of the purest reflections of authentic Thai culture as it has gradually developed over the past seven centuries.

163

SALADS AND VEGETABLES

A FARMER CARRIES BUNCHES OF GREEN ONIONS, JUST PULLED FROM THE FIELDS

SALADS AND VEGETABLES

THAI FOODS ENTRANCE THE EYE as well as the palate—qualities well displayed in Thailand's appealing and appetizing variety of salads. These salads combine fresh raw vegetables with protein such as shrimp, squid or charcoal-broiled, thinly sliced beef. The paradigmatic salad resonates with three taste notes: a hint of sourness, followed by saltiness, then sweetness.

In preparing salads, one strives for a mix of colors to tantalize the diner, complementing the warm reds of peppers and tomatoes with the green of green onions. Salads are often presented on a bed of green leaf lettuce.

One of the most popular Thai salads is beef salad *(yam nuea)*. Beef strips are tossed with a dressing made of lime juice, minced Thai chili peppers, minced garlic and chopped green onions. The dish is embellished with a sprig of cilantro and slivers of green onions. So the salad not only tastes good but looks good too.

Another popular dish, papaya salad *(som tam Esan)*, originated in northeast Thailand. The salad is made from under-ripe, firm papaya that is peeled and shredded; raw, long string beans cut into 1-inch (2.5-centimeter) sections; and tomatoes. Seasonings include garlic, Thai

chili peppers, and lime juice or tamarind juice. Papaya salad can be assembled in a large mortar in which the vegetables and papaya are slightly crushed together, a technique that helps release the flavors and juices. The version cooked in the Bangkok style uses ground peanuts, fish sauce, palm sugar and, sometimes, fresh shrimp. In the Northeast style, anchovy sauce is used instead of fish sauce.

Regional variations in Thai cuisine echo the abundance or scarcity of certain ingredients. One finds that the cooking of the Bangkok area and the southern region of the country relies upon seafood to a larger extent than the cooking of the North and Northeast. The cuisine of these northern areas draws upon freshwater fish and freshwater shrimp.

Cooked vegetable dishes vary greatly. Some, like ten vegetable stew *(tom jabchai)*, are quite substantial, containing beef, pork, chicken, seafood or tofu as well as a variety of vegetables. Other dishes, like stir-fried Chinese broccoli with sun-dried fish *(pad kanaa pla kem)* and long string beans with egg *(pad tua fak yow kai)*, are quick, light and easy, using spicy sauces to complement the flavor of a particular vegetable.

PREVIOUS PAGES: SHRIMP SALAD NORTHEAST STYLE (LEFT, RECIPE PAGE 181), CRISPY FRIED EGG SALAD (BOTTOM, RECIPE PAGE 186) AND YOUNG CHILI SAUCE WITH VEGETABLES (RIGHT, RECIPE PAGE 181)

A PROFUSION OF CRISP, NEWLY PICKED VEGETABLES ON DISPLAY AT THE MARKETS IN PAK KLONG DALAT

The Northeast

SOOP NAW MAI

ซุปหน่อไม้

Bamboo Shoot Salad

There is an abundance of bamboo recipes in northeastern Thailand, and many are now also served elsewhere in the country. Bamboo shoot salad originated in the Northeast and is now popular in Bangkok.

2 cups (16 fl oz/500 ml) water
1 lb (500 g) young bamboo shoots (see glossary), shredded
6 bay leaves
¼ cup (2 oz/60 g) sticky rice
¼ cup (2 fl oz/60 ml) water
¼ cup (2 fl oz/60 ml) anchovy sauce
¼ cup (2 fl oz/60 ml) fish sauce (*nam pla*)
⅓ cup (3 fl oz/90 ml) lime juice
2 tablespoons toasted sesame seeds
1 teaspoon ground Thai chili pepper (*prik khee noo pon*)
¼ cup chopped green onions/scallions/spring onions
¼ cup mint leaves
¼ cup chopped cilantro/coriander leaves (*bai pak chee*)
1 bunch Chinese lettuce

Heat the water to boiling in a large saucepan. Add the shredded bamboo and bay leaves and cook for 10 minutes. Drain and set aside. Discard the bay leaves.
Heat a small skillet on medium-high heat and add the rice. Toast the rice, adding 1 tablespoon of water at a time to aid in the cooking. Continue to toast the rice in the dry pan until it is golden brown. Remove and grind in a mortar with a pestle.
Place the ground rice, drained bamboo, fish sauces, lime juice, toasted sesame seeds and ground chili pepper in a large saucepan. Heat to almost a boil. Add half of each of the green onions, the mint leaves and the cilantro leaves. Serve on a bed of Chinese lettuce and garnish with the remaining green onions, mint leaves and cilantro leaves. Serve cold.

SERVES 4

Bangkok and the Central Plains

MOO PAD TUA NGOK

หมูผัดถั่วงอก

Bean Sprout Pork

A favorite for a quick meal, this is an easy and simple recipe to make. Bean sprouts and green onions give it an attractive appearance.

3 tablespoons oil
4 garlic cloves (*kratiem*), minced
8 oz (250 g) ground/minced pork
¼ teaspoon white pepper
3 tablespoons fish sauce (*nam pla*)
1 lb (500 g) bean sprouts
1 teaspoon sugar
2 green onions/scallions/spring onions, cut into 1-in
   (2.5-cm) lengths

Heat a large skillet and add the oil, garlic and ground pork. When the pork is cooked, add the pepper and fish sauce and cook for 2 minutes to reduce the sauce. Add the bean sprouts, sugar and green onions and cook for 30 seconds on high.
Transfer to a serving dish and serve immediately.

SERVES 4

169

NORTHEAST SALAD WITH PORK SKIN (LEFT, RECIPE PAGE 171),
BEAN SPROUT PORK (TOP) AND BAMBOO SHOOT SALAD (RIGHT)

The Northeast

PHLA NANG MOO ESAN
พล่าหนังหมูอีสาน

Northeast Salad with Pork Skin

In the Northeast every part of the pig is put to good use, showing the Thais' creativity with recipes. This is an interesting and delicious recipe.

4 cups (1 qt/1 l) water
8 oz (250 g) pork skin/pork rind, cut into 2-in x ½-in
   (5-cm x 1-cm) strips
4 oz (125 g) ground/minced pork
¼ cup (2 fl oz/60 ml) fish sauce (*nam pla*)
¼ cup (2 fl oz/60 ml) lime juice
2 tablespoons ground roasted rice (see glossary)
4 stalks lemon grass/citronella (*ta-krai*), thinly sliced
½ cup mint leaves
¼ cup chopped green onions/scallions/spring onions
¼ cup chopped cilantro/coriander leaves (*bai pak chee*)

❊ Heat the water to boiling and cook the pork skin for about 20 minutes or until tender. Drain and set aside.
❊ In a medium skillet, cook the ground pork on medium-high heat with the fish sauce, lime juice and pork skin. Add the roasted rice and toss with the remaining ingredients. Remove to a serving plate and serve with a few fresh vegetables of your own choice.

SERVES 4   *Photograph pages 168–169*

Bangkok and the Central Plains

TOM JABCHAI
ต้มจับฉ่าย

Ten Vegetable Stew

A very hearty dish, this can also be served as a complete meal.

1 tablespoon oil
6 garlic cloves (*kratiem*), minced
1 lb (500 g) pork, cut into cubes
½ cup minced cilantro/coriander leaves (*bai pak chee*)
1 teaspoon salt
1 teaspoon white pepper
4 cups (1 qt/1 l) water
½ cup (4 fl oz/125 ml) light soy sauce
⅓ cup (3 oz/90 g) sugar

VEGETABLES

4 oz (125 g) bok choy
4 oz (125 g) cabbage
4 oz (125 g) Chinese broccoli
4 oz (125 g) napa cabbage
4 oz (125 g) celery
4 oz (125 g) green onions/scallions/spring onions
4 oz (125 g) sweet chard
4 oz (125 g) swamp cabbage
4 oz (125 g) carrots
4 oz (125 g) spinach

❊ Heat a large pot and add the oil and garlic. Add the pork and stir-fry for 3 minutes. Add all the ingredients except the vegetables. Heat to boiling, cover, and cook for 15 minutes.
❊ Slice all the vegetables, add them to the pot and cook for 10 minutes longer. Serve in a large soup tureen.

SERVES 4

TEN VEGETABLE STEW

The North

NAM PRIK ONG

น้ำพริกอ่อง

Vegetables with Chiang Mai Dipping Sauce

In the North most meats are barbecued and vegetables are served fresh on the side. This hearty sauce is a favorite among those used to add variety to the meals.

1 tablespoon oil
½ cup chopped garlic cloves (*kratiem*)
¼ cup chopped shallots
1 lb (500 g) diced red tomatoes
8 oz (250 g) ground/minced pork
⅓ cup (3 fl oz/90 ml) fish sauce (*nam pla*)
3 tablespoons sugar
2 tablespoons lime juice
1 cup cucumber slices
¼ cup cilantro/coriander leaves (*bai pak chee*)
4 green onions/scallions/spring onions

VEGETABLES

broccoli flowerets
carrots, sliced
cauliflower flowerets
shallots, cut into 2-in (5-cm) sections
sugar peas/snow peas

Heat a large skillet and add the oil, garlic, shallots and tomatoes. Cook for 3 minutes and add the pork. Add the fish sauce, sugar and lime juice and cook for 4 minutes or until the pork is done.

Remove to a serving dish with the cucumber, cilantro and green onions on the side. Serve with the vegetables for dipping.

SERVES 4

The Northeast

SOM TAM ESAN

ส้มตำอีสาน

Papaya Salad

This salad is delicious served with steamed sticky rice (khao neow), on page 98. The papaya must be dark green and firm.

1 medium dark green papaya/pawpaw
4 garlic cloves (*kratiem*)
6 green Thai chilies (*prik khee noo*)
2 tomatoes, cut into wedges
½ cup chopped green beans, in 1-in (2.5-cm) pieces
2 tablespoons anchovy sauce
½ teaspoon salt
¼ cup (2 fl oz/60 ml) lime juice or tamarind juice (*ma-kaam piag*) (see glossary)

Peel the papaya and rinse with running water to remove the acid. Remove the seeds and shred the papaya with a grater. Set aside.

Place the garlic cloves and the chilies in a mortar and mash with a pestle until crushed into chunks. Place the papaya and the remaining ingredients in the mortar and gently combine all ingredients by mixing with the pestle and a spoon. Serve cold.

SERVES 4

PAPAYA SALAD (LEFT) AND VEGETABLES WITH
CHIANG MAI DIPPING SAUCE (RIGHT)

RICE SALAD

The South

KHAO YAM

ข้าวยำ

Rice Salad

Like many salads from the South, khao yam is a very light salad. Jasmine rice is used to complement the flavors of the many herbs, making this a very delicious light meal.

SALAD

2 cups steamed jasmine rice *(khao suay)* (see page 98)
¼ cup thinly sliced ginger
½ cup ground dried shrimp/prawns
1 cup bean sprouts
1 cup chopped grapefruit flesh, in ½-in (1-cm) pieces
½ cup thinly sliced cucumber
2 stalks lemon grass/citronella *(ta-krai)*, thinly sliced
6 fresh lime leaves, thinly sliced
6 shallots, thinly sliced

SAUCE

½ cup (4 fl oz/125 ml) fish sauce *(nam pla)*
2 tablespoons sugar
¼ cup (2 fl oz/60 ml) lime juice

Place all the salad ingredients in a large bowl. Thoroughly combine the ingredients for the sauce in a separate bowl. Pour the sauce over the salad and toss well just before serving.

SERVES 4

The North

PAK LUAK NAM PRIK

ผักลวกน้ำพริก

Vegetables with Dipping Sauce

While vegetables can be the highlight of any meal, dipping sauces make the vegetables more spicy and flavorful.

½ cup (1 oz/30 g) dried shrimp/prawns
1 lb (500 g) eggplant (long slender purple ones if available)
¼ cup (2 fl oz/60 ml) fish sauce *(nam pla)*
¼ cup (2 fl oz/60 ml) lime juice
2 tablespoons sugar

VEGETABLES

1 cup string beans, cut into 4-in (10-cm) lengths
4 oz (125 g) swamp cabbage
4 oz (125 g) spinach
1 cup sliced cucumber
4 baby eggplants

Soak the shrimp in warm water to cover for 10 minutes and drain.
Heat some water to boiling in a medium saucepan and cook the unpeeled eggplant until just soft and tender.
Drain, cool in cold water and peel the skin. Roughly dice the eggplant.
Put the eggplant, shrimp, fish sauce, lime juice and sugar in a mortar and gently mash with the pestle until all ingredients are combined and a coarse paste is formed. Spoon into an attractive serving bowl.
Arrange the raw or blanched vegetables on a platter and serve with the dip.

SERVES 4

Bangkok and the Central Plains

GAI PAD YOD KHAO POD

ไก่ผัดยอดข้าวโพด

Young Corn Chicken

A very easy recipe to prepare, this is especially delicious when served with hot steamed jasmine rice (khao suay), on page 98.

3 tablespoons oil
1 lb (500 g) boned chicken, thinly sliced
3 garlic cloves *(kratiem)*, crushed
1 cup baby corn
½ cup halved straw mushrooms
2 tablespoons oyster sauce
2 tablespoons fish sauce *(nam pla)*
2 tablespoons sugar
½ teaspoon freshly ground peppercorns
2 green onions/scallions/spring onions, cut into 1-in (2.5-cm) pieces

Heat a medium skillet on high heat and add the oil, chicken and garlic. Stir-fry for 2 minutes and add all the remaining ingredients.
Continue to cook until the chicken is done and all ingredients are combined (about 2 minutes).
Remove to a serving plate and serve with steamed rice.

SERVES 4

174

Bangkok and the Central Plains

YAM GOON CHIANG

ยำกุนเชียง

Chinese Sausage Salad

Offerings of plump, juicy and flavorful Chinese sausages can be found in many food markets in Bangkok. This salad is a favorite among them, although the vegetables can be varied.

DRESSING

2 tablespoons vinegar
1 tablespoon sugar
¼ teaspoon salt

2 cups (16 fl oz/500 ml) water
3–4 Chinese sausages
1 small onion, sliced
1 cup cucumber slices
½ cup cilantro/coriander leaves (*bai pak chee*)
3 tablespoons chopped green Thai chili peppers (*prik khee noo*)
green leaf lettuce/Chinese lettuce, for garnish
cilantro/coriander leaves (*bai pak chee*), for garnish

▨ Mix together the dressing ingredients and set aside.
▨ Heat the water to boiling and cook the Chinese sausages, covered, for 3 minutes. Remove and slice in ¼-in (6-mm) thick slices.
▨ Arrange the sausages decoratively on a platter with the other ingredients, then trickle the dressing over.
▨ Garnish with the green leaf lettuce and cilantro leaves.

SERVES 4

The Northeast

TAM TAENG

ตำแตง

Northeast Cucumber Salad

Many of the broiled and barbecued meats of this region are complemented by this light salad.

1 lb (500 g) cucumbers
6 garlic cloves (*kratiem*), minced
3 green Thai chili peppers (*prik khee noo*), chopped
6 tablespoons tamarind juice (*ma-kaam piag*) (see glossary)
¼ cup (2 fl oz/60 ml) fish sauce (*nam pla*)
2 tablespoons sugar
6 cherry tomatoes, cut into quarters

▨ Peel the skin from the cucumbers, cut them in half lengthwise and remove the seeds. Cut into shreds the size of matchsticks.
▨ Mix together the remaining ingredients except the tomatoes, then mix with the cucumber shreds and tomatoes.

SERVES 4

NORTHEAST CUCUMBER SALAD (BOTTOM) AND
CHINESE SAUSAGE SALAD (TOP)

SHRIMP PASTE DIPPING SAUCE

The Northeast

SOOP NAW MAI PLA-RAA

ซุปหน่อไม้ใส่ปลาร้า

Bamboo Shoot Salad with Pickled Fish

The subtle flavor of bamboo shoots combines well with pickled anchovy. Served with its accompaniment of vegetables and with steamed sticky rice (khao neow), on page 98, this dish becomes a nutritious meal.

1 cup (8 fl oz/250 ml) water
1 lb (500 g) bamboo shoots (see glossary), shredded or in strips
5 bay leaves
4 oz/125 g pickled anchovy fish
¼ cup (2 fl oz/60 ml) fish sauce (nam pla)
¼ cup (2 fl oz/60 ml) lime juice
½ cup mint leaves
¼ cup chopped green onions/scallions/spring onions
1 teaspoon toasted sesame seeds
¼ teaspoon ground Thai chili pepper (prik khee noo pon)
1 tablespoon ground roasted sticky rice (see glossary)

ACCOMPANIMENT (OPTIONAL)

4 long string beans or snake beans, cut into 4-in (10-cm) lengths
8 leaves swamp cabbage or spinach
¼ head of cabbage, sliced into 1-in (2.5-cm) sections
4 stems of sweet basil leaves (bai horapa)

▨ Pour the water into a large saucepan. Add the bamboo shoots and bay leaves and heat to boiling. Cook for 1 minute. Drain the water and remove the bay leaves. Add the remaining ingredients to the bamboo shoots, mix well and reheat. Remove to a serving dish.
▨ If serving the accompaniment, mix the ingredients together and serve in a separate dish.

SERVES 4

The South

NAM PRIK GOONG SIAP

น้ำพริกกุ้งเสียบ

Shrimp Paste Dipping Sauce

Add your favorite vegetables to this recipe to make it even better.

8 green Thai chili peppers (prik khee noo)
6 garlic cloves (kratiem)
2 tablespoons shrimp paste (gapi)
¼ cup (2 fl oz/60 ml) fish sauce (nam pla)
⅓ cup (3 fl oz/90 ml) lime juice
3 tablespoons palm sugar (nam taan peep)
10 whole large dried shrimp/prawns, rinsed in warm water

VEGETABLES

snake beans or long string beans
green onions/scallions/spring onions
tomatoes
broccoli
sugar peas/snow peas

▨ Place the chilies, garlic and shrimp paste in a mortar and mash with a pestle until the garlic is crushed and combined with the other ingredients. Add the fish sauce, lime juice and sugar and gently mash together. Alternatively, use a blender.
▨ Add the whole dried shrimp and combine. Remove to a serving bowl and allow the shrimp to soak in the sauce for about 15 minutes.
▨ Serve as a dip for the raw or steamed vegetables.

SERVES 4

Bangkok and the Central Plains

YAM PLA SARDINE

ยำปลาซาร์ดีน

Sardine Salad

This combination of seafood and fresh vegetables is very popular.

8 oz (250 g) canned sardines
4–6 leaves green leaf lettuce/Chinese lettuce

TOPPING

8 shallots, sliced
2 stalks lemon grass/citronella (ta-krai), thinly sliced
4 garlic cloves (kratiem), sliced
¼ cup chopped green Thai chili peppers (prik khee noo)
¼ cup (2 fl oz/60 ml) fish sauce (nam pla)
¼ cup (2 fl oz/60 ml) lime juice

½ cup mint leaves
¼ cup cilantro/coriander leaves (bai pak chee)
2 green onions/scallions/spring onions, sliced in 1½-in (3.5-cm) pieces

▨ Split each sardine in half lengthwise. Remove the backbone.
▨ Cut the lettuce in 4-in (10-cm) sections and arrange on a plate. Place a sardine half on top of each piece of lettuce.
▨ Combine the topping ingredients and pour over the sardines. Garnish with the mint, cilantro and green onions.
▨ To eat, wrap each sardine in its piece of lettuce, including some of the topping and garnish ingredients.

SERVES 4

SARDINE SALAD (TOP) AND BAMBOO SHOOT SALAD WITH PICKLED FISH (BOTTOM)

The North

NAM PRIK NOOM

น้ำพริกหนุ่ม

Young Chili Sauce with Vegetables

This dipping sauce is always included in the traditional Khantoke dinner of Chiang Mai.

15 green jalapeño peppers *(prik chee fa)*
10 garlic cloves *(kratiem)*
8 shallots
2 large tomatoes
1 oz (30 g) dried anchovies
2 tablespoons fish sauce *(nam pla)*
1 green onion/scallion/spring onion, chopped
2 tablespoons cilantro/coriander leaves *(bai pak chee)*

VEGETABLES

green beans, sliced
cabbage, chopped
cucumbers, sliced
baby eggplant, sliced

◾ Barbecue or broil/grill the peppers, garlic, shallots and tomatoes until they are slightly charred on the outside.
◾ Place the anchovies in a small pan with enough water to cover. Heat the water to boiling and cook the anchovies for 10 minutes at a slow boil, until the liquid is reduced to 2 tablespoons. Strain the juice and discard the anchovies.
◾ Combine the barbecued vegetables, the anchovy juice and the fish sauce in a blender and blend until the vegetables are coarsely chopped, or pound in a pestle and mortar.
◾ Pour the resulting dipping sauce into a serving dish and garnish with the chopped green onion and cilantro leaves. Serve with the vegetables.

SERVES 4

The Northeast

PHLA GOONG

พล่ากุ้ง

Shrimp Salad Northeast Style

The fresh, sweet, crisp taste of the shrimp will be lost if they are overcooked. The lemon grass and lime leaves add a delightful subtle flavor.

2 cups (16 fl oz/500 ml) water
1 lb (500 g) shrimp/prawns, shelled and deveined
2 stalks lemon grass/citronella *(ta-krai)*, thinly sliced
4 kaffir lime leaves *(bai ma-grood)*, thinly sliced
¼ cup mint leaves
2 tablespoons chopped green onion/scallion/spring onion
1 tablespoon chopped cilantro/coriander leaves *(bai pak chee)*
1 teaspoon ground Thai chili pepper *(prik khee noo pon)*
¼ cup (2 fl oz/60 ml) fish sauce *(nam pla)*
¼ cup (2 fl oz/60 ml) lime juice

◾ Heat the water to boiling in a large saucepan and add the shrimp. Blanch for 30 seconds and remove. Place in a bowl.
◾ Add the lemon grass, lime leaves, mint leaves, green onion and cilantro leaves, and mix. Sprinkle the ground chili pepper over the mixture, then pour in the fish sauce and lime juice.
◾ Gently toss to combine, then serve.

SERVES 4

SEAFOOD SALAD

The South

YAM PO TAEK

ยำโป๊ะแตก

Seafood Salad

The interesting combination of herbs and spices used in this dish creates an appetizing fresh taste. Alternative types of seafood can be used to give variation to this popular recipe.

1 cup (8 fl oz/250 ml) water
4 oz (125 g) shrimp/prawns, shelled and deveined
4 oz (125 g) white fish fillets, sliced
4 oz (125 g) clean squid, sliced into 2-in (5-cm) pieces
4 oz (125 g) clams or mussels

DRESSING

1 tablespoon black chili paste *(nam prik pow)* (see page 241)
¼ cup (2 fl oz/60 ml) fish sauce *(nam pla)*
¼ cup (2 fl oz/60 ml) lime juice
2 tablespoons sugar
6 garlic cloves *(kratiem)*, sliced
1 teaspoon minced green Thai chili peppers *(prik khee noo)*
2 stalks lemon grass/citronella *(ta-krai)*, thinly sliced
4 kaffir lime leaves *(bai ma-grood)*, thinly sliced

green leaf lettuce/Chinese lettuce for garnish (optional)

◾ Heat the water to boiling in a large skillet and cook the seafood until done. Drain and set aside.
◾ Mix together the dressing ingredients and gently toss with the seafood just before serving. Serve on a large platter and garnish with green leaf lettuce if desired.

SERVES 4

VEGETARIAN DELIGHT

Bangkok and the Central Plains

PAD KANAA PLA KEM

ผัดคะน้าปลาเค็ม

Stir-Fried Chinese Broccoli with Sun-Dried Fish

This delicious recipe is a quick and easy accompaniment for a rice soup, or it can be served with steamed jasmine rice (khao suay), on page 98.

3 tablespoons oil
4 oz (125 g) sun-dried fish, cut into 1-in (2.5-cm) pieces
6 garlic cloves (*kratiem*), crushed
1 tablespoon yellow bean sauce or black bean sauce
1 lb (500 g) Chinese broccoli, cut into 1-in (2.5-cm) pieces

▓ Heat a large skillet and add the oil. Add the fish and stir-fry for 2 minutes on medium-high heat. Add the other ingredients and cook for 2 more minutes.

SERVES 4

Bangkok and the Central Plains

YAM YAI

ยำใหญ่

Thai Chef Salad

Salads are among the favorite foods of the Thai people. This recipe allows for the creativity of each individual chef, because any vegetable or cooked meat can be added for a change of flavor.

DRESSING

2 tablespoons minced cilantro/coriander leaves (*bai pak chee*)
4 garlic cloves (*kratiem*), minced
3 tablespoons lime juice
1 tablespoon sugar

4–6 leaves green leaf lettuce/Chinese lettuce
4 hard-cooked/hard-boiled eggs, quartered
½ cup sliced white onion
1 tomato, cut into wedges
½ cup sliced cucumber
½ cup sliced red jalapeño pepper (*prik chee fa daeng*)
sprigs of cilantro/coriander (*pak chee*), for garnish
sprigs of mint, for garnish

▓ Combine the ingredients for the dressing and set aside.
▓ Arrange the green leaf lettuce attractively on a large platter with the eggs, onion, tomato, cucumber and pepper slices placed on top of the lettuce. Pour the dressing over and garnish with the sprigs of cilantro and mint.

SERVES 4

Bangkok and the Central Plains

PAD PAK RUAM MIT

ผัดผักรวมมิตร

Vegetarian Delight

The variety of vegetables used in this dish gives it an attractive colorful appearance. It is very easy to prepare.

2 tablespoons oil
2 garlic cloves (*kratiem*), minced
¼ cup sliced onion
½ cup sliced carrots
1 cup sliced cabbage
1 cup broccoli flowerets
½ cup cauliflower flowerets
½ cup sliced red bell pepper/capsicum
¼ cup sugar peas/snow peas
¼ cup sliced mushrooms
¼ cup bean sprouts
1 tablespoon soy sauce
1 tablespoon sugar

▓ Heat a large skillet and add the oil and garlic.
▓ Add all the other ingredients. Stir-fry for 4 minutes, until the vegetables are crisp tender.
▓ Serve with steamed jasmine rice (*khao suay*), on page 98.

SERVES 4

STIR-FRIED CHINESE BROCCOLI WITH SUN-DRIED FISH (LEFT)
AND THAI CHEF SALAD (RIGHT)

Bangkok and the Central Plains

Pad Tua Fak Yow Kub Kai

ผัดถั่วฝักยาวกับไข่

Long String Beans with Egg

This dish can be made very quickly and can be eaten before going to school or work. Serve it over rice.

3 tablespoons oil
8 oz (250 g) boned pork, sliced
1 lb (500 g) long string beans or snake beans, cut into 2½-in (6-cm) lengths
4 garlic cloves (*kratiem*), minced
¼ cup (2 fl oz/60 ml) water
3 tablespoons fish sauce (*nam pla*)
1 tablespoon Maggi seasoning
2 tablespoons sugar
¼ teaspoon white pepper
2 eggs, beaten

▨ Heat a large skillet and add the oil. When the oil is hot, add the pork, beans and garlic and stir-fry until the pork is done.
▨ Add all the remaining ingredients except the eggs, then cover and cook for 2 minutes. Remove the lid, add the eggs, and stir until the eggs are cooked (about 1 minute).

SERVES 4

Bangkok and the Central Plains

Kanaa Namman Hoi

คะน้าน้ำมันหอย

Chinese Broccoli with Oyster Sauce

Almost any fresh vegetable can be used in this recipe, which uses a simple cooking method and seasoning to provide a delicious dish.

2 tablespoons oil
4 garlic cloves (*kratiem*), minced
1 lb (500 g) Chinese broccoli, cut into 1-in (2.5-cm) pieces
¼ cup (2 fl oz/60 ml) water
3 tablespoons oyster sauce
1 tablespoon fish sauce (*nam pla*)
3 green jalapeño peppers (*prik chee fa*)
1 tablespoon sugar

▨ Heat a medium skillet on high heat then add the oil and garlic. Add the broccoli and the other ingredients. Stir-fry, cooking until the broccoli is crisp but tender. Remove to a serving dish.

SERVES 4

Bangkok and the Central Plains

Pad Pak Tow-Hoo

ผัดผักเต้าหู้

Tofu with Vegetables

Tofu, which is extremely nutritious, tends to absorb the flavors of the various ingredients with which it is cooked.

3 tablespoons oil
3 garlic cloves (*kratiem*), minced
¼ cup sliced onions
¼ cup bean sprouts
¼ cup sugar peas/snow peas
¼ cup sliced carrots
¼ cup sliced red bell pepper/capsicum
¾ cup cauliflower flowerets
¾ cup broccoli flowerets
¼ cup sliced mushrooms
2 cups fried tofu (see glossary)

CHINESE BROCCOLI WITH OYSTER SAUCE (TOP LEFT),
LONG STRING BEANS WITH EGG (BOTTOM LEFT)
AND TOFU WITH VEGETABLES (RIGHT)

2 tablespoons fish sauce *(nam pla)*
2 tablespoons oyster sauce
2 tablespoons sugar
¼ teaspoon white pepper

Heat a large skillet over high heat, then add the oil and garlic. Add all the vegetables and the fried tofu.

Add the fish sauce, oyster sauce, sugar and pepper and mix thoroughly. Reduce heat to medium and cook slowly for a further 2 minutes, until the vegetables are crisp but tender.

SERVES 4

185

GROUND BEEF SALAD

The Northeast

LAAB NUEA

ลาบเนื้อ

Ground Beef Salad

The blend of fresh herbs and lime juice makes this salad very refreshing. This laab recipe was taken to Bangkok by the people of the Northeast and is one of the favorite dishes of Thailand. Other meats such as chicken or pork can also be used.

1 lb (500 g) ground/minced beef
¼ cup (2 fl oz/60 ml) lime juice
2 tablespoons fish sauce (nam pla)
½ teaspoon galangal powder (kha pon)
6 shallots, thinly sliced
2 tablespoons chopped green onion/scallion/spring onion
2 tablespoons chopped cilantro/coriander leaves (bai pak chee)
2 tablespoons ground roasted sticky rice (see glossary)
1 teaspoon ground red Thai chili pepper (prik khee noo pon), optional
15 mint leaves

▨ Combine the ground beef with the lime juice, fish sauce, galangal powder and shallots.
▨ Heat a skillet and cook the ground beef mixture on medium-high heat for 5 minutes or until the beef is cooked.
▨ Remove the skillet from the heat and add the chopped green onion and cilantro and the ground roasted rice. Mix thoroughly so that everything is well combined.
▨ Remove to a serving plate, spoon the ground pepper on the side of the plate if desired, and garnish with the mint leaves.
▨ Serve with an accompaniment of raw vegetables, such as long string beans or snake beans, sliced cabbage, green leaf lettuce/Chinese lettuce, basil leaves and swamp cabbage or spinach.

SERVES 4

Bangkok and the Central Plains

YAM KAI DOW

ยำไข่ดาว

Crispy Fried Egg Salad

A delicious salad made from fried eggs, in which the eggs are fried until the whites of the eggs are golden brown and crispy. A very tasty way of cooking eggs.

SAUCE

8 garlic cloves (kratiem), minced
2 tablespoons chopped cilantro/coriander leaves (bai pak chee)
6 green Thai chili peppers (prik khee noo), minced
¼ cup (2 fl oz/60 ml) fish sauce (nam pla)
¼ cup (2 fl oz/60 ml) lime juice
2 tablespoons sugar

½ cup (4 fl oz/125 ml) oil
4 eggs
¼ cup sliced carrots
¼ cup sliced tomato
¼ cup sliced green bell pepper/capsicum
¼ cup sliced onion
¼ cup sliced red cabbage
6 leaves green leaf lettuce/Chinese lettuce, sliced

▨ Mix together all the ingredients for the sauce, and set aside.
▨ Heat the oil in a small skillet to 350°F (180°C). Fry the eggs individually until puffy and light golden brown. Remove and allow to cool. Then cut each fried egg into quarters.
▨ Arrange all the sliced vegetables on top of the sliced lettuce and top with the fried eggs.
▨ Serve the sauce on the side or toss it with the salad.

SERVES 4

CRISPY FRIED EGG SALAD

Bangkok and the Central Plains

PAD PREW WAN MOO

ผัดเปรี้ยวหวานหมู

Sweet and Sour Pork

Unlike other styles of sweet and sour pork, the lean meat in this dish does not require coating and deep-frying. It is still delicious, but has fewer calories.

SAUCE

½ cup (4 fl oz/125 ml) vinegar
½ cup (4 oz/125 g) sugar
½ teaspoon salt
¼ cup (2 fl oz/60 ml) tomato paste

1 tablespoon oil
4 garlic cloves (*kratiem*), minced
8 oz (250 g) pork, cut into ¼-in x 2-in x 2-in
  (6-mm x 5-cm x 5-cm) pieces
½ cup tomato wedges
½ small onion, sliced
¼ cup chopped green jalapeño peppers (*prik chee fa*)
½ cup pineapple chunks
1 green onion/scallion/spring onion, cut into 1-in (2.5-cm) pieces
2 tablespoons cornstarch/cornflour, in 3 tablespoons water

▦ Mix the sauce ingredients in a small skillet and heat to boiling. Reduce to a simmer, cook for 3 minutes and set aside.
▦ Heat a large skillet and add the oil, garlic and pork. Cook for 30 seconds and add the sauce. Heat to boiling, add the remaining ingredients, except the green onion and the cornstarch mixture, and cook for 2 minutes, stirring intermittently.
▦ Add the green onion then stir in enough cornstarch mixture to thicken the sauce to a medium thickness.

SERVES 4

MUSTARD LEAF CHICKEN

Bangkok and the Central Plains

GAI PAD KIAMCHAI

ไก่ผัดเกี้ยมไฉ่

Mustard Leaf Chicken

The pickled mustard leaf is preserved in salt and should be rinsed before cooking. Its salty flavor is complemented by the chicken and the spiciness of the fresh ginger root.

3 tablespoons oil
4 garlic cloves (*kratiem*), minced
1 tablespoon slivered fresh ginger
8 oz (250 g) boned chicken, thinly sliced
1 cup mustard leaf pickle, cut into 1-in (2.5-cm) lengths
2 eggs, beaten
3 tablespoons fish sauce (*nam pla*)
2 tablespoons sugar

※ Heat a medium skillet and add the oil with the garlic and ginger. Add the chicken and stir-fry for 2 minutes. Add the mustard pickles and the eggs and stir to combine. Stir in the fish sauce and sugar and cook for 2 more minutes until the sauce thickens. Serve hot.

SERVES 4

Bangkok and the Central Plains

Yam Nang Moo

ยำหนังหมู

Pork Skin with Lemon Grass Salad

The skin of the pork in this salad has a unique texture resembling that of a translucent and elastic noodle. This is a popular salad in Bangkok.

4 cups (1 qt/1 l) water
1 lb (500 g) pork skin/pork rind
¼ cup (2 fl oz/60 ml) black chili paste (*nam prik pow*)
   (see page 241)
2 stalks lemon grass/citronella (*ta-krai*), thinly sliced
5 kaffir lime leaves (*bai ma-grood*), thinly sliced
1 cup mint leaves
½ cup (4 oz/125 g) ground roasted peanuts
2 tablespoons fish sauce (*nam pla*)
2 tablespoons lime juice
1 tablespoon sugar
green leaf lettuce/Chinese lettuce, for garnish
mint leaves, for garnish

※ Heat the water to boiling, add the pork skin and simmer for 30 minutes to soften and tenderize it. Drain the skin then slice into thin 2-in (5-cm) long strips. Set aside.
※ Mix the black chili paste with all the remaining ingredients except the lettuce and mint, and toss with the pork skin pieces. Garnish with the green leaf lettuce and mint before serving.

SERVES 4

PORK SKIN WITH LEMON GRASS SALAD (LEFT)
AND SWEET AND SOUR PORK (RIGHT)

BEEF SALAD

Bangkok and the Central Plains

YAM NUEA

ยำเนื้อ

Beef Salad

In Bangkok, this recipe is one of the favorites in restaurants and home kitchens alike.

1 lb (500 g) tender beef steak

SALAD

¼ cup sliced onions
1 tomato, cut into wedges
¼ cup sliced cucumber
¼ cup thinly sliced red and green Thai chili peppers (*prik khee noo*)

SAUCE

¼ cup (2 fl oz/60 ml) fish sauce (*nam pla*)
¼ cup (2 fl oz/60 ml) lime juice
2 tablespoons minced garlic (*kratiem*)
2 tablespoons chopped cilantro/coriander leaves (*bai pak chee*)
¼ cup chopped green onions/scallions/spring onions, in 1-in (2.5-cm) pieces

Barbecue the beef over charcoal or broil/grill until medium to well done. Slice thinly and set aside.

Combine all the salad ingredients and add the sliced beef.

Make the sauce by mixing together all the ingredients, and toss with the salad just before serving.

SERVES 4

Bangkok and the Central Plains

PAD PAK BOONG FI DAENG

ผัดผักบุ้งไฟแดง

Flamed Swamp Cabbage

This light dish tastes just as good with spinach, if swamp cabbage is not available.

2 tablespoons oil
1 lb (500 g) swamp cabbage or spinach, cut into 1-in (2.5-cm) pieces
6 garlic cloves (*kratiem*), minced
2 tablespoons black bean sauce
1 tablespoon fish sauce (*nam pla*)
1 teaspoon sugar
¼ cup sliced green jalapeño pepper (*prik chee fa*)

Heat a large skillet until very hot; add the oil and all the remaining ingredients. Quickly stir-fry for 30 seconds and serve.

SERVES 4

Bangkok and the Central Plains

YAM PLA MUK

ยำปลาหมึก

Calamari Salad

Those who enjoy squid will want to eat this dish at every meal. Charcoal-broiling instead of sautéeing will provide added flavor.

8 oz (250 g) squid, thinly sliced (mantle/hood portion only)
1 teaspoon cornstarch/cornflour
1 teaspoon white wine
1 garlic clove (*kratiem*), minced
1 teaspoon grated fresh ginger
1 tablespoon oil

DRESSING

1 teaspoon red curry paste (*nam prik gaeng ped*) (see page 236)
1 teaspoon minced garlic (*kratiem*)
¼ cup (2 fl oz/60 ml) fresh lime juice
¼ cup (2 fl oz/60 ml) fish sauce (*nam pla*)
2 tablespoons sugar
1 tablespoon ground roasted sticky rice (see glossary)
¼ cup minced fresh cilantro/coriander leaves (*bai pak chee*)

2 cups shredded lettuce
¼ cup sliced red bell pepper/capsicum
¼ cup sliced green bell pepper/capsicum
¼ cup sliced mushrooms
¼ cup sliced sugar peas/snow peas
¼ cup sliced onions
⅛ cup mint leaves
¼ cup sliced lemon grass/citronella (*ta-krai*)
1 tomato, cut into wedges
¼ cup sliced cucumber

green onions/scallions/spring onions, sliced, for garnish
cilantro/coriander leaves (*bai pak chee*), for garnish
fresh ginger, grated, for garnish

Marinate the squid slices in the combined cornstarch and white wine, and garlic and ginger for about 10 minutes.

Heat a medium skillet and add the oil. Sauté the squid quickly and remove. Set aside.

Mix together the dressing ingredients.

Combine the squid with the vegetables and toss with the dressing just before serving. Garnish with the green onions, cilantro leaves and grated ginger.

SERVES 4

CALAMARI SALAD (TOP) AND FLAMED SWAMP CABBAGE (BOTTOM)

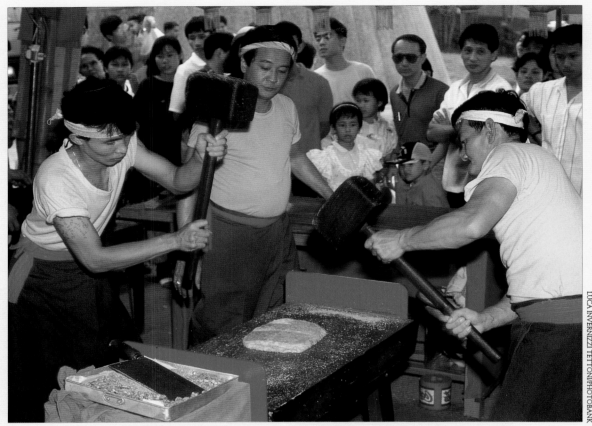

BEATING NUTS WITH A HAMMER TO MAKE A KIND OF CHINESE HARD CAKE

 # DESSERTS

THAI DESSERTS OFFER a soothing finale to a spicy meal. Usually a simple meal will conclude with fresh fruit of some kind, with the more elaborate desserts reserved for special occasions.

Many of the dessert recipes can double as sweet snacks, for eating at any time. Puréed banana *(gluay guan)*, coconut delight *(ma-prow kaew)*, and crisp sweet taro *(puek chaap)* all fall in this group.

At midday a cold dessert is preferred, such as short noodles rolled in coconut *(kanom duang)*, an attractive tricolored noodle dish. Crispy water chestnuts *(tab-tim grob)* is another particularly refreshing dish, with chilled water chestnuts being topped with coconut cream.

Egg desserts like Thai custard *(sangkaya)* reflect the Portuguese influence on Thai cuisine. Thai custard is probably the best known Thai dessert, but there is a great diversity of desserts in the different regions.

In the Northeast sticky rice squares *(khao neow tad)* are popular, with the rice being steamed with coconut milk. In the North, sweet rice pudding with longan *(khao neow piag lamyai)* is a regional specialty when longans are in season. Sticky, or sweet, rice is a short-grain glutinous rice used all over Thailand for desserts but as a staple in the North and Northeast. In the South, pudding with coconut topping *(ta-gow)* served in banana leaf cups is a favorite. The popular desserts of Bangkok include baked mung bean cake *(kanom naw gaeng)* and black glutinous

A CHILD SIPPING COCONUT MILK THROUGH A STRAW—
THE FRESHEST AND SIMPLEST OF DRINKS

rice pudding *(khao neow dam piag)*, with its distinctive velvety plum color.

Another favorite dessert combines sticky rice with crescent slices of mango *(khao neow ma-muang)*. The fruit makes a tempting, sweetly tart complement to the sticky rice, all presented on a bright green banana leaf.

Dessert can also be as simple as a platter of fresh fruits that are in season. They are peeled, sliced and ready to eat: papayas, watermelons, jackfruits, longans, lychees and mangoes are just some of the huge variety available.

One fruit that disdains the company of any other is the magnificent durian. It makes a strong statement with "a smell like hell and a taste like heaven". Durian, an oval-shaped fruit with spikes, signals its presence with its aroma during Thailand's summer—April through June—when durian is in season. As the fruit ripens, the flavor becomes richer. The choicest durians are found in the province of Nonburi, on the periphery of Bangkok.

Thailand's wealth of fruits, as well as vegetables, also play another role during major celebrations such as national holidays when intricately carved fruit and vegetable sculptures add luster to a banquet setting. The embellishment of dishes with such sculptures is a purely Thai signature.

This style of presentation, which elevates any food to one fit for royalty, is another way of showing special regard for one's guests—and this is always an important part of Thai hospitality.

EXOTIC TROPICAL FRUIT FORMS THE BASIS OF MOST THAI DESSERTS

JOHN HAY

FRIED BANANAS

Bangkok and the Central Plains

KRONG KRAENG GROB

ครองแครงกรอบ

Sweet Clam Shells

The "clam shells" are made by using a wooden mold, available in Thailand, which resembles a wooden spatula with fine grooves. The fine teeth of a comb can be used to achieve the same grooves. This dessert should have a sweet and salty taste.

2 cups (8 oz/250 g) all-purpose/plain flour
pinch of salt
1 tablespoon sugar
½ teaspoon baking soda/bicarbonate of soda
1 tablespoon oil
3 eggs
3 cups (24 fl oz/750 ml) oil, for deep-frying

SAUCE

1 teaspoon garlic *(kratiem)*
1 tablespoon cilantro/coriander root *(raak pak chee)*
1 tablespoon cilantro/coriander leaves *(bai pak chee)*
3 tablespoons oil
1 teaspoon white pepper
⅓ cup (2 oz/60 g) palm sugar *(nam taan peep)*
3 tablespoons fish sauce *(nam pla)*

clam shell mold

▨ Mix the flour, salt, sugar and baking soda together. Beat the oil with the eggs and gradually add to the flour mixture until all the ingredients are well blended.
▨ Pinch off a small piece of dough and roll it into a ball about ½ in (1 cm) in diameter. Press the ball onto the clam shell mold. Then press the piece of dough away from you, making it curl. (It should resemble a ridged potato chip, only thicker and more rounded.) Place on a cookie tray/baking tray lined with waxed paper. Continue until all of the dough is used.
▨ Heat the oil in a deep skillet. Deep-fry the pieces of shaped dough until golden brown. Remove and drain well.
▨ In a blender, chop the garlic, cilantro root and leaves. Heat the 3 tablespoons of oil in a small saucepan and sauté the blended ingredients on medium heat for 30 seconds. Add the pepper, sugar and fish sauce, stir to combine, and boil for 3 minutes to the glaze stage. Remove from heat.

▨ Drop the fried "clam shells" into the sauce and remove them immediately. Let them cool and then store in a tightly sealed container.

SERVES 4   *Photograph pages 202–203*

Bangkok and the Central Plains

GLUAY KAEG

กล้วยแขก

Fried Bananas

These treats are found in many areas of Bangkok at street food stalls. They are bought as snacks throughout the day and night.

1 lb (500 g) small green bananas, about 6

BATTER

1 cup (4 oz/125 g) rice flour
1 cup (4 oz/125 g) all-purpose/plain flour
1 teaspoon baking soda/bicarbonate of soda
1 cup (8 fl oz/250 ml) water
½ cup (4 fl oz/125 ml) coconut milk
½ teaspoon salt
¼ cup (1¼ oz/45 g) sesame seeds
3 tablespoons sugar
¾ cup (1¼ oz/40 g) flaked/shredded coconut

4 cups (1 qt/1 l) oil, for deep-frying

▨ Peel and slice each banana lengthwise into four slices. Combine all the batter ingredients and stir just to mix together.
▨ Heat the oil in a wok to 375°F (190°C). Dip each piece of banana into the batter and then deep-fry until golden brown. Remove from the oil and drain. Serve as a snack or dessert.

SERVES 4

Bangkok and the Central Plains

GLUAY GUAN

กล้วยกวน

Puréed Bananas

A sweet to be enjoyed anytime as a snack. The abundance of this fruit encouraged the creation of a variety of different recipes, and bananas are used in many desserts and snacks throughout Thailand. If they are available Thai candied fruits make a good accompaniment.

6 ripe bananas
¾ cup (6 fl oz/185 ml) coconut milk
½ cup (4 oz/125 g) sugar
½ cup (3 oz/90 g) palm sugar *(nam taan peep)*
pinch of salt

▨ Peel the bananas. Use a beater or food processor to process the coconut milk and bananas until creamy.
▨ Spray a large non-stick skillet with a non-stick coating. Sauté the creamy banana mixture on medium-high heat until the mixture is dry, about 10 minutes.
▨ Add both the sugars and the salt and continue to mix and cook until the mixture caramelizes. Spread on a cookie sheet/baking sheet to a thickness of 1 in (2.5 cm) and allow to cool.
▨ Cut into 1-in (2.5-cm) pieces and serve as a snack.

SERVES 4

Bangkok and the Central Plains

KANOM MAW GAENG

ขนมหม้อแกง

Baked Mung Bean Cake

This dessert is a favorite with the people of Bangkok—the best recipe is from Petchaburi province.

1 cup (8 oz/250 g) dried mung beans
¼ cup shallots, sliced
½ cup (4 fl oz/125 ml) oil, for deep-frying
1 cup (8 fl oz/250 ml) water
6 eggs
1½ cups (12 fl oz/375 ml) coconut cream
1 cup (8 oz/250 g) white sugar or ¾ cup (5 oz/155 g) palm
  sugar (*nam taan peep*)

Soak the mung beans overnight in water to cover. Drain.

Using a small saucepan, deep-fry the shallots in the oil until golden brown, then drain and set aside.

Heat the water to boiling in a medium saucepan and simmer the mung beans until they are soft. Drain and put in a blender. Process until smooth.

Add the eggs, coconut cream and sugar to the blender and process with the mung beans for 2 minutes.

Pour the mixture into an 8-in x 8-in (20-cm x 20-cm) baking pan, sprinkle the shallots on top, and bake at 350°F (180°C) for 45 minutes.

Allow to cool, and cut into 2-in (5-cm) squares to serve.

MAKES 16 PIECES   *Photograph pages 202–203*

Bangkok and the Central Plains

GLUAY CHAAP

กล้วยฉาบ

Crisp Sweet Bananas

Green bananas are firmer and so easier to handle for deep-frying. The crispy texture takes the syrup coating readily and makes for a very tasty dessert or snack.

1 lb (500 g) green bananas
4 cups (1 qt/1 l) oil, for deep-frying

SYRUP

1 cup (8 oz/250 g) sugar
1 cup (8 fl oz/250 ml) water
1 drop jasmine flavoring
pinch of salt

Slice the bananas into long pieces about 4 in (10 cm) long and ¼ in (6 mm) thick.

Heat the oil to 375°F (190°C) in a large deep pan. Deep-fry the bananas for 10 minutes or until golden and crispy. Remove and set aside.

Combine all the ingredients for the syrup, heat to boiling and cook the syrup for 3 minutes.

Dip the fried bananas into the syrup and remove immediately.

These can be served hot, warm or cool, as either a snack or dessert.

SERVES 4

CRISP SWEET BANANAS

Bangkok and the Central Plains

MA-PROW KAEW

มะพร้าวแก้ว

Coconut Delight

Food coloring can be used to give this any color of the rainbow.

1 cup (8 fl oz/250 ml) water
1½ cups (12 oz/375 g) sugar
⅛ teaspoon salt
1 teaspoon jasmine extract
1–2 drops food coloring
2 cups (3 ½ oz/105 g) flaked/shredded coconut

▨ Place the water in a medium saucepan and add the sugar and salt. Heat on medium-high heat. Stir, and continue cooking until the mixture thickens like syrup.
▨ Add the jasmine extract and food coloring. If desired, divide the mixture and add different colors to each half. Mix in the flaked coconut and stir until all of the syrup is absorbed.
▨ Drop by teaspoonfuls onto a tray lined with a sheet of waxed paper. Allow 2 in (5 cm) space between each piece. Allow to cool, then serve.

SERVES 4

Bangkok and the Central Plains

SANGKAYA

สังขยา

Thai Custard

One of the best known Thai desserts, this traditional dish is sometimes served with steamed sticky rice (khao neow), *on page 98.*

6 eggs
1 cup (8 fl oz/250 ml) coconut cream
1 cup (8 oz/250 g) sugar
½ teaspoon jasmine extract

▨ Combine the eggs, coconut cream, sugar and jasmine extract. Beat together with a fork for 2 minutes.
▨ Heat a 9-in (23-cm) cake pan in a steamer. Pour the egg mixture into the cake pan. Cover the steamer and steam for approximately 30 minutes.
▨ Allow the custard to cool and then cut into slices.

SERVES 4

COCONUT DELIGHT

CRISP SWEET TARO (TOP, RECIPE PAGE 212)
AND THAI CUSTARD (BOTTOM)

Bangkok and the Central Plains

PUEK CHAAP

เผือกฉาบ

Crisp Sweet Taro

A favorite among the Thai people, this dessert or snack is readily available in markets and food stalls. The glaze on the outside is almost like candy, complementing the tender taro on the inside.

1 lb (500 g) taro/sweet potato
2½ cups (20 fl oz/625 ml) oil, for deep-frying
1¾ cups (14 oz/440 g) sugar
3 tablespoons water
pinch of salt

▓ Peel the brown outer skin from the taro and discard. Rinse the taro and wipe dry.
▓ Cut the taro in half lengthwise. Slice it lengthwise again, leaving four equal quarters. Slice each quarter diagonally into ¼-in (3-mm) thick pieces, which are about 2 in (5 cm) long by 1–1½ in (2.5–3.5 cm) wide.
▓ Heat the oil and deep-fry the taro slices in small batches at 375°F (190°C) until golden brown on all sides.
▓ Heat the sugar, water and salt to boiling in a small saucepan. Continue to boil for 3 minutes.
▓ Dip the fried taro slices in the sugar solution so that they are coated all over. Set aside to cool.

SERVES 4 *Photograph page 211*

The North

KHAO NEOW PIAG LAMYAI

ข้าวเหนียวเปียกลำไย

Sweet Rice Pudding with Longan

When longans come into season, this dessert tastes extra special. However if fresh longans are not available, canned longans can be substituted, or rambutans.

1 cup (8 oz/250 g) sticky rice
3 cups (24 fl oz/750 ml) water
¾ cup (6 oz/185 g) sugar
1 cup fresh seeded longans
½ cup (4 fl oz/125 ml) coconut cream
pinch of salt

▓ Rinse the sticky rice then place in a medium saucepan and add the water. Cook until the rice is soft, stirring occasionally. Add the sugar and continue to stir.
▓ Add the longans and stir into the rice. Remove from heat and allow to cool.
▓ Add the salt to the coconut cream and stir until the salt is fully dissolved.
▓ Garnish the cooked rice and fruit with the coconut cream mixture.

SERVES 4

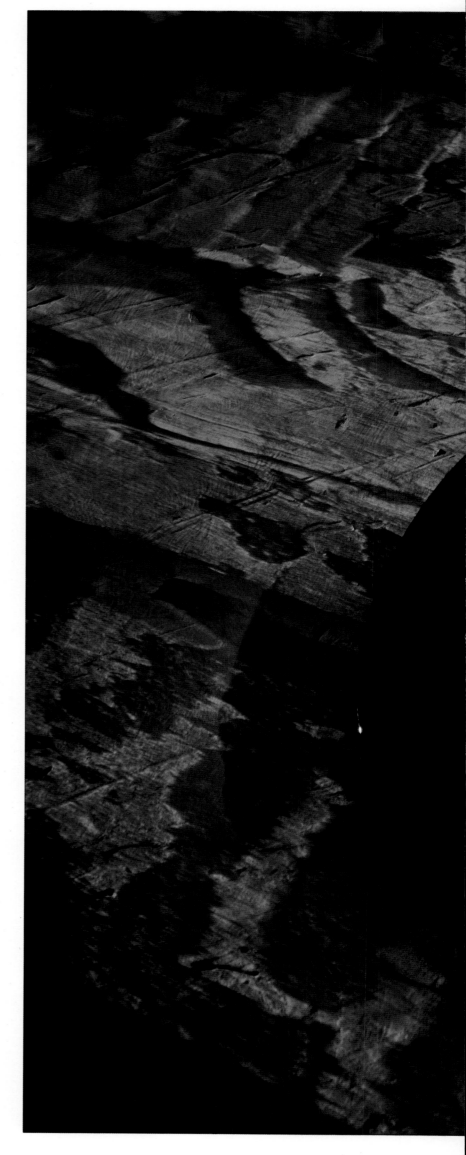

SWEET RICE PUDDING WITH LONGAN, GARNISHED WITH RAMBUTAN

SWEET STICKY RICE

Bangkok and the Central Plains

KANOM DUANG

ขนมด้วง

Short Noodles Rolled in Coconut

In the early morning hours in Bangkok the vendors sell this favorite sweet snack to the waiting customers. This light and tasty dish provides energy for the morning, ready for a day's work. It is also popular as a sweet ending to a meal.

1½ cups (6 oz/185 g) rice flour
1½ cups (6 oz/185 g) tapioca flour
1¼ cups (10 fl oz/310 ml) scented jasmine water (see glossary)
1 drop of pandanus extract for green color
1 drop red coloring
¾ cup (6 fl oz/180 ml) chilled coconut cream
1 cup (1½ oz/45 g) flaked/shredded coconut
½ cup (4 oz/125 g) sugar
pinch of salt
¼ cup (1¼ oz/40 g) toasted sesame seeds

▧ Combine the rice flour and 5 oz (155 g) of the tapioca flour together in a large bowl. Heat the scented jasmine water to boiling in a small saucepan and immediately pour into the bowl of flour. Stir to mix until the flour resembles a very thick dough. Knead until smooth.
▧ Divide the dough into three equal parts. Add the green coloring to one of the portions and knead into the dough until the color is even. Add the red coloring to another portion, leaving one batch white. You should have dough in three colors—green, pink and white.
▧ Dust your hands with the rest of the tapioca flour and pinch off a ball of dough about ½ in (1 cm) in diameter. Roll it in the palm of your hand to form a thin noodle about 2¼ in (5.5 cm long). Repeat until all the dough is used. Heat a large pot of water to boiling and boil the noodles for 1 minute.

▧ Drain the noodles, then place in a bowl containing the chilled coconut cream. Drain, then roll the noodles in the flaked coconut. Set aside the noodles on a serving plate.
▧ Combine the sugar, salt and toasted sesame seeds. Place in a serving bowl. To eat, place a portion of the noodles in a dish and sprinkle the sugar mixture over the noodles.

SERVES 4

Bangkok and the Central Plains

KHAO NEOW KAEW

ข้าวเหนียวแก้ว

Sweet Sticky Rice

Usually fresh pandanus leaves are used to color and flavor the rice for this delicious dessert. Similar results are achieved using pandanus extract or commercial food colorings.

1 cup (8 oz/250 g) sticky rice
3 cups (24 fl oz/750 ml) water
2 teaspoons pandanus extract
⅛ teaspoon salt
¾ cup (6 fl oz/180 ml) coconut cream
⅔ cup (5 oz/155 g) sugar

▧ Soak the rice in the water with the pandanus extract overnight. The next day, drain and place in a steamer. Cover and steam for 20 minutes on high heat.
▧ Combine the salt with the coconut cream and stir into the hot steamed rice. Cover the rice and leave in the steamer for another 10 minutes. Remove to a bowl and thoroughly mix in the sugar. Serve in small cups or bowls.

SERVES 4

Bangkok and the Central Plains

SA-KOO PIAG

สาคูเปียก

Tapioca Pudding

Used to balance the palate after a fiery Thai meal, this dessert is not very sweet. Toasted sesame seeds can be sprinkled on top.

1 cup (6 oz/185 g) small tapioca pearls
6 cups (1½ qt/1.5 l) water
1½ cups (12 oz/375 g) sugar
2 cups (16 fl oz/500 ml) coconut cream
pinch of salt
2 cups assorted sliced canned Thai fruit, such as jackfruit, longan, lychee, coconut meat, rambutan or palm seed

Rinse the tapioca then place in a large saucepan and add the water. Heat to boiling, stirring constantly. Reduce heat to medium and simmer for 15 minutes, or until all the pearls are soft and clear.

Add 1 cup (8 oz/250 g) of the sugar and half the coconut cream and salt. Stir to combine, then add the sliced fruit.

Mix together the rest of the coconut cream and sugar to make a topping. Divide the fruit mixture into individual bowls and pour some of the topping over each. Serve warm.

SERVES 4

Bangkok and the Central Plains

TAB-TIM GROB

ทับทิมกรอบ

Crispy Water Chestnuts

This is a very light and refreshing dessert which is perfect for summer.

8 oz (250 g) peeled water chestnuts (fresh if possible, otherwise use canned)
1 cup (8 fl oz/250 ml) water tinted with red food coloring
½ cup (2 oz/60 g) tapioca starch/tapioca flour
1 cup (8 oz/250 g) sugar
1 cup (8 fl oz/250 ml) water
pinch of salt
½ cup (4 fl oz/125 ml) coconut cream
1 cup ice cubes

Cut each peeled water chestnut into a square by trimming the edges. Place the water chestnuts in the colored water and allow to soak for 30 minutes to pick up the color of the water. Drain and set aside.

Heat a large saucepan of water to boiling. Roll the water chestnuts in the tapioca starch and drop them into the boiling water. Boil until they float to the top, or for 4–5 minutes. Canned water chestnuts will not require boiling. Remove them with a strainer and drop immediately into a large pan of cold water. Hold at this stage until ready to serve.

Dissolve the sugar in the cup of water and heat to boiling. Allow to cool.

Mix the salt with the coconut cream and set aside.

When ready to serve, drain the water chestnuts and place in a glass bowl with the sugar water, and add the ice cubes.

Each guest is served a portion of the chilled water chestnuts in a smaller glass bowl and this is then topped with the coconut cream mixture.

SERVES 4

TAPIOCA PUDDING (LEFT) AND CRISPY WATER CHESTNUTS (TOP RIGHT)

SWEET RICE WITH SYRUP

Bangkok and the Central Plains

GAENG BUAD TUA DAM

แกงบวดถั่วดำ

Black Beans in Coconut Milk

These black beans are cooked until tender and combined with a creamy coconut sauce. This sauce can also be served alone or over sticky rice.

1 cup (6 oz/185 g) dried black beans
5 cups (1¼ qt/1.25 l) water

SAUCE

1¾ cups (14 fl oz/440 ml) coconut milk
¼ cup (2 oz/60 g) sugar
¼ cup (1½ oz/45 g) palm sugar (*nam taan peep*)
pinch of salt

▩ Soak the black beans overnight in water. Drain them and cook in the 5 cups of water until soft. Drain.
▩ Combine the remaining ingredients in a large saucepan, and add the beans. Heat to boiling and serve.
▩ If you would like a more creamy texture, add some coconut cream. This will make a richer dessert.

SERVES 4

The North

KANOM NEOW

ขนมเหนียว

Sweet Rice with Syrup

This tasty dessert makes a very nice ending to a Thai meal. It can be made in advance and is a favorite dessert of the North where sticky rice is more popular.

DOUGH

2 cups (8 oz/250 g) sticky rice flour
1 cup (4 oz/125 g) rice flour
1 cup (8 fl oz/250 ml) hot water
1 teaspoon pandanus extract

SYRUP

1 cup (8 fl oz/250 ml) hot water
¾ cup (5 oz/155 g) palm sugar (*nam taan peep*)

extra rice flour for dusting
5 cups (1¼ qt/1.25 l) water
1½ cups (2 1/2 oz/75 g) flaked/shredded coconut
½ cup (4 oz/125 g) sticky rice

▩ Combine the rice flours in a large bowl. Add the hot water and pandanus extract. Knead the dough until smooth. Set aside.
▩ For the syrup, combine the hot water with the sugar and heat to boiling in a small saucepan. Continue to boil until it reaches the syrup stage (just before it sets). Remove and allow to cool. Set aside.
▩ Roll the dough out into a ½-in (1-cm) thick sheet. Cut into ½-in x ½-in x 2-in (1-cm x 1-cm x 5-cm) pieces. Use more rice flour to dust the dough pieces.
▩ Heat the water to boiling. Drop in the pieces of dough and boil until they float to the top. Remove the cooked dough pieces and sprinkle with the flaked coconut.
▩ Sauté the rice in a skillet until golden brown.
▩ Before serving the dumplings, drizzle with the syrup and sprinkle with the roasted rice.

SERVES 4

Bangkok and the Central Plains

KHAO NEOW MOON

ข้าวเหนียวมูล

Sweet Glutinous Rice

This steamed sticky rice is the basis of many Thai desserts. It has the delicate scent of jasmine and imparts a flavor which is enhanced by many of the ingredients in the various dessert recipes.

2 cups (1 lb/500 g) sticky rice

SAUCE

2 cups (16 fl oz/500 ml) coconut milk
pinch of salt
½ cup (4 oz/125 g) sugar

▩ Soak the rice in water overnight, or in warm water for 2 hours. Drain, then place the rice in a steamer and steam for 15 minutes.
▩ Combine the sauce ingredients in a large bowl. Add the steamed sticky rice and stir to combine. Cover the bowl and allow to stand for 10 minutes before serving.

SERVES 4

SWEET GLUTINOUS RICE (BOTTOM) AND
BLACK BEANS IN COCONUT MILK (TOP)

The South

KANOM TUAY FOO

ขนมถ้วยฟู

Puffy Cups

The cake's delicate taste is very similar to a sponge cake and is perfect as a dessert after a spicy Thai meal. It is very pleasing to the eye as well as the palate.

¾ cup (3 oz/90 g) rice flour
⅓ cup (3 oz/90 g) sugar
½ teaspoon baking soda/bicarbonate of soda
1 drop of red or yellow food coloring
½ cup (4 fl oz/125 ml) scented jasmine water (see glossary)

▓ Combine the rice flour, sugar and baking soda thoroughly in a bowl. Add the food coloring to the jasmine water and stir to combine thoroughly, then add to the bowl of dry ingredients and stir until the batter is smooth.
▓ Arrange eight tea cups in a large steamer or use a muffin pan that fits into the steamer. The cups or muffin pan can also be lined with cupcake liners.
▓ Steam the cups uncovered for 2 minutes to heat them then pour in the batter and cover the steamer. Steam on high heat for 15 minutes. Remove them from the steamer and allow to cool for 5 minutes. Turn the steamed cakes out of the cups and serve warm or cool.

SERVES 4

Bangkok and the Central Plains

KANOM TUA-PAEP

ขนมถั่วแปบ

Mung Bean Stuffing

Mung beans are steamed, encased in dough and rolled in shredded coconut for this dish, creating a light dessert or snack.

1 cup (8 oz/250 g) dried mung beans
2 cups (8 oz/250 g) sticky rice flour
1 cup (4 oz/125 g) rice flour
1 cup (8 fl oz/250 ml) boiling water
⅖ cup (1 oz/30 g) flaked/shredded coconut
½ cup (4 oz/125 g) sugar
pinch of salt
¼ cup (1¼ oz/40 g) toasted sesame seeds

▓ Soak the mung beans overnight in water to cover. Drain, and steam the mung beans for 20 minutes or until tender. Set aside.
▓ Combine the sticky rice flour and rice flour in a large bowl. Gradually add the boiling water and knead until a smooth dough forms.
▓ Pinch off a 2-in (5-cm) piece of dough and roll it with a rolling pin until a 3½-in (9-cm) circle is formed. Place 1 tablespoon of cooked mung beans on the dough circle, fold the dough over, then seal the edges by pinching all around to form a filled crescent. Continue until all of the dough is used.
▓ Spray the bottom of a steamer with water and evenly space the filled dough in the steamer. Cover and steam for about 20 minutes.
▓ Remove the dumplings and roll them in the flaked coconut. Place on a tray.
▓ Combine the sugar with the salt. Sprinkle the sugar and salt mixture over the dumplings and then sprinkle with toasted sesame seeds.

SERVES 4

PUFFY CUPS (TOP) AND MUNG BEAN STUFFING (BOTTOM)

The Northeast
KHAO NEOW TAD

ข้าวเหนียวตัด

Sticky Rice Squares

When sticky rice is steamed with coconut milk the resulting flavor combines well with the texture of the steamed rice. This dessert can be cut into decorative shapes for presentation.

⅓ cup (3 oz/90 g) dried black beans
2 cups (1 lb/500 g) sticky rice
1 cup (8 fl oz/250 ml) coconut milk
pinch of salt
¼ cup (2 oz/60 g) sugar

TOPPING SAUCE

1 cup (8 fl oz/250 ml) coconut cream
pinch of salt
½ cup (4 oz/125 g) sugar
1 tablespoon tapioca starch/tapioca flour

▧ Soak the black beans overnight in warm water to cover. Also cover the sticky rice with water and soak overnight.
▧ The next day, drain the black beans then cover them with fresh water and simmer for 1 hour. Drain and set aside. Drain the rice and place it in a square pan 8 in x 8 in x 2 in (20 cm x 20 cm x 5 cm).
▧ Combine the coconut milk, salt and sugar together, stir to dissolve, and pour over the rice in the pan. Place the pan of rice in a steamer, cover, and steam for 30 minutes or until soft throughout.
▧ While the rice is cooking, thoroughly combine all the ingredients for the topping sauce. Pour the sauce over the steamed sticky rice. Then cover the steamer and continue steaming on high heat for 5 minutes.
▧ Uncover the steamer and sprinkle the cooked drained black beans on the surface. Cover the steamer and continue steaming for another 5 minutes.
▧ Allow the sticky rice to cool and then cut into squares before serving.

SERVES 4

The Northeast
GLUAY TAAK

กล้วยตาก

Sun-Dried Bananas

Drying the bananas in the sun was a way of preserving the fruit for later use. A favorite snack food in Thailand.

1 lb (500 g) small bananas, about 6
1 cup (10 oz/315 g) honey

▧ Peel the bananas, slice thinly and lay on a tray. Allow to dry in the sun for 5 days, turning occasionally to allow for even drying. The bananas will be dark when they are ready. On the fifth day, dip into the honey and dry for 1 more day.
▧ A faster way of achieving the same effect is to lay the banana slices on an oven rack and bake at 300°F (150°C) for 40 minutes or until golden brown. Then dip them into the honey and bake for 20 minutes more.
▧ Store in a jar with a tight lid and eat when desired.

SERVES 4

SUN-DRIED BANANAS

Bangkok and the Central Plains
KHAO NEOW DAM
NAA GRACHEEK

ข้าวเหนียวดำหน้ากระฉีก

Black Rice with Coconut

This variety of rice is naturally black and the texture is firm. It is usually grown away from other varieties of rice so that the color does not blend with the other rice grown in nearby fields. This favorite Thai dessert has a rich color.

2 cups (1 lb/500 g) black rice
2 cups (16 fl oz/500 ml) coconut milk
½ cup (4 oz/125 g) sugar
1½ cups (2½ oz/75 g) flaked/shredded coconut
½ cup (3 oz/90 g) palm sugar (*nam taan peep*)
pinch of salt

▧ Soak the black rice in warm water overnight. Drain, place the rice in a steamer and steam for 20 minutes on high heat.
▧ Combine half the coconut milk with the sugar and mix thoroughly into the hot steamed rice. Set aside.
▧ Place the flaked coconut, the rest of the coconut milk, the palm sugar and salt in a medium saucepan and cook on high heat to reduce until almost dry. Use as a topping for the black rice. Serve warm.

SERVES 4

STICKY RICE SQUARES (TOP)
AND BLACK RICE WITH COCONUT (BOTTOM)

The North

KANOM TIEN

ขนมเทียน

Mung Beans in Banana Leaf

Wrapping the sticky rice flour dough filled with mung beans in a banana leaf gives the typical triangular shape. This can be served either as a dessert or snack. The banana leaf is not eaten.

1½ cups (12 oz/375 g) dried mung beans
3 cups (12 oz/375 g) sticky rice flour
½ cup (3 oz/90 g) palm sugar (*nam taan peep*)
2 cups (16 fl oz/500 ml) hot water
3 tablespoons oil
2 tablespoons chopped cilantro/coriander root (*raak pak chee*)
2 garlic cloves (*kratiem*), minced
pinch of salt
1 lb (500 g) banana leaves (available frozen)

▧ Soak the mung beans in water overnight. The next day, drain, then place the mung beans in a steamer and steam for 30 minutes. Remove, allow to cool, and mash to form a paste. Set aside and keep covered.
▧ Combine the sticky rice flour and sugar in a large bowl. Add the hot water and blend well. Mix to form a smooth dough.
▧ Heat a large skillet and add the oil. Sauté the cilantro root, garlic and salt for 30 seconds. Mix in the mashed mung beans.
▧ Cut sections from the banana leaves and cut a 10-in (25-cm) circle from each section.
▧ Pinch off a 2-in (5-cm) ball from the dough. Press the ball out to a 5-in (12.5-cm) diameter circle. Fill with 1 tablespoon of the mung bean filling and enclose the filling with the dough.
▧ Pick up a banana leaf circle using both hands, positioned as if on the numbers 4 and 8 on a clock face. Push both hands together to form a funnel shape, making sure the fold is in the inside of the funnel-shaped container.
▧ Drop the filled dough in the center part of the banana leaf funnel. Holding the folded side close to you, fold this part up. Fold the other two sides in to overlap. Fold the top down and tuck under the first fold. Pin with a piece of bamboo or a toothpick, or tie with twine. It should resemble a triangle.
▧ Repeat until all the dough is used. Place the filled triangles in a steamer and steam for 15 minutes. Allow to cool. Serve at room temperature.

SERVES 4

Bangkok and the Central Plains

BUA LOI

บัวลอย

Floating Lotus Seeds

"Lotus seeds" floating in a pool of coconut milk make a favorite winter dessert. Sometimes an egg is added to the coconut milk to give a richer taste.

1½ cups (6 oz/185 g) sticky rice flour
½ cup (2 oz/60 g) tapioca starch/tapioca flour
2 cups (16 fl oz/500 ml) hot water
2½ cups (20 fl oz/625 ml) coconut milk
½ cup (3 oz/90 g) palm sugar (*nam taan peep*)
1 teaspoon jasmine extract
pinch of salt
5 cups (1¼ qt/1.25 l) water

▧ Combine the rice flour and tapioca starch and gradually add the hot water to the mixture. Continue to mix until the dough is completely blended, using a spoon and kneading with hands. Cover and set aside.
▧ Heat the coconut milk in a large saucepan and add the palm sugar, jasmine extract and salt. Heat to boiling, stirring to dissolve the sugar. Remove from heat and set aside.

224

The South
GAENG BUAD FAK THONG

แกงบวดฟักทอง

Squash in Coconut Sauce

The color of winter squash (fak thong) is similar to that of Thai monks'
robes. This dessert is commonly made at home for offering to the monks at
temple ceremonies. It also makes a delightful finish to an elegant meal.

2 cups (16 fl oz/500 ml) coconut milk
¼ cup (2 oz/60 g) sugar or coconut sugar
2 cups sliced winter squash/pumpkin, in
    1 in x 1 in x ¼ in (2.5 cm x 2.5 cm x 6 mm) pieces

▨ Heat the coconut milk to boiling and add the sugar. Stir and
boil again. Add the sliced squash and simmer for 15 minutes.
Serve cold.

SERVES 4   *Photograph page 227*

The South
TA-GO

ตะโก้

Pudding with Coconut Topping

In Thailand small containers made of banana leaves are used for a
beautiful presentation which contrasts green with the white dessert. This is
a slightly sweet dessert which can be eaten any time of day.

1 cup (4 oz/125 g) rice flour
¾ cup (6 oz/185 g) sugar
2¼ cups (18 fl oz/560 ml) scented jasmine water (see glossary)

PUDDING WITH COCONUT TOPPING

TOPPING

⅓ cup (1½ oz/45 g) rice flour
2 cups (16 fl oz/500 ml) coconut cream
2 tablespoons sugar
pinch of salt

▨ Combine the rice flour and sugar with the water and set
aside for 15 minutes, then heat to boiling in a medium
saucepan. Simmer, stirring constantly, for 15 minutes. After
cooking, half-fill twelve ⅓-cup capacity molds or small banana
leaf cups.
▨ Combine the topping ingredients in a small saucepan and
bring to a slow boil. Cook, stirring constantly, on low heat
for 20 minutes. Spoon carefully into the molds on top of the
first layer and allow to cool. The top layer should be thinner
than the bottom layer. If using molds, unmold to serve.

SERVES 4

Bangkok and the Central Plains
KRONG KRAENG GA-THI

ครองแครงกะทิ

Clam Shell Delight

The picture of clams floating in a sea of coconut milk is as appealing
to the eye as it is to the palate. Using the proper wooden mold,
which resembles a paddle with fine line grooves, makes this dessert
much more delightful.

1½ cups (6 oz/185 g) rice flour
¾ cup (3 oz/90 g) tapioca starch/tapioca flour
1 cup (8 fl oz/250 ml) hot water
3 cups (24 fl oz/750 ml) coconut milk
1 cup (8 oz/250 g) sugar
pinch of salt
¼ cup (1¼ oz/40 g) toasted sesame seeds

1-in (2.5-cm) clam mold or a fine-tooth comb (the fine teeth of
    the comb resembles the outside surface of a clam)

▨ Combine the rice flour with ½ cup (2 oz/60 g) of the tapioca starch in a bowl. Add the hot water a little at a time and
mix to make a pliable dough. Knead until smooth. Keep the
dough covered to prevent it from drying out.
▨ Using the leftover tapioca starch to dust your fingers, pinch
off pieces of the dough to form ½-in (1-cm) diameter balls. Dust
your fingers and the clam mold, or the fine teeth of the comb,
with the starch and press the dough into the mold. Roll the
dough off with your thumb, pushing and rolling the dough at
the same time into the shape of a clam. Remove onto a surface
dusted with tapioca starch.
▨ Heat a large pot of water to boiling and drop in the clam
shapes. Try not to crowd them while cooking and stir to keep
them separated. Cook in stages if necessary to avoid crowd-
ing. Continue to cook until the clam shapes float to the surface
(about 30 seconds), then remove them with a slotted spoon
and set aside.
▨ Meanwhile, combine the coconut milk, sugar and salt in a
medium saucepan. Bring to a simmer and stir intermittently.
▨ Gently drop the clam shapes into the coconut sauce. Simmer
to heat through, and serve with a sprinkling of toasted sesame
seeds.

SERVES 4

CLAM SHELL DELIGHT

228

Bangkok and the Central Plains

MED KA-NOON

เม็ดขนุน

Jackfruit Seeds

Although this dessert looks like the jackfruit seeds for which it is named, it also resembles nuggets of gold. This golden appearance makes it a very appealing dessert, which is delicious served with fruit.

8 oz (250 g) split mung beans
4 cups (1 qt/1 l) water
2½ cups (1¼ lb/625 g) sugar
4 egg yolks

Place the mung beans in a medium saucepan and add half the water. Bring to a slow simmer and cook until the beans are soft. Drain, then place the beans in a mortar and grind until smooth. A blender can be used for this process. Mix in thoroughly ½ cup (4 oz/125 g) of the sugar and allow the mixture to cool.

Take about 1 tablespoon of the mixture and shape into an oblong piece resembling a jackfruit seed or nugget. Continue until all of the mixture is used.

Heat the rest of the water to boiling in a large saucepan and add the rest of the sugar. Simmer.

Mix the egg yolks in a bowl and carefully dip a nugget into the egg yolks. Drop the nugget into the simmering syrup and cook for 5 minutes. Repeat with the remaining nuggets. Remove to a rack and allow to cool.

SERVES 4

JACKFRUIT SEEDS

SWEET RICE WITH MANGO

Bangkok and the Central Plains

Khao Neow Ma-Muang

ข้าวเหนียวมะม่วง

Sweet Rice with Mango

A favorite Thai dessert—the firm texture of the sweet rice paired with slices of fresh mango with coconut cream topping is an irresistible taste experience.

2 cups (1 lb/500 g) sticky rice, soaked overnight in water
    to cover
2 mangoes

SAUCE 1

1 cup (8 fl oz/250 ml) coconut cream
½ cup (4 oz/125 g) sugar
pinch of salt

SAUCE 2

1 cup (8 fl oz/250 ml) coconut cream
½ cup (4 oz/125 g) sugar

1 12-in (30-cm) section of banana leaf
1 teaspoon toasted sesame seeds

⁂ Drain the rice and place in an even layer in a steamer lined with cheesecloth so the rice does not fall through the holes. Steam the rice on full steam or high heat for 15 minutes.
⁂ While the rice is cooking combine the ingredients for Sauce 1. Remove the rice to a bowl and mix with Sauce 1 while the rice is still hot. Set aside.
⁂ Peel the mangoes carefully so as not to bruise the fruit. Slice in half as close to the seed as possible, then slice each half into ½-in (1-cm) slices.
⁂ Cut the banana leaf attractively and lay it on a serving plate. Arrange the sticky rice and mango slices on top of the leaf.
⁂ Combine the ingredients for Sauce 2 and either serve it separately or pour over the sticky rice. Garnish with a sprinkling of sesame seeds and perhaps an orchid or other flower on the side.

SERVES 4

231

Bangkok and the Central Plains

SANGKAYA FAK THONG OR SANGKAYA MA-PROW

สังขยาฟักทอง หรือ สังขยามะพร้าว

Baked Custard in Squash or Coconut

This is a beautiful and delicious dessert served in many Bangkok restaurants. Sometimes a small coconut is hollowed out and used as a container instead of a winter squash: both methods of presentation are equally acceptable.

2 small winter squash/pumpkins

CUSTARD

3 eggs
¾ cup (6 fl oz/180 ml) coconut cream
½ cup (3 oz/90 g) palm sugar (*nam taan peep*)
⅛ teaspoon jasmine extract

Cut the top off each squash, retaining it to act as a lid. Scoop out the seeds and some of the flesh from the squash.
Combine all the custard ingredients. Be careful not to over beat the eggs, causing too much foam. Pour carefully into the squash containers and cover with the lids. Place in a steamer over rapidly boiling water.
Cover the steamer and steam on high heat for 45 minutes. Make sure the steamer has enough water to boil for 45 minutes. Remove the steamer lid carefully and lift out the squash. Allow to cool before serving. Garnish with golden threads (*foithong*), on page 226.

SERVES 2

Bangkok and the Central Plains

KHAO NEOW NAA GOONG

ข้าวเหนียวหน้ากุ้ง

Sweet Yellow Rice with Shrimp

The sticky yellow rice makes this a very colorful dish.

2 cups (1 lb/500 g) sticky rice
4 cups (1 qt/1 l) water
1 teaspoon turmeric
1 cup (8 fl oz/250 ml) coconut milk
½ cup (4 oz/125 g) sugar
4 oz (125 g) shrimp/prawn meat, minced
1 cup (1½ oz/45 g) flaked/shredded coconut
2 drops orange food coloring
1 tablespoon oil
8 garlic cloves (*kratiem*), chopped
pinch of salt
3 tablespoons sugar
½ teaspoon white pepper
2 tablespoons chopped cilantro/coriander leaves (*bai pak chee*)
5 kaffir lime leaves (*bai ma-grood*), thinly slivered

Soak the sticky rice in the water with the turmeric overnight. Drain and steam in a steamer on high heat for 15 minutes. Remove and set aside.
Combine the coconut milk with the sugar and mix into the hot rice. Place on a large serving plate and set aside.
Combine the minced shrimp meat with the flaked coconut and food coloring very thoroughly, so the mixture is even.
Heat the oil in a skillet and fry the garlic, shrimp mixture, salt, sugar, pepper and cilantro until the mixture is reduced so much that it is almost dry. Remove to a serving dish and sprinkle the lime leaves on top.
Spread the shrimp mixture over the sticky rice and serve.

SERVES 4

SWEET YELLOW RICE WITH SHRIMP

BAKED CUSTARD IN SQUASH OR COCONUT

Sauces, Dips and Curry Pastes

Sauces, Dips and Curry Pastes

Thai cuisine relies upon a wealth of sauces and dips
to enhance the flavor of any dish. Fish sauce (*nam pla*) is
considered an essential ingredient in many of these recipes,
imparting a distinctive saltiness. Peppers of different
varieties impart the distinctive hotness, and the other herbs
and spices provide the varieties of flavors.

Nam Prik Gaeng Keow Wan

น้ำพริกแกงเขียวหวาน

Green Curry Paste

Green curry paste is used to make the hottest of all Thai curries.

10 green jalapeño peppers (*prik chee fa*)
5 green Thai chili peppers (*prik khee noo*)
1/2 cup sliced cilantro/coriander root (*raak pak chee*) or stems
    (*pak chee*)
8 garlic cloves (*kratiem*)
1/4 cup chopped shallots or purple onions
1/4 cup chopped lemon grass/citronella (*ta-krai*) or 1 tablespoon
    dried lemon grass (*ta-krai haeng*)
5 thin slices fresh galangal (*kha*) or 1 teaspoon dried galangal
    powder (*kha pon*)
1 teaspoon cumin
1 teaspoon shrimp paste (*gapi*)

Combine all the ingredients in a blender and process until smooth.

MAKES 2½ CUPS

Nam Prik Ma-Muang

น้ำพริกมะม่วง

Green Mango Dip

A good dip with seafood and fish, fresh vegetables, and boiled eggs.

8 oz (250 g) shredded green mango
6 garlic cloves (*kratiem*), minced
2 tablespoons shrimp paste (*gapi*)
1/4 cup (2 fl oz/60 ml) fish sauce (*nam pla*)

2 tablespoons lime juice
2 tablespoons sugar

Place the shredded mango, garlic and shrimp paste in a
mortar and gently mash with the pestle so that the mango is
bruised but is still in shreds. Add the remaining ingredients
and stir to combine. Remove to a serving bowl and use as a
dip for grilled meats or fresh vegetables.

MAKES 2 CUPS   *Photograph pages 234–235*

Nam Prik Gaeng Ped

น้ำพริกแกงเผ็ด

Red Curry Paste

Red and green curry pastes are the basis for most Thai curries.

1/2 cup chopped onions
8 garlic cloves (*kratiem*)
10 dried red jalapeño chilies (*prik chee fa daeng haeng*)
4 thin slices fresh galangal (*kha*)
2 tablespoons chopped lemon grass/citronella (*ta-krai*)
1 tablespoon chopped cilantro/coriander root (*raak pak chee*) or
    stems (*pak chee*)
1/2 teaspoon cumin
1 teaspoon shrimp paste (*gapi*)
1 teaspoon salt
3 tablespoons oil

Combine all the ingredients except the oil in a blender and
process until smooth.
Heat a small skillet on medium-high heat and add the oil.
Slowly fry the curry paste for 5 minutes until it is fragrant.
Remove and store in a jar for future use.

MAKES 2½ CUPS

GREEN CURRY PASTE (TOP) AND RED CURRY PASTE (BOTTOM)

HELL DIPPING SAUCE

Nam Prik Na-Rok

น้ำพริกนรก

Hell Dipping Sauce

Because it keeps well, this sauce was traditionally used by travellers.

2 cups (16 fl oz/500 ml) oil, for deep-frying
2 lb (1 kg) freshwater fish fillets
1 cup dried green Thai chili peppers (*prik khee noo haeng*)
½ cup garlic cloves (*kratiem*), unpeeled
½ cup whole shallots, unpeeled
2 tablespoons shrimp paste (*gapi*)
¼ cup (2 fl oz/60 ml) fish sauce (*nam pla*)
3 tablespoons palm sugar (*nam taan peep*)

Heat the oil in a large skillet to 375°F (190°C). Deep-fry the fish fillets until very crispy and golden brown.

Charcoal-broil/grill the chilies, garlic and shallots until their outsides are charred. Remove the garlic and shallot skins.

Place the fried fish, chilies, garlic and shallots in a mortar and mash with the pestle until smooth, or use a blender.

Place the shrimp paste, fish sauce and palm sugar in a small saucepan and cook for about 15 minutes on medium-high heat, so that the mixture is reduced to a paste.

Thoroughly combine the mashed ingredients with the reduced sauce ingredients. Store in a jar with a tight-fitting lid and use as a dipping paste or for cooking.

MAKES 4 CUPS

Nam Jim Satay

น้ำจิ้มสะเต๊ะ

Peanut Sauce

This richly flavored sauce is usually served with satays.

1¾ cups (14 fl oz /440 ml) coconut milk
2 tablespoons red curry paste (*nam prik gaeng ped*) (see page 236)
¼ cup (2 fl oz/60 ml) fish sauce (*nam pla*)
3 tablespoons sugar
1 cup (8 oz/250 g) ground roasted peanuts

Combine all the ingredients in a medium saucepan and simmer for 15 minutes, stirring constantly.

MAKES 2½ CUPS

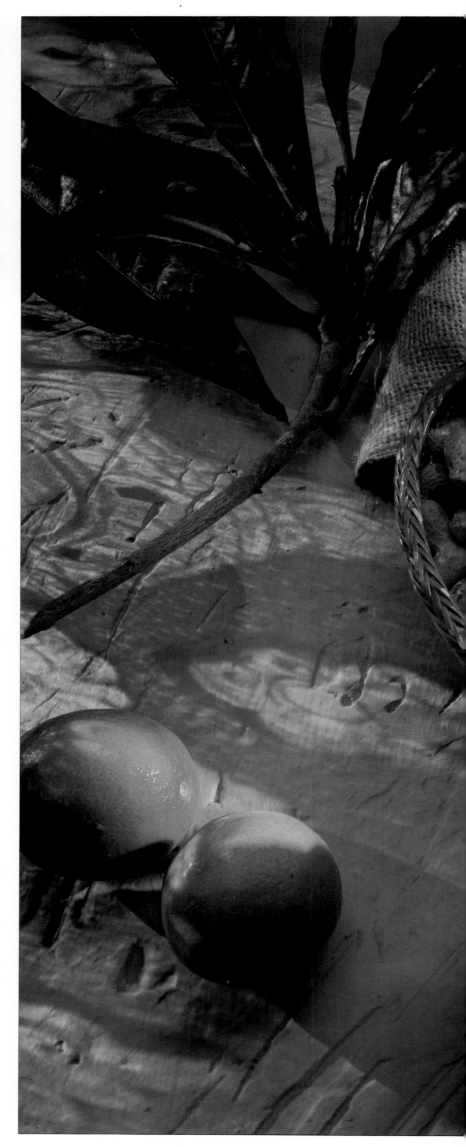

PEANUT SAUCE

Nam Prik Gaeng Massaman

น้ำพริกแกงมัสมั่น

Massaman Curry Paste

A different style of curry paste, this reflects an Indian influence.

5 tablespoons (2½ fl oz/75 ml) oil
4 dried jalapeño peppers (*prik chee fa haeng*)
½ cup chopped onions
½ cup chopped garlic cloves (*kratiem*)
1 tablespoon chopped lemon grass/citronella (*ta-krai*)
2 thin slices galangal (*kha*)
2 shallots
¼ teaspoon kaffir lime skin (*piew ma-grood*)
2 tablespoons dried cilantro/coriander (*pak chee pon*)
1 tablespoon cumin
1 teaspoon cinnamon powder
1 tablespoon star anise powder

▨ Heat a small skillet on medium heat and add the oil. Fry the peppers, onions and garlic until golden brown.
▨ Combine the fried ingredients and all remaining ingredients in a blender and process until thoroughly mixed.

MAKES 2 CUPS

Nam Prik Panaeng

น้ำพริกพะแนง

Panaeng Curry Paste

The name of this curry paste shows its Malaysian origin.

4 oz (125 g) dried green jalapeño peppers (*prik chee fa haeng*)
¼ cup coriander seed (*med pak chee*)
½ cup chopped onions or shallots
½ cup chopped garlic (*kratiem*)
2 tablespoons chopped galangal (*kha*)
2 tablespoons kaffir lime skin (*piew ma-grood*)
¼ cup chopped lemon grass/citronella (*ta-krai*)
2 tablespoons shrimp paste (*gapi*)
1 teaspoon salt

▨ Place all the ingredients in a mortar and crush with the pestle to form a thick paste, or process in a blender. Store in a jar with a tight-fitting lid for future use—it will keep indefinitely.

MAKES 3 CUPS

Nam Prik Pow

น้ำพริกเผา

Black Chili Paste

This dip will give any food a much richer taste, and add spiciness.

1 cup (8 fl oz/250 ml) oil, for deep-frying
4 oz (125 g) dried green jalapeño peppers (*prik chee fa haeng*)
1 cup chopped shallots
1 cup chopped garlic (*kratiem*)
8 oz (250 g) dried shrimp/prawns

BLACK CHILI PASTE

2 tablespoons shrimp paste (*gapi*)
⅓ cup (3 fl oz/90 ml) fish sauce (*nam pla*)
¼ cup (2 oz/60 g) sugar

▨ Heat a small pan with the oil and deep-fry the dried peppers, shallots and garlic until dark brown. Place the fried ingredients with all the others in a blender, and process until a smooth mixture forms.
▨ Pour the entire mixture into a medium skillet and fry on medium heat for 5 minutes. Remove, cool, and place in a jar with a tight lid and use as needed. It will keep indefinitely.

MAKES 4 CUPS

Prik Dong

พริกดอง

Chili in Vinegar

This very simple sauce adds flavor to any dish.

6 green jalapeño peppers (*prik chee fa*), sliced in rounds
⅓ cup (3 fl oz/90 ml) vinegar

▨ Combine the peppers with the vinegar. Use as a sauce or dip for noodles or to improve or change the flavor of other dishes.

MAKES ⅔ CUP *Photograph page 242*

Nam Pla Prik

น้ำปลาพริก

Fish Sauce with Chili

Most popular of all the sauces, this can be served with most dishes.

¼ cup (2 fl oz/60 ml) fish sauce (*nam pla*)
5 tablespoons (2½ fl oz/75 ml) lemon or lime juice
2 garlic cloves (*kratiem*), minced
5 green Thai chili peppers (*prik khee noo*), chopped

▨ Combine all the ingredients and use as a dipping sauce. This sauce can also be used in curries or stir-fried dishes.

MAKES ¾ CUP

Jaew Bong

แจ่วบอง

Northeast Anchovy Paste

This paste is a very popular dip, used in the Northeast to add flavor to any fresh vegetable or cooked meat.

8 oz (250 g) fresh/frozen anchovy fish (use canned
  if unavailable)
1 banana leaf

SAUCE

¼ cup chopped lemon grass/citronella (*ta-krai*)
¼ cup chopped shallots
¼ cup chopped galangal (*kha*)
2 tablespoons chopped green Thai chili peppers (*prik khee noo*)
¼ cup (2 fl oz/60 ml) tamarind juice (*ma-kaam piag*)
  (see glossary)
5 lime leaves, sliced
4 garlic cloves (*kratiem*)

▨ Remove the head and bones of the anchovy fish. Cut the banana leaf in 12-in (30-cm) pieces. Neatly wrap the anchovy fish together using the banana leaf sections.
▨ Cook the wrapped anchovy fish over charcoal for 4 minutes on each side. The fish can also be broiled/grilled, or baked in the oven at 350°F (180°C) for 15 minutes. If using canned anchovies just drain away the oil.
▨ Remove the fish from the banana leaves and place them in a mortar with the sauce ingredients and mash with a pestle until all ingredients are combined.
▨ Serve the paste as a dip for barbecued fish and steamed or fresh vegetables.

SERVES 4

FISH SAUCE WITH CHILI (LEFT) AND CHILI
IN VINEGAR (RIGHT, RECIPE PAGE 241)

Nam Prik Jaew

น้ำพริกแจ่ว

Spicy Anchovy Dip

*The charcoal-broiled lemon grass and shallots give this dip a richer flavor
ideal for barbecued meats such as barbecued chicken (gai yang), on
page 130, and tiger cry beef (seua rong hai), on page 134.*

2 cups (16 fl oz/500 ml) water
8 oz (250 g) anchovy fish (2 fish)
¼ cup chopped roasted lemon grass/citronella *(ta-krai)**
¼ cup chopped roasted shallots*
¼ cup chopped roasted galangal *(kha)**
15 roasted green Thai chili peppers *(prik khee noo)**
6 garlic cloves *(kratiem)*
½ cup (4 fl oz/125 ml) tamarind juice *(ma-kaam piag)*
  (see glossary)
2 tablespoons fish sauce *(nam pla)*

Boil the water in a medium saucepan. Add the fish to the pan and
boil for 5 minutes, leaving at least ½ cup (4 fl oz/125 ml) of stock.
Place the roasted lemon grass, shallots, galangal, chilies and
garlic in a mortar and mash until all ingredients are finely ground.
Strain the fish stock and add to the mashed mixture. Add the
tamarind juice and fish sauce and mix all the ingredients together.
Use as a dip for barbecued meats.
* *Charcoal broil/grill, or burn over a gas flame, whole lemon grass,
shallots, galangal and chili peppers for a few minutes, until barbecued but not black. Measure required amounts after cooking.*

MAKES 2 CUPS

Nam Prik Pla-Raa

น้ำพริกปลาร้า

Pickled Fish Dipping Sauce

*The pickled fish and fresh fish together make this thicker dipping sauce
suitable for any selection of fresh vegetables.*

8 oz (250 g) pickled fish
2 cups (16 fl oz/500 ml) water
8 oz (250 g) firm-fleshed freshwater fish
2 stalks lemon grass/citronella *(ta-krai)*, chopped
6 garlic cloves *(kratiem)*, minced
¼ cup chopped green Thai chili peppers *(prik khee noo)*
6 shallots, chopped
2 teaspoons chopped galangal *(kha)*
⅓ cup (3 fl oz/90 ml) fish sauce *(nam pla)*
⅓ cup (3 fl oz/90 ml) lime juice

Boil the pickled fish in the water for 10 minutes. Strain,
pressing as much liquid through as possible. Reserve only the
liquid, discarding the pickled fish.
Broil/grill the freshwater fish until done, then remove all
the bones, reserving the cooked flesh.
Put the lemon grass, garlic, chilies, shallots and galangal in
a mortar and pound with a pestle until ground to a coarse
mash.
Add the fish sauce, lime juice and strained fish juice. Combine thoroughly with the finely chopped cooked fish flesh and
remove to a bowl. Use as a dip for any fresh vegetables.

MAKES 3 CUPS

243

YOUNG TAMARIND PASTE

❋ Place the dried shrimp, young tamarind, garlic and shrimp paste in a mortar and gently pound with the pestle until all the ingredients are mashed. Add the fish sauce, lime juice and sugar and carefully stir to combine. Alternatively, all the ingredients can be blended in a blender.

❋ Heat a medium skillet and add the oil. Stir-fry the mixture on medium heat until it has reduced to a medium-thick paste.

* *Young tamarind is still green and the seeds are not hard so it can be blended to form a paste. Do not use the outer peel.*

MAKES 2 CUPS

MA-MUANG DONG

มะม่วงดอง

Mango Pickle

Not just a condiment, this dish can be eaten as a snack before lunch or dinner and whets the appetite for the remainder of the meal. It can be kept indefinitely.

PICKLING SOLUTION

4 cups (1 qt/1 l) water
1 cup (8 oz/250 g) salt
½ cup (4 oz/125 g) sugar

2½ lb (1.25 kg) green mangoes

❋ Combine all the ingredients for the pickling solution in a medium enamel or stainless steel saucepan, heat to boiling, then set aside and allow to cool.

❋ Peel the mangoes and slice into sections, leaving in large pieces.

❋ Place in a large container (glass is best) and pour the pickling solution over the mango pieces to cover.

❋ Allow to sit for at least 2 weeks before eating.

MAKES 4 CUPS

KHING DONG

ขิงดอง

Ginger Pickle

If young tender ginger is available, it need not be peeled as its skin is translucent. If using regular ginger the outer skin must be peeled. Pickled ginger can be eaten with roasted meats or poultry.

PICKLING SOLUTION

2 cups (16 fl oz/500 ml) vinegar
2 cups (16 fl oz/500 ml) water
¼ cup (2 oz/60 g) salt
1 lb (500 g) sugar

2 lb (1 kg) fresh ginger
½ teaspoon baking soda/bicarbonate of soda

❋ Combine the ingredients for the pickling solution in an enamel or stainless steel pan, heat to boiling then allow to cool.

❋ Peel the ginger if necessary and slice very thinly. Rub the ginger slices with the baking soda and allow to sit for 5 minutes.

❋ Place the ginger in a jar and pour the pickling solution over the slices to cover. Keep for 2 weeks in the refrigerator and then it is ready to use.

MAKES 4 CUPS

NAM PRIK MA-KAAM

น้ำพริกมะขาม

Young Tamarind Paste

Another of the interesting and flavorful dips that team with the natural flavors of meat and vegetables to give Thai cuisine its variety of tastes.

¼ cup (½ oz/15 g) dried shrimp/prawns
8 oz (250 g) young tamarind,* peeled and chopped
6 garlic cloves (kratiem), peeled
2 tablespoons shrimp paste (gapi)
¼ cup (2 fl oz/60 ml) fish sauce (nam pla)
2 tablespoons lime juice
3 tablespoons sugar
3 tablespoons oil

MANGO PICKLE (TOP), GINGER PICKLE (BOTTOM LEFT)
AND GARLIC PICKLE (RIGHT)

KRATIEM DONG

กระเทียมดอง

Garlic Pickle

Whole clusters of garlic cloves are pickled in this solution and allowed to sit for at least a week after which they can be kept indefinitely. These cloves of garlic can be eaten with any dish or used in cooking.

2 cups (16 fl oz/500 ml) water
1 lb (500 g) garlic (*kratiem*)

PICKLING SOLUTION

2 cups (16 fl oz/500 ml) vinegar
1 lb (500 g) sugar
¼ cup (2 oz/60 g) salt

▓ Heat the water to boiling in a medium saucepan and simmer the clusters of garlic for 10 minutes. Drain and set aside to dry for 5 minutes.
▓ Heat the pickling solution to boiling in a medium enamel or stainless steel saucepan, then remove from the heat and drop in the clusters of garlic. When cool transfer to a glass jar and allow to pickle for at least a week. Peel the garlic before eating or using for cooking.

MAKES 5 CUPS

FOLLOWING PAGES: NORTHERN THAIS IN COLORFUL
TRADITIONAL COSTUME GATHER AT A FESTIVAL
LUCA INVERNIZZI TETTONI/PHOTOBANK

GLOSSARY

BAMBOO SHOOTS: A vegetable which is widely used in Thai cooking, canned bamboo shoots are to be found in most Asian food stores. Even in Thailand it is simpler to use the canned shoots. If the fresh vegetable is used it needs considerable boiling to soften.

BASIL
Bai ga-prow: This is the hot form of basil. If it is unavailable then sweet basil can be substituted but the taste will not leave the burning sensation on the palate. It is sometimes called white basil or light green basil.
Bai horapa: The variety which is most commonly used in Thai curries, this type of basil is similar to sweet basil, but it has a slight aniseed flavor and a reddish purple color. Ordinary sweet basil makes a good substitute.
Bai manglak: A plant which has smaller leaves but a similar taste to sweet basil, which can be used as a substitute, it can be sprinkled in soups and salads. It is sometimes called Greek basil or bush basil.

BEAN SPROUTS: The fresh sprouts of the mung bean are very crunchy and are available in most vegetable markets. If unavailable, canned bean sprouts from Asian food stores can be substituted.

BEANS
LONG STRING BEANS or snake beans: These can measure up to 2 feet (60 cm) in length. If unavailable, green string beans can be used.
SOUTHERN BEANS (*sa-taw*): These are small round green beans available only in Thailand. Use ordinary green beans as a substitute.

BLOODY CLAMS: These are sold at Asian seafood shops. If they are not available ordinary clams or mussels may be used instead.

CARDAMON: The pods or large black seeds of the cardamon plant are used to flavor and garnish many Thai dishes. They can be bought fresh or in the spice section of Asian food stores. They are also used in ground form.

CHILI (*prik*)
There are several chilies used in Thai cooking. They come in a number of sizes and colors. If the type of chili specified in a particular recipe is unavailable, substitute with care. The smaller the chili, the hotter it is, and green chilies are hotter than red ones of the same size. The quantity of chili used depends on the palate—always start with a little, and add more.
THAI CHILI PEPPERS (*prik khee noo*): These are tiny red or green chilies used to add heat to the dish.
  Dried chilies are also used in cooking and are called *prik khee noo haeng.*
  Ground chili pepper is called *prik khee noo pon.*
  Tinned chilies may not be as hot as fresh ones, so check after adding.
JALAPEÑO PEPPERS (*prik chee fa*): These are larger red or green chilies used in milder dishes. Remove the seeds to reduce the heat further.
  The large pale green chilies are not hot and can be used like capsicums.

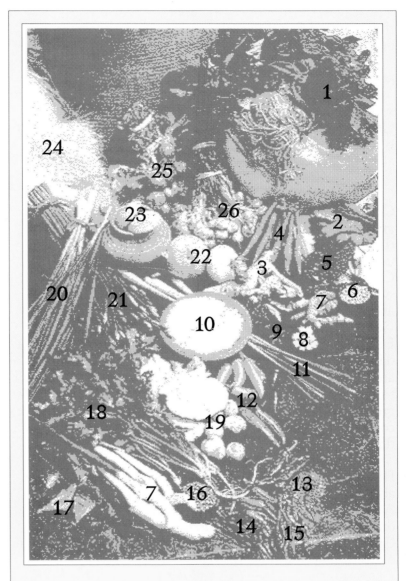

KEY

1	basil	15	Thai chili peppers
2	tamarind pods	16	coriander seeds
3	galangal	17	fresh and dried kaffir
4	lesser ginger		lime leaves
5	green peppercorns	18	coriander
6	white peppercorns	19	mushrooms
7	ginger	20	green onions/scallions/
8	cardamon		spring onions
9	star anise	21	garlic chives
10	jasmine rice	22	brown onions
11	lemon grass	23	palm sugar
12	jalapeño peppers	24	cellophane noodles
13	ground chili	25	shallots
14	dried chilies	26	garlic

CHINESE BROCCOLI: Chinese broccoli has a smaller flower head than broccoli, but the flavors are similar, so that they can be used interchangeably.

CHIVES: Chives belong to the same family as the onion, leek, garlic and shallot. Available in both flat and hollow forms, they are very pungent, and are used as garnishes as well as in cooking.

CILANTRO/CORIANDER (*pak chee*): This herb is essential to Thai cooking and is also known as Chinese parsley. There is no substitute for its distinctive flavor and not only are the leaves used in many dishes but also the stems, roots, and seeds. All have a different flavor and use. The leaves, fresh or dried, are used to garnish many dishes, the roots add flavor to curry pastes, while the seeds are ground into powder.

Cilantro leaves are called *bai pak chee* and the roots are *raak pak chee*.

To grind your own cilantro powder, take whole cilantro seeds and saute lightly in pan until brown and aromatic. Grind in a blender or food processor until a coarse powder is produced. 1 teaspoon of cilantro powder is the equivalent of 2 tablespoons of fresh leaves.

COCONUT
COCONUT MILK: Coconut milk can either be obtained by grating the coconut flesh, soaking it in boiling water and then squeezing out the liquid using a fine sieve, or by using cans of coconut milk from Asian food stores.
COCONUT CREAM: Coconut cream is the thick top layer which forms after making coconut milk. This is also available in Asian food stores and some supermarkets.

EGGPLANT (*ma-khue puang*): These tiny eggplants have a different texture to that of the Western vegetable. There are several forms of Thai eggplants which may be difficult to find outside Thailand. There are small types like a baby green tomato, others are round with stripes. If unavailable, common eggplants or peas can be substituted, but the flavor may vary.

FISH: If the particular fish specified in a recipe is unavailable substitute with any firm-fleshed fish.
ANCHOVIES: If fresh or frozen anchovies are not available drained canned ones can be used.
CRISPY FISH: Prepare crispy fish by deep-frying fish fillets in oil until crisp. Remove from pan and drain well.
DRIED FISH BELLY: Dried fish belly/maw is available from Asian food stores.
PICKLED FISH: Pickled fish are sold in Asian food stores.

FISH SAUCE (*nam pla*): A salty, pale brown liquid used widely in Thai cooking, this is made from fermented small fish or shrimp. The fish are salted and fermented in jars and then the liquid is collected. It adds salt to many dishes and is essential for authentic Thai flavors—and is available from Asian food stores.

GALANGAL (*kha*): A relative of the ginger root, galangal is pale yellow and has a unique, delicate flavor. In Indonesia it is called *laos*. It has rhizomes which are similar to but narrower than those of common ginger, and can be obtained as a root knob or in dried or powdered form from Asian food stores. Fresh young ginger root, but not dried ginger, is an adequate substitute, but does not properly replace the unique flavor.

Kha orn is young galangal, *kha haeng* is dried galangal, *kha pon* is powdered galangal.

GARLIC (*kratiem*): In Thailand the garlic cloves are much smaller and sweeter than the Western variety and have a purple tinge. They can be difficult to find outside the country. These recipes will work with ordinary garlic.

GINGER, LESSER: Another relative of the ginger root, lesser ginger (*krachai*) is milder-flavored than ginger and galangal. The tubers are yellow with a brown skin, and are shaped like fingers hanging from the main body.

JASMINE WATER: Used to add a delicate flavor to some desserts, scented jasmine water can be made by adding ¼ teaspoon of jasmine extract to 1 cup of water.

KAFFIR LIME (*ma-grood*): This fruit is widely used in Thailand and adds a sour, sharp flavor. Dried and frozen leaves are sold in Asian food stores. If dried kaffir lime leaves are all that are available, soak them in water to prepare them for use. The skin, juice, and leaves of this green lime are all used, the rind especially in curry pastes. If unavailable, there is no real substitute but lemon is the closest flavor.

LEMON GRASS/CITRONELLA (*ta-krai*): This tall plant resembles a grass with a small bulbous root. Its flavor and aroma are very lemony. The bulb and base leaves are chopped and pounded for use in a variety of dishes. It is available fresh in markets and Asian food stores and also comes in frozen and dried forms.

MAGGI SEASONING: A sauce which is used in many Asian and Southeast Asian dishes, Maggi seasoning is found in Asian food stores.

MUSHROOMS
ABALONE OR OYSTER MUSHROOMS: Appropriately named, oyster mushrooms have a distinct oyster flavor. They are available from Asian food stores.
DRIED CHINESE BLACK MUSHROOMS: These are soaked in boiling water for 20 minutes before using in Chinese-style clear soups and stir-fried dishes. Their flavor is a fairly bland mushroom one. Asian food stores stock them.
STRAW MUSHROOMS: These are more delicately flavored and have a small brown round cap. They can be bought in cans from Asian food stores.

NOODLES
CELLOPHANE NOODLES (*woon sen*) or glass noodles: These are made from mung beans and are thin and almost transparent in appearance.
RICE VERMICELLI (*sen mee/sen lek/sen yai*): Rice noodles or rice sticks are made from rice and used in such dishes as mee grob. They have a subtle distinct flavor of their own.
THIN EGG NOODLES (*ba mee*): Egg and wheat noodles are used in soups and stir-fried dishes. Most Asian food stores stock a wide variety.
SOFT NOODLES: Fresh wheat flour noodles are used in soups.

ONIONS
SHALLOTS: Small brown or red onions in a bulb form. Red Spanish onions give a similar taste. In some parts of the world (especially Australia), green onions are mistakenly called shallots.
GREEN ONIONS/SCALLIONS/SPRING ONIONS: Mild, long-stemmed, slim onions. Both the green and the white portions are used.
WHITE, BROWN, RED, OR YELLOW ONIONS: These are the large, bulbous, common variety.

OYSTER SAUCE: A brown salty sauce, oyster sauce is made from oysters boiled in salted water and soya sauce. It adds flavor to a number of dishes and is widely available.

PALM SUGAR (*nam taan peep*): This is obtained from a species of palm tree, the Palmyra tree. It comes in dry cubes and a thick paste form. If unavailable, then demerara, light brown or coconut sugar can be substituted.

PEPPERCORNS: These are hot and pungent and used in many dishes for flavor. Canned peppercorns can be bought at Asian food stores. Dried white and black peppercorns are used whole and also in ground form.

PORK
PORK NECK: A boned pork neck can be obtained by making a special request of your butcher or from a specialist Asian food supplier.
PORK STOMACH: Specialist Asian butcher shops are the best source of supply for this.
SIDE PORK: Side pork is also known as pork flap. Pork belly is a slightly different cut but can be used if necessary.

RICE (*khao*)
BLACK GLUTINOUS RICE: A dark rice, black glutinous rice is most often used in desserts.
JASMINE WHITE RICE: The most popular rice in Thailand is fragrant or jasmine white rice, a long-grain white fluffy rice with a distinctive fragrance.
ROASTED STICKY RICE: Prepared by adding raw sticky rice to a hot skillet and cooking until it is golden brown. Add a tablespoon of water to the pan at occasional intervals.
   Grind in a mortar with a pestle if ground roasted sticky rice is needed.
STICKY OR GLUTINOUS JASMINE RICE: A short-grain rice which becomes very sticky when cooked. This is popular in the North and Northeast and is used in many desserts.

SALTED DRIED TURNIP: Salted turnip is available from Asian food stores. It is available in soft shreds or strips and looks like dried banana.

SHRIMP PASTE (*gapi*): This can be bought in a jar from Asian food stores and has a pungent fish taste. Use in small quantities and keep refrigerated.

STAR ANISE: A spice which is a feature of most Asian cuisines, star anise has a distinctive sweet liquorice taste.

SUN-DRYING: Only attempt to sun-dry foods if the weather is very hot and dry. Otherwise follow the alternative instructions, which use an oven.

SWAMP CABBAGE: A vegetable found in Thailand, swamp cabbage may not be available everywhere. Although not the same taste, English spinach, silverbeet or green chard can be substituted.

TAMARIND (*ma-kaam*): Tamarind juice adds a sharp, sour flavor without the tartness of lemon. It comes from the tamarind tree, which has fine fern-like leaves. The fruit is eaten green, but the brown pulp is used for cooking.
   Tamarind juice can be prepared at home or can be bought in bottles in Asian food stores. Lemon or lime can act as a substitute, but the delicate flavor is lost.
   To make tamarind juice add 1 tablespoon of tamarind paste to 1/2 cup of hot water and stir.
   Commercial tamarind sauce can be bought in bottles and can be substituted for tamarind juice but the quantity needs to be reduced and then diluted with water to bring back up to the required quantity.

TAPIOCA FLOUR: Cornstarch/cornflour can be substituted for tapioca flour if it is unavailable.

TOFU: Also known as beancurd, tofu is made from soya beans and is very nutritious. It is sold by healthfood stores and Asian food stores in square blocks packed in water.
FRIED TOFU: Chop the tofu into 1/2-in (1-cm) squares and fry in oil on both sides until it turns golden brown.

TURMERIC: A yellow colored rhizome used for flavor and coloring, it is a perennial plant of the ginger family. The dried root is used in curry powders and is bright yellow in appearance. It has a mellow fragrance.

THE SUN SHINING THROUGH DRIED FISH AT A BANGKOK MARKET

JOHN HAY

251

ACKNOWLEDGMENTS

The Publishers would like to thank the following people and organizations for their support and assistance in the production of this book.

Thai Airways International
Tourism Authority of Thailand
The Regent of Bangkok
Nestlé Products (Thailand) Inc.
Tetra Pak
AT&T
Italthai
Ogilvy & Mather
Bangkok Post
Presko Public Relations Company

The Editorial Board in Thailand was especially helpful in guiding us through the complexities of Thai cuisine and language. We would like to thank Dr Suvit Yodmani, who chaired the meetings, for the outstanding job he did in selecting the members comprising M. L. Tooi Xoomsai, M. R. Thanadsri Svasti, M. L. Tuang Snidvongs, Mrs Chancham Bunnag, Mrs Charunee Bhumidit, and also for his own generous contribution of time and support.

In addition, we would like to thank those people in Bangkok who assisted in making the book a reality: Adisorn Charanachitta, Chertchai Methanayanonda, Dharmnoon Prachuabmoh, Didier Millet, Garth M. Britton, Glenn R. Nelson, John Englehart, Louie Morales, Nadaprapai Sucharitkul, Nares Howatanakul, Nigel Oakins, Norman Pajasalmi, Rusty Kekuewa, Steve Tsitouris, William D. Black, William L. Zentgraf and Yibpan Promyoti.

A number of companies kindly donated their goods and services to facilitate the location photography in Thailand: Mrs Naphali Areesorn, props, Thai Celadon, 18/7 Sukhumvit 21 Road, Bangkok 10110; Mrs Marisa Viravaidya from the Thai House Co. Ltd for the use of the guesthouse as a location, tel (662) 2589651, fax (662) 2588426; Mr Tinakorn Asvarak, props; Ms Worawon Ongkrutraksa, Chiang Mai Honorary Guide; Siam Exclusive Tours Limited kindly allowed us to use their Bangkok to Ayutthaya river cruise boat, the *Mekhala*, as a photographic platform, tel (662) 2567168-9, fax (662) 2556065. At the Ancient City, or Muang Boran, we were able to photograph the recreated traditional Thai architecture. Visitors can obtain further information from 78 Democracy Monument Circle, Ratchadamnoen Avenue, Bangkok 10200.

We would also like to thank John Dunham and Jimmy Shu. The fruit and vegetables shown in the desserts section were expertly carved by Miss Kuson Japeng.

This book was inspired by Somnuk Phadchan who first introduced us to the joy of Thai cuisine.

MONKS AT WAT THAMMAKAI IN BANGKOK

252

Index

GOLDEN BUDDHAS ARE FOUND IN TEMPLES THROUGHOUT THAILAND